W9-BBA-154

The Destruction of Slonim Jewry

From the Library of
Carol M. Cohen
KU Class of 1972

Department of Religious Studies
Moore Reading Room
University of Kansas

Holocaust Library

Statement of Purpose

The Holocaust spread across the face of Europe almost fifty years ago. The brutality then unleashed is still nearly beyond comprehension. Millions of innocents—men, women and children —were consumed by its flames.

The goal of Holocaust Library, a non-profit organization founded by survivors, is to publish and disseminate works on the Holocaust. These will include survivors' accounts, testimonies and memoirs, historical and regional analyses, anthologies, archival and source documents and other relevant materials that will help shed light on this cataclysmic era.

These books and studies will be made available to the general public, scholars, researchers, historians, teachers and students. They will be used in Holocaust Resource Centers, libraries and schools, synagogues and churches. They will help foster an increased awareness of the Holocaust and its implications. They will help *to preserve the memory* for posterity and to enable this awesome time to be better understood and comprehended.

Holocaust Library
216 West 18th Street
New York, NY 10011

Nachum Alpert

The Destruction of Slonim Jewry

The Story of the Jews of Slonim During the Holocaust

Translated from the Yiddish by Max Rosenfeld

Holocaust Library
New York

© 1989 Nachum Alpert

Translated from the Yiddish by Max Rosenfeld

Library of Congress Cataloging-in-Publication Data

Alpert, Nachum, 1913-1989.
  The destruction of Slonim Jewry: the story of the Jews of Slonim during the Holocaust / by Nachum Alpert; translated from the Yiddish my Max Rosenfeld.
        p.   cm.
  ISBN 0-89604-136-0: $18.95.—ISBN 0-89604-137-9 (pbk.): $10.95
  1. Jews—Byelorussian S.S.R.—Persecutions. 2. Holocaust, Jewish (1939-1945)—Byelorussian S.S.R.—Slonim—Personal Narratives. 3. Alpert, Nachum, 1913-1989. 4. Slonim (Byelorussian S.S.R.)—Ethnic relations. I. Title
DS135.R93S542   1990   90-81303
940.53'18'094765—dc20   CIP

Cover Design by The Appelbaum Company

Printed in the United States of America

Published by
Holocaust Library
216 W. 18th St.
New York, NY 10011

Last Will and Testament of Nachum Alpert

Because of my extremely weakened physical condition, resulting from two serious operations on my heart and stomach, I do hereby declare that in the event of my death I empower Holocaust Publications (also known as Holocaust Library), located at 216 W. 18th Street, New York City, to publish the English translation of my Yiddish manuscript, *Der Umkum fun Yidishn Slonim* (The Destruction of Slonim Jewry) and to distribute it.

June 17, 1988

This book appears thanks to Mel Dubin, who himself stems from the town of Smolevici in Byelorussia. His abiding friendship to me as artist, writer and human being greatly encouraged me in writing this book.

The story is about a vanished world of 25,000 Jews, their Jewish learning and their love of Zion; it is about the heroic fight of Jewish partisans against the Nazis in the forests of Western Byelorussia.

—Nachum Alpert

SPONSOR'S DEDICATION

This book is dedicated to the memory
of the beloved martyred members of our family,
and to the many thousands of our people who were brutally slain
when the Nazis destroyed the city of Slonim
in the Grodno province of Byelorussia.

Eleanor and Mel Dubin

Contents

Contents

Part II
In the Forest

On the History of This Book

Yes, this book has its own sad forty-year history, typical of the time and conditions in which it was born. This book has two dates of birth. The first was in 1947, in Slonim, when I had to write in accordance with the spirit and the demands of the Stalin regime. Then it was born a second time in the free world, without the interference of Soviet Party requirements.

Of the more than 25,000 Jews whom the Hitlerites caught in Slonim on June 24, 1941, only about a hundred went back there immediately after the war. For several days they wandered about its burned out ruins, then they ran back to wherever they had come from. To recreate a new life on that mass grave made no sense. Nevertheless, a few dozen stubborn "Slonimer" stayed in the city—"patriots" who overcame all the moral and economic difficulties and replanted their roots in the familiar soil. But they had to begin all over again from the beginning.

While no Jews survived in Slonim, hundreds of grim stories about their torment and their tragic destruction were preserved by individuals who were miraculously saved from the fearful bloodbath. During the deadly years in the ghetto, Jews would often comment despairingly that the Germans would murder them all

and no one would be left to write about their pain and suffering. Some eyewitnesses, however, did survive.

It was early in 1946 when I returned to my native Slonim. The city had been cleansed of the Hitler abomination by the Red Army. But when I had left, Slonim had a normal, pulsating, full-blooded Jewish life. Now it was barren, with only skeletons of buildings. At every step one found only traces of a Jewish community that had been cut down root and branch.

Immortalizing the history of Jewish Slonim—the anguish of the Jewish victims, its heroic partisans—became my life's purpose in those woeful postwar years. I took upon myself the task of recording what the Germans had done to the Jews of Slonim; I considered it my sacred duty to erect a memorial to our martyrs. With youthful energy I began gathering the materials. I listened to the testimony of more than a hundred Jewish and non-Jewish witnesses. I checked and rechecked every fact. By the end of 1947 I had completed a lengthy manuscript, of which I sent out three copies: one to the Jewish Museum in Vilna, one to the Jewish Anti-Fascist Committee in Moscow, and one to the Yiddish publishing house, *Emes* (Truth) in that same city.

Early in 1949 the editor of the Yiddish almanac *Heymland*, Aaron Kushnirov, had promised to publish "In the Forest," the second part of my book, because, according to the publisher's Five Year Plan, they were no longer permitted to put out anything on the "ghetto" theme, since they had already published books about the ghettos in Vilna, Kovno, Minsk and Warsaw. So far they still had permission to publish material about the Jewish partisans.

However, "man proposes and God disposes." The all-powerful god in the Kremlin laughed sardonically at all the Jewish plans and his divine laughter demolished *Emes* publishers, the almanac *Heymland*, the newspaper *Eynikayt*, the Jewish Anti-Fascist Committee, and the Yiddish theaters in Moscow, Minsk, Kiev, Odessa and Vilna. The Jewish Museum in Vilna was closed. The Yiddish elementary schools in Vilna and Kovno were closed, as were all the other Jewish cultural organizations that were still breathing any-

where. Then came the arrest of the most outstanding Yiddish writers, artists and cultural leaders. Some of them were shot, some were sent to labor camps.

During the early 1960s Nikita Krushchev, in a gesture toward the Jews, permitted the publication of one orphaned literary magazine, *Sovetish Heymland,* to replace all the Jewish cultural institutions that had existed up until the pogrom of 1949-1953.

Then—in 1977, thirty years after the war—my manuscript suddenly "turned up" in the offices of *Sovetish Heymland.* I asked the new editors if they were going to publish it. The reply was a long, instructive letter. Here are some significant excerpts:

"This thing is 30 years too late. It should have been published right after the war, when it would have sounded totally different than now. It cannot be published in its present form. It must be fundamentally reworked, starting from the most important, basic chapters. . . . It would be good to present more fully the main heroes of the resistance movement, as well as the traitorous and cowardly role of the Judenrat. . . . Obviously it is a very complicated matter. . . . It creates the impression that the Germans carried out their horrible crimes, almost all their massacres, with the help of the local nationalities. There are fewer facts about the humane attitude of their neighbors toward the Jews. . . . If you rework this, we must come closer to the Slonim of today, to the survivors, to the veterans of the war and the partisan movement."

Commentary would be superfluous.

Despite my endeavors to write that book in the spirit of the Soviet government—so that it could see the light of day—it was still not enough; it had to be "planed down" even more, in order to fit better into the framework of the official Party censorship, which allows generous portions of anti-Semitic poison to be pumped into the Soviet atmosphere every day of the week.

For the sake of the Party line I was supposed to whitewash and even transform into "friends of the Jews" the anti-Semites and the fascist helpers of Hitler, many of whom actually wormed their way into Soviet institutions. I was also supposed to accuse the three

Jewish Councils (Judenrate) of being informers and traitors (also in accordance with the long-standing Soviet line), when in reality the first two Jewish Councils of Slonim (a total of 16 people), were killed by the Germans in the first five months of the occupation.

I had no choice, therefore, but to wait for "better times." A year and a half later those times knocked at my door and I walked out into freedom, where I did indeed rework my book, but this time in consonance with my Jewish conscience. I added many new details which—during the 1970s—I had dug out of various Soviet archives, museums and libraries, in a number of cities. I had accumulated files of supplementary materials, particularly on the resistance movement in Byelorussia. I also found new eyewitnesses to the struggle of the partisans. During 1979-1982 I met twice in Israel with people who had participated in the events.

Almost forty years have passed from the time I made my first notes in 1946 to the present rewriting of the book. I have tried to reflect and illuminate the road which the Jewish community of Slonim traveled during the last three years of its existence, from September 1, 1939 to September 21, 1942.

I am especially grateful to Dr. Noah Kaplinsky for his advice and consultation in arranging the first section of the book, "Behind Barbed Wire."

Nachum Alpert
New York, 1988

Part I
Behind Barbed Wire

Introduction

Slonim is a large Byelorussian city which is now part of Grodno province. In ancient times both sides of the Szczara River were populated by an eastern Slavic tribe known as Dregowiczi. (Even today you still come across many names of cities and villages in Byelorussia with the suffix *wiczi* or *vici*; for example, Smolevici, Skoizici, Dereviancici, Puzevici, Baranovici.) As early as the year 1040 Slonim is mentioned in the chronicles in connection with the victory of the Russian Prince Jaroslaw Vladimirovich over the Lithuanians, who lived in proximity to the Dregowiczi and made frequent forays against this Slavic tribe.

The word "Slonim" itself apparently stems from "Slenis" or "Slenumas," meaning valley or lowland. Slonim actually lies in a valley on both sides of the Szczara River and is surrounded by rolling hills of varying heights. As early as the 12th century there was a princely court here, with a castle that served as a fortress against surprise attacks. In 1241, during the Tatar-Mongol invasion led by Khan Fatia, the court and castle were pillaged and burned to the ground. In the 14th century the area was ruled by the Lithuanian Prince Gedimin, and Slonim was incorporated into his domain. His oldest son Monvid became ruler over Slonim. It was around that time that Jews began settling in the area, although the Jewish community there was not established until the 16th century.

3

In the 15th century, Slonim became a regional city of Novogrod province. In 1633, when Liev Sapeha became *starosta* (governor) of Slonim, marketplaces were constructed and trade developed in the city itself. Contributing to this development was the *starosta* Kazimir-Leon Sapeha, with the help of Jews who introduced handicrafts. During the period of the Moscow wars in the mid-17th century, Slonim was destroyed and was not developed again until the second half of the 18th century, when the Polish Prince Michael Kazimir Oginski became *starosta*. Prince Michael settled here with his court, erected a large castle, an opera house, an inn and many other buildings. Around 1777 he opened the first print-shop. At his own expense he dug a canal to connect the Jaselda River with the Szczara, thereby creating a waterway between the Dnieper and Nieman Rivers, which also meant connecting the Black Sea and the Baltic Sea. This canal runs partly through Slonim and straightens out a large loop in the Szczara River.

The Oginski Canal and the Szczara divide Slonim into two parts—"the city and Zamoshche" (the city and across the bridge), as the inhabitants of Slonim say.

In 1795 Slonim became the capital city of the province, but only one year later, after that province was combined with the Lithuanian province, it again became a regional city in the Czarist empire, a status that continued until 1920.

In 1812 Slonim became the battleground for hostilities between the Czarist army and the Third Regiment of the French Guard.

From 1920 to 1939 Slonim was part of Poland as a regional city of the Novogrod province. At various times Slonim was visited by the Polish kings Wladislaw IV, Jan Kazimir, Jan Sobeski and his son Jakub, August II and Stanislaw August Poniatowski. Bogdan Chmielnitski and his murderous bands also passed through Slonim, pogromizing Jews and sowing destruction among the Poles.

The city of Slonim rests spaciously along the banks of the Szczara River and the Oginski Canal, along the River Issa and the Zamoscie Lake, whose waters softly lap the edges of the city with a lovely murmuring sound. The old churches, as well as the Great Synagogue, which grew up centuries ago on the slopes of the city, are reflected in these waters upside down, as though they were trying to get to the bottom of the secrets buried in the depths.

Slonim was not built according to a plan. Its old narrow streets and alleys turn and twist, uphill and down, sometimes growing wider when least expected. Surrounding the city is a chain of pretty hills and mountains covered with primeval blue-green forests. In the valleys lie colorful sleepy fields, lush meadows, and through them snakes the silvery Szczara. On both sides of the Oginski Canal stretch long dams, overgrown with old trees. The "city and Zamoshche" are joined together by a dozen bridges across the Szczara, the Canal, the Issa River and the lake.

Before the Nazi destruction Slonim had a Jewish Quarter—the old courtyard with the Great Synagogue in the center, a baroque building that goes all the way back to 1642. The synagogue was encircled by a dozen Study Houses with names like The Building, The Shoemakers Synagogue, The Tailors Synagogue, the Lubavitcher *shtiebl,* and a few others. Near the Great Synagogue sprawled the "Old Marketplace," full of butcher shops, herring stalls, flour stores and the workshops of various Jewish craftsmen. Always there was a din there: Jewish women with big baskets on their shoulders, porters, coachmen, peasants, buyers and sellers. There was a little street called "Rubinovski's" that led from the old marketplace to the new marketplace, which again was lined with Jewish stores, workshops, inns and taverns. And wherever you looked you saw friendly Jews, always busy and absorbed in the pursuit of earning a livelihood.

Directly ouside the synagogue courtyard, between the Tailors Synagogue and the Slaughterhouse, the street led uphill to "The Mountain," a densely populated working-class neighborhood where, in a dozen crooked, narrow little streets the Jewish poor huddled together in their crowded little homes.

In the low-lying streets along the banks of the Szczara and the canal there was more Jewish poverty and overcrowding. Between the Szczara and the canal, on an elongated island, there were two streets, Balione and Zhabinke, and two more synagogues. A third synagogue was located on Breger Street. This island is crossed by six bridges that lead to Zamoshche. There were also neighborhoods with a mixed population, such as "Poniatowska and the Rezkes," Skrobive with its army barracks, Zamoscie with its railroad station, Ruzany Street up the hill, with its Jewish and Christian cemeteries.

Exotic and fascinating was the Hassidic court on Skrobive Street. In the center of the yard was the *shtiebl,* from which came a constant stream of fervent melodies. Their Rebbe was beloved and respected by the rapturous and ecstatic Hasidim in Slonim. The great majority of the Jews in Slonim, however, were *misnagdim,* opponents of Hasidism.

The main street, which was in the exact center of the city, on the spine of a big hill, had four names: the Russians under the Tsar called it Nievsky Prospect; the Germans, when they occupied the city in 1914-1918, called it Paraden Strasse; the Poles called it Adam Mieckewicz Street; the Soviets called it *First of May Street.* Whatever its name, it was broad and remarkably straight, and its beautiful, well kept buildings gave it a majestic, aristocratic look. It was not a very long street. Its beginning was at Rutkovski's two-story building with a balcony and a large clock. It ended at Zeli-kovski's rectangular two-story building. Jews called it either *Paradne* or *Nievsk.*

From Paradne-Nievsk a network of crooked little streets and alleys branch off and run downhill to the river, then climb back up again. Streets cross each other with long rows of shops and trees; overhead are cupolas with crucifixes, and the Great Synagogue with its Star of David.

Slonim's tremendous expanse of forests and its cheap water transportation aided the development of its lumber industry. The Szczara is always crowded with long rafts of pine logs. Part of the lumber was reworked in the local sawmills; the rest floated through the city all the way to the great Prussian locks and the Baltic Sea. This contributed greatly to Slonim's commerce. The production of several brick factories and tile kilns filled the needs of the city and the region. The tanneries produced high quality shoe and boot leather for export. Carloads of grain, mushrooms and eggs went by rail from Slonim to all parts of Poland.

Three kilometers from the city, in a picturesque area of pine trees, lay the resort town of Albertin. On the banks of large Lake Albertin lay a working class neighborhood; in the opposite direction, the beautiful palace of Baron Puslawski glistened in the sun. In Albertin too the manufacturer Gurvich constructed a large, modern box factory that produced largely for export.

Jewish children in Slonim received their education in more than ten private and public schools. A particularly important role in the city was played by the Yiddish Folkshul and the Hebrew Tarbut school; together they educated thousands of children of working- and lower-middle-class families. For the wealthy families there was a Jewish high school where Polish was the language of instruction. The "Slonimer yeshiva" had a well deserved reputation throughout the Jewish world.

Every Friday you could buy the weekly *"Slonimer Vort"* edited by Kalman Lichtenstein. There were Jewish sports clubs—Maccabee, Morning Star; there were Zionist youth organizations—Gordonia and Hashomer Ha-tsair. The trade unions played a leading role in the lives of the working people. Many of Slonim's Jews were self-educated and well read—a "working-class intelligentsia."

In the Polish language there was a teachers' seminary (with separate instruction for men and women) and a state secondary school with a few wealthy Jewish students. In the town of Zyrowicy, ten kilometers from Slonim, there was a monastery with an agricultural school. There were also some Polish elementary schools in Slonim that had a few Jewish students. The Byelorussian school system was strictly forbidden in Western Byelorussia.

With Hitler's rise to power and with the adoption of Goebbel's Nuremberg laws, the anti-Semitic winds began blowing harder in Poland. Polish fascists aped Hitler's anti-Semitic policies. Throughout Poland there was a wave of anti-Jewish "excesses," pogroms, blood libels, picketing of Jewish businesses with the slogan *Swoi*

Do Swego (Buy From Your Own). The universities introduced "ghetto benches" for Jewish students. When Jewish students protested by standing during classes, some of the Polish professors demanded that they sit on the ghetto benches or leave. When the students left, they were set upon by Polish students.

This tense atmosphere became even more strained when Polish Foreign Minister Beck began paying "social calls" on Hitler in Berlin and the Nazi leaders reciprocated by taking part in fox hunts in the Bialowieski forest.

Though things had been relatively calm in Slonim up to this time, with no "anti-Jewish excesses," on the eve of World War II the Polish government feverishly began Polonizing the "eastern provinces." Polish handicraftsmen and petty tradesmen showed up in Slonim. All public places were flooded with poisonous anti-Semitic literature. The new "Christian" enterprises—with government subsidies—began competing successfully with Jewish businesses.

When Hitler suddenly ended his cunning flirtation with Poland and began demanding that Poland return Pomerania and Upper Silesia, the Polish fascists grew no wiser; they did not unite the people, but continued their anti-Jewish policies, which further divided the people. Finally, with Hitler already at the gates of Warsaw, the anti-Semitic Polish government picked up its treasury and ran off to London.

Even before the Nazi attack on Poland, Slonim's national composition was already different. The Russian census of 1897 counted almost 16,000 inhabitants in Slonim, 12,000 (70%) of whom were Jews. This proportion continued up until the infamous Polonization campaign which increased the non-Jewish percentage to more than forty. But after the attack on September 1, 1939, when Germany swallowed up large chunks of Polish territory and installed its barbaric rule, refugees began streaming into Slonim from these captured areas. Most of them were Jews, who stood on the streets of the city talking to crowds of people about the brutalities being perpetrated under the swastika.

The Jews of Slonim found shelter for thousands of these refugees in private homes and in synagogues. The population of Slonim doubled. By mid-September 1939 there were 45,000 people in the city. Day and night the main streets were jammed with people. The mood was nervous, dejected. The two Polish regiments—the 79th and 80th—which had always been stationed in the Skrobive barracks, simply vanished. German aircraft flew unhindered over the city, spreading panic down below. The authorities declared a state of emergency and ordered a blackout after dark. They also ordered trenches dug outside all the buildings. The populace began hoarding food, which only intensified the panic. But people continued to believe that Stalin would never permit Hitler to seize the western Byelorussian territories.

On September 17th Molotov reported over the radio that the Red Army was on its way to liberate Byelorussia and the western Ukraine. The government in Slonim, on the last day of its life, distributed a few dozen old inoperable rifles to the fire brigades— to maintain order during the transition. They themselves ran like rats from a sinking ship. At dawn on September 19th a small group of "heroes" set fire to the wooden bridge from Baranovici, in order to halt the advance of the Red Army! That same afternoon the Red Army entered Slonim by way of the Vilna highway.

The Jews of Slonim welcomed the Red Army with joy and relief, as if they sensed an end to Polish anti-Semitism. No more discrimination and demeaning of Jews. No more degradation of Jewish honor. No more "anti-Jewish excesses," pogroms, blood libels. And, most important, no more danger of falling into the hands of the murderous Hitlerites. Even more relieved than the Jews were the Byelorussians, because for the Poles they were ignorant louts who could be oppressed, assimilated and exploited like beasts of burden. Now suddenly they felt like masters of their own land and their own destiny.

The Soviet tanks and motorized troops sparkled in the sunshine that lit up the triumphant liberation-march of the Red Army. The Jews of Slonim greeted the Soviet tanks with flowers. In those happy moments we dreamed and hoped that the "Stalin sun" would forever warm and illuminate the life of the poor working people and lead them out on the bright highway of true national and social justice.

With the disappearance of the Polish "pannes" it seemed that the barriers between Poles, Jews and Byelorussians had also fallen, as well as the barrier between the most oppressed toilers and the educated, cultured class. In only a few short hours, all had become *tovarishchi*—comrades.

There were some people, however, whose enthusiasm was somewhat tempered. They were afraid that as soon as the Bolsheviks got around to investigating their biographies, they would be found lacking in the proper credentials for "proletarian status."

A provisional city administration was organized in Slonim, headed by Matvei Kolotov, a Jew from Minsk. Kolotov, in his army uniform, and with a pistol strapped to his right hip, had a rather coarse appearance. He installed his office in the *starosta* and in private conversations he could not conceal his elation about having been born into a proletarian family. "My father is an *izvostchik* (coachman)!" he would boast at the top of his voice. And that was nothing to be sneezed at. The whole world was in his hands. It is the main standard by which they judge people over there, even today. Whoever does not measure up to that "pedigree" lives in constant peril of having every nook and cranny of his life gone over with a fine-tooth-comb.

Kolotov immediately began organizing a "Workers Guard" (a temporary militia) whose function was to maintain order in the city. Heading this Guard was Chaim Chomsky, a veteran Communist. Gradually Kolotov introduced order into the chaos that followed the transfer of power and it did seem that a just order had been established. Education and medical services were now free. They opened several new hospitals, a clinic, a woman's consultation center, several new Yiddish schools, kindergartens, evening courses for adults. The handicraftsmen organized large artels—but the quality of the work soon declined. In place of private business they opened large stores (with very little merchandise) which always had long lines outside. In one large bookstore the only books available were a History of the Communist Party and Stalin's "Problems of Leninism." Every few days a Byelorussian newspaper, *Volna Fratsa* (Free Labor) appeared, but hardly anyone, even the Byelorussians, could read it and understand it, because the Byelorussian language had been forbidden in Poland. And when the working people received their first wages they wondered how they were going to live on so little money.

The previous enthusiasm and the hope for better times began to cool off; even among former Communists and underground activists there was dissatisfaction. And no sooner did the NKVD arrive than it made itself felt everywhere. First they deported merchants, manufacturers, Polish officers and police; then Bundists, Zionists, Trotskyites and Polish "colonists" and "kulaks" from the villages. Many innocent people were caught in this dragnet.

At the end of 1939 elections were held to the Bialystok "People's Convention." Slonim chose Chaim Chomsky as delegate to the convention, which unanimously agreed to nationalize all the factories, all the land that had belonged to the nobility and all private dwellings larger than 106 square meters. Every day the public was fed political propaganda lauding the "Great Stalin" in a thousand different ways.

This was the situation when Slonim fell into the claws of Hitler — the deadliest enemy the Jews—and all humanity—ever had to face.

Hitler's Treacherous Attack

The morning of Sunday, June 22, 1941 was unusually sunny. Through the open window of my room came a cool, fresh aroma, accompanied by the cheerful chatter of the birds in the willows by the spring in back of the house. The rosy sun, which had just appeared over the horizon, began its climb up the azure sky with a promise of pleasant warmth.

I was still stretched out in my bed, hands clasped behind my head, making plans for my day off, when my sister Tsirl suddenly ran in from the kitchen. Close behind her was a Red Army soldier carrying a rifle. From a list in his hand he read my name along with an order for me to report, with all my documents, to the military unit to which I had been assigned the year before. Having completed his mission, he brought two fingers smartly up to the peak of his green cap, did an about face and left.

A year earlier about sixty of us reservists from Slonim had gone through a month's course in which we were trained in the art of observing the sky through binoculars, so that we could identify German and Soviet planes, their classifications, their markings, their silhouettes and their position, and then report all this information accurately and quickly to our company headquarters.

On that Sunday morning, concealing my thoughts from everyone,

I came to some conclusions: The previous good relationship between Stalin and Hitler had lately been going sour. A continuous stream of Soviet heavy military equipment had been rolling past our house on the way to Bialystok and the German border. Add to all this the sudden visit by the Red Army man, instead of the customary written "invitation," and it began to smell suspiciously of gunpowder.

Twenty minutes later I crossed the threshold of my house for the last time. Reporting to my company in Zamoshche, near the railroad station, I found many friends, along with some newly mobilized soldiers. I also found my brother Leybe. They were all feverishly digging trenches.

Political Commissar Niaradze explained the new war situation to us and analyzed the international political situation as well, encouraging us all with the promise that the great Stalin, in his wisdom, would lead the Soviet people to a speedy victory over Hitlerism. A little while later we all had our new haircuts, had been outfitted with Red Army uniforms, with rifles and gas masks, and been assigned to various units.

Around one o'clock Zavel Gendzelevitch came from the city with the news that Molotov had just reported over the radio to the Soviet people that Hitler had violated the nonaggression pact between the two countries and had treacherously attacked the Soviet Union, bombarding Bialystok, Kiev, Vilna, Kovno, Brisk and other cities. Molotov had finished his report with these words: "Our cause is just! The enemy will be smashed! Victory will be ours!"

Toward evening our commander gave me my first duty. I climbed up to the high observation point, which was camouflaged in a tree. There I found a regular Army man who was expecting me. At first he wasn't sure he could trust me, since I was a greenhorn, but he soon learned that I had been well trained for this particular job and his attitude toward me softened.

Thus passed my first day at war. That night, in the tent, I couldn't fall asleep.

At dawn I relieved the watch on the tower and returned to my sacred duty of guarding the skies over the city, which was still asleep. On my left, across the Szczara River, against the background of the clear morning sky, I could see the long silhouette of the Baranovici highway bridge. But I couldn't believe my eyes. Only yesterday, long lines of our military equipment were rolling westward; now almost all of it was racing back toward the east. Already? Only yesterday the radio had reported that our air force was puliverizing Berlin and that in some places the Germans had been beaten back scores of kilometers. I was confused by feelings of bitterness and disappointment. I rubbed my eyes—perhaps it was only a mirage. I put my binoculars to my eyes. It was painfully true. They were retreating in panic. Our heroic army was showing its heels to the enemy.

Then I thought I saw something else. On the dreamy western horizon—aircraft, but not ours! I broke out in a cold sweat. I had to report this at once to our command post. Every second was precious. But whose planes were they—ours or theirs? I took a quick look at the German silhouettes on the chart. There was no doubt about it. They were light German bombers—D-D-17's. At that moment my ears distinguished their peculiar sound, not continuous, like ours, but staccato-like. My voice trembling, I yelled into the telephone: "Three D-D-17's approaching, 45 degrees left, altitude 800 meters, time: 5:20. Alpert."

Immediately came the brusque question: "Are you sure?"

In that 15-20 seconds the bombers had grown larger. Now I could recognize them with the naked eye. My reply was even more certain: "They're heading for the Derewianczycy airport!"

A few minutes later, through my binoculars, I could already see the fiery clouds over the airport. Our Zenith anti-aircraft guns were counter-attacking, but our planes were no longer there. Count Jelski's palace, which housed the Aviation School, must be burning. I was feeling pretty important—hadn't I just warned the anti-aircraft gunners to be ready? Being an aircraft observer is "light work" with a heavy responsibility. The slightest error can result in a disaster—and then the observer will be in hot water himself.

But a few hours later Nathan Rabinowitch (now Haim Kleinman) came up to my post to relieve me, and when I showed him what was happening on the bridge, he said calmly: "What! You mean you've just discovered that we're getting out of here? Go down below and see how they're piling everything into the trucks."

We were particularly affected by the arrival of soldiers who had been stationed at various observation posts like Ozernitza, Zelve, Kaslowczini, Czemeri and other towns and villages, from which they had barely escaped with their lives, because in some places German troops had already broken through. Our newly mobilized men were still in civilian clothes. The situation was beginning to look catastrophic.

That afternoon a squadron of German D-D-17's reached our position. We barely managed to sound the alarm and dive into our trenches before these air-pirates with the black crosses on their wings raked the air above us. Arrogantly, without any fear of being hit, they swooped so low that they almost caught their wings in the branches of the tree that was our observation post. Their jackal-like howling deafened our ears and battered our spirits. The metallic roar of their motors, accompanied by a dense hail of bullets, spread terror and an awareness of death among us.

In order not to expose our protective cover, we did not return their fire. Overhead, the swastika-marked planes dropped little black bombs that whistled insanely as they tore up the railroad station. A mixture of bricks, boards, stones and black earth whirled all around us. Eventually our Zeniths on the heights around the cemetery in Ruzany drove the German planes from the Slonim sky.

But that was only the beginning, a baptism in the bloody waters of war, an inhalation of gunpowder, in the approaching struggle with the relentless, inhuman forces of Hitlerism. The Russians called it: "Boyovoya Kreshchenye" (baptism of fire).

During the entire attack by the German planes, our Captain

Tishkov issued orders from his headquarters in a trench. He was furious with two men from Czemeri who, with their white shirts, had given away our position.

The second night brought us face to face with the battle-front. The stillness of the night was shattered by the partial retreat of the Byelorussian garrison from Slonim. The clanging of the equipment and the incessant roaring of the motors became unbearable. Suddenly two tremendous streaks of light lit up the sky; their long tongues, licking the heavens, had caught a silvery "Junker-U" in their crossfire. The plane could not get out of the grip of the projectors as our Zeniths sent up a steady salvo of tracer bullets. But none of this seemed to bother the Junker. It continued on its course, safe in its impenetrable bullet-proof suit.

The next morning, June 24th, many relatives and friends came to the gate of our company post to say goodbye; somehow they had learned of our imminent retreat. Among them was my sister Tsirl, her face dark with foreboding. During our last agonizing moments together, neither of us dared utter a word, the dreadful blow having come so brutally and so unexpectedly. Finally she said:

"They always boasted about the invincibility of the Red Army. But now that the time has come to prove their heroism they are running like scared rabbits, leaving the people behind to the winds of fate."

I tried to cheer her up. "Our retreat is only temporary. Napoleon was also lured in—all the way to Moscow, where they ripped him to shreds. Wait for us—(I whispered through my clenched teeth) —we're leaving the enemy in pursuit, but we'll return victorious, as Molotov said."

The guards began dispersing the visitors; it was time for us to line up. We parted with half-words. Tsirl could no longer restrain her tears . . .

"Enemy aircraft!" came the sudden alarm, and almost before the word was out we could hear their beastly howling. Tsirl ran down the street, weeping. I could see her shoulders shuddering. She ducked behind a gate. And that was the last time I ever saw her.

In an instant, the trenches swallowed us up. The war was raging over the whole city. Again our unit intercepted an air attack. Now we could also hear the growling of the German artillery, hitting the city from the Bialystok road, near the Jewish cemetery. Flames blazed up everywhere. Fire and thunder split the air, sowing death and destruction.

Not until the Nazi planes had fired their quota of shells did they fly off to sow death in other places.

One of our scouts came galloping up with the news that the Germans were well inside the city. But Captain Tishkov still spoke calmly into the telephone. Suddenly he ran out of the head-quarters. Apparently he had just received the order to retreat. He ordered the automobiles to ride out to the Baranovici Road with several officers; then he instructed us infantrymen to brace up the defenses around the railroad station.

Before we got to the little bridge across the Issa River we were greeted by machine-gun fire. Someone shouted: "German troops on the bridge!" but it was too late to put up any resistance. Lt. Dagestanski gave the order: "Go left through the water to the Albertin woods."

My brother Leybe and I, along with Zavel, holding on to each other, crossed the swiftly flowing river under a hail of fire from the bridge and from a Messerschmidt 109 in the sky. Soaking wet, our heads down and almost crawling on our knees, we reached the cornfields at the same time as the other men in our company.

Crouched on all fours, we dried out our clothing as bullets whistled around us and buried themselves deep in the ground. Zavel, who had fought in the German-Polish conflict of 1939, shouted at us: "Hit the dirt! They can see your heads!" We followed his instructions and the Germans must have assumed they had finished us off. Nearby, a wounded man groaned. Covered by the golden waves of corn, we crawled on our bellies to the woods. Together with our people, our bread had also fallen into the enemy's hands.

Suddenly came Tishkov's curses in the direction of the captured bridge: "*Svolatchi!* Cut-throats! Firing at your own people!" His justified anger erupted in the form of double-barreled Russian swear-words.

A little while later we carried our wounded comrade—our company cook—into a peasant cottage near the river. The rustling pine trees sighed sympathetically.

In the woods we took count—37 of us. A second group had gone off with Lt. Volochin. A large number of Slonim's citizens had chosen Hitler's paradise over the Soviet Union and deserted en masse. In the very first days of the German occupation it became clear who had made the right choice. They deserted for various personal reasons: some simply hated the Soviets, some couldn't leave their relatives, some thought they could play it safe and sit out the war in the comfort of their own homes.

In the shadowy forest a few kilometers from Slonim the tragic reality gnawed at me, throwing me into a hopeless silence. A squadron of German planes flew low overhead, no doubt searching for us. Our commander conferred with a Red Army man from the Soviet Union. Apparently they didn't trust those of us who had come from "the west"—they considered us sheep who had strayed into an unfamiliar flock and would desert at the first opportunity. Very soon, however, they discovered that their suspicions were groundless.

After catching our breath we retreated through the dense forest around Albertin Lake, heading southeast. When we reached the Polanka Highway we realized at once that we could not use that road—German planes were flying overhead in an endless wave. From Polanka we could see Slonim and Baranovici in flames. It was a heartbreaking sight.

As prearranged, we met the 2nd platoon in Polanka and Lt. Volodin took over general command of both groups. On the Minsk

Highway we found many other retreating units and in the blackness
of the night, to which our eyes became accustomed, we marched
along both edges of the road. During the day we took cover under
the trees and bushes that lined the road.

On June 27, after a three-day exhausting retreat, hungry, dirty
and unshaven, we reached Stolbcy at dawn. It had been a classic
forced march with all our gear—about 125 kilometers in 72 hours.

By sheer accident, our entire 5th Regiment, which had been
scattered over various points of the compass, gathered at Stolbcy.
We also met Captain Tishkov here with the rest of the Slonim
company. It could have been worse, we thought. Our army units,
our equipment and—most vital—our provisions, were all intact.
For three days we had eaten practically nothing.

But before we could even catch our breath, we were forced to
defend ourselves against an enemy "tankette" unit that had evi-
dently been parachuted down during the night by U-78 Junkers.
Well camouflaged in the forest, it had purposely allowed us to get
through to Stolbcy, so that it could launch a surprise attack on the
town. A full-scale battle developed. The Germans swarmed around
our little hill like starving hyenas on a corpse. Their small tanks
were sharpshooters. The first victim was our observation post,
which they blew to bits.

From the exploding shells and from the debris the air grew dark
and suffocating. In the early morning sky a dozen planes were
locked in a dog-fight. After a twenty minute battle during which
one of the enemy tanks was blown up, we were forced to retreat
again.

A red rocket signal and the command, *"Into the trucks!"* ended
our part in the battle. In the confusion we lost my brother Leybe
and Pikelne the Watchmaker, plus several Byelorussians who apparently had not noticed the retreat signal or who had been
wounded.

Our retreat was covered by a cannon into which Captain Tishkov
loaded the shells and our Colonel Khoroshilov triggered the firing
mechanism. When we halted at the cannon, Tishkov ordered us to

ride out to the collective farm at Djerzinski and wait there for the rest of the company.

In this manner, fighting all the way, Zavel Genzelevich, Khaim Bitenski, Khaim Kleiman, Kalman Gertsowski, Joseph Derechinski, myself, and several Jewish refugees from Poland, joining up with units of the Red Army, got through to the badly hit cities of Minsk and Mohilev. We took part in the defense of Smolensk and Vyazma, where Derechinski was taken prisoner, and finally, in the dramatic defense of Moscow, where the Nazi "blitzkriegers" were given a good drubbing and pushed back for miles and miles. After Moscow our regiment was transferred through Stalingrad to the Caucasian front.

*In Slonim After
the Outbreak of the War*

It took only a few minutes for the alarming news of Hitler's treacherous invasion to rush through Slonim like a spring flood. The normal routine of life was instantly transformed into a state of war. Military patrols, battle-ready, moved through the streets. With their stern looks and their tight lips they quickly put everyone into a mood of the strictest discipline. The loudspeakers on the main streets blared continuously with warnings to maintain order.

The radio, meanwhile, was broadcasting frequent bulletins assuring the populace that the heroic Red Army would halt the enemy and drive him back. From the loudspeakers came popular Soviet military songs and high-spirited marches.

As is customary in such situations, the government ordered a general mobilization. After-dark traffic through the city was restricted. Because of the influx of wounded soldiers brought from the front, several schools were turned into field hospitals. Slonim began writing a new, bloody chapter in its long history.

The population understood the practical consequences of the new situation. Long lines formed around stores of all kinds, but especially food stores. Crowds stormed the few peasant wagons that showed up in the marketplace. The farmers, in turn, took

advantage of the situation to raise their prices. Many of them, suspecting that Soviet currency would depreciate, closed up shop and
went back home.

Army trucks kept evacuating the families of the military. On
June 23rd the last trainload of Soviet citizens working in Slonim
left the city. Outside of Slonim there was a Pioneer Camp; those
children also went into this train. Among them was my brother
Karpel's son Leyzer, whom I found after the war in Magnitagorsk
in the Urals. It became obvious that the Soviets were leaving
Slonim.

The uneasiness of the population grew to feverish proportions.
There were various interpretations of the events, but one question
plagued everyone: "To leave or to stay?" The Jews knew very well
what Hitler meant for them, they knew what the Polish Jews were
suffering, but most of them hated the Soviet "comrades" with their
ready prescriptions for everyone's life. Young people of the middle
and working classes whose family circumstances permitted followed close on the heels of the Red Army.

Among the latter was a group of 26 people, including Anshl
Delyaticki, Moshe Ogushevich, Pesach Alpert, Alter Kletzkin,
Chaim Gazetchik, Pesach Rizakov and Moshe Yankelevich. Wandering over dozens of roads, weary, unwashed and hungry, but
with fire in their eyes, they reached Stolbcy on June 26th and reported at once to the mobilization office. But the very next day,
even before they were inducted into the army, a German tank
column attacked the city and they had to retreat.

When they got to Minsk, it was already in flames. The dead lay
in the streets. The living were fleeing the city. From Minsk the
group headed for Smoliewiczi, but on June 30th they learned to
their dismay that the "Heil Hitlers" were moving a "little faster" on
their wheels than the exhausted Jews on foot.

In an old abandoned cottage on an outlying street the group
gathered to consider their alternatives. Unkempt and unshaven,
barely recognizable, dispirited and painfully aware of the catastrophic dimensions of what was happening, they cursed the

Germans, their military might and their *Drang Nach Osten*. Bone weary, they sat or sprawled on whatever broken furniture was left in that foul-smelling hut; others sat on the window-sills or curled up on the filthy floor. Desperate people at a fateful crossroads.

In that whispered discussion, Anshl spoke up:

"From now on we are exposed to the German fascists. If they discover us, especially if they realize we're trying to get to the front, we're dead—at the very least, we end up in a concentration camp. I therefore propose that we split up into small groups of three or four and begin a retreat to Slonim. There we'll at least be able to do underground work in the German hinterland."

Moshe Ogushevich disagreed. He proposed instead that they continue on our way through forests and along the back roads until we reached the Red Army lines. "Double our efforts and get rid of the feeling that there's no way out except to go back where we came from."

The sleepy, apathetic eyes and the weary faces bore witness to the fact that the majority had accepted Anshl's proposal. Encouraged, he began giving orders:

"Choose the guys you want to go with and let's not waste any more time! Every additional minute we stay here could be fatal!"

Sighing and groaning, they swallowed their pain like condemned prisoners. Slowly they got up and began leaving the hut in small groups. This time they would measure the Byelorussian earth from east to west.

Anshl Delyaticki, Alter Kletzkin and Moshe Yankelevich cautiously started on their way back toward Slonim. On July 3, not far from the Djerzinski kolkhoz, near Stolbcy, Stalin's voice came over the radio: A government defense committee had been formed and all power had been placed in their hands. He appealed to that part of the population that had temporarily fallen under the fascist yoke to form cavalry and infantry detachments; to organize diversionary groups that would blow up bridges, roads, cut telephone and telegraph lines, set fire to forests, warehouses, trains; to make life for the enemy in the captured territories unbearable. Pursue the enemy and his traitorous helpers and kill them. Destroy their facilities. "Comrades! Our forces are innumerable—the enemy will soon learn that for himself! Onward to victory!"

The first to comment was Anshl. "Now you can see, *khevra,* that we're doing the right thing. We'll open a second, invisible front and attack the fascists from behind. We'll do everything that Stalin said—except one thing: we won't set fire to the forest. The forest will be our cover and our protection! It will be our base and our home. If anyone sets fire to the forest, it will be the enemy, to try and smoke us out of there."

Their tasks were now clear to them. It raised their spirits, gave them the strength to fight for their lives.

Another group—Pesach Alpert, Chaim Gazetchik, Pesach Rizakov and Moshe Ogushevitch—were caught and got a taste of the Minsk jail. From there, they and hudreds of others were squeezed into a roped off area on the bank of a stream. On the other side of the rope stood the "pure Aryans," displaying their racist spirit in its purest form—shooting at defenseless men. At night they lit up the area with floodlights. Anyone who made the slightest movement was rendered motionless forever by a bullet from a German automatic.

The camp was continually enlarged by new arrivals of civilian prisoners. No food was distributed. Water was available only from the stream.

Two days later the Nazis divided this "open-air camp" into two— with another rope. Then came the command: "All Jews move to the left side of the rope—on the double!"

To make this command more effective the Nazis began wielding their rifle butts, clubs and blackjacks. A dozen Jews were shot through the head. To add zest to their game, the Nazis circulated the "news" that it was the Jews who were responsible for the war. This useful information was accompanied by an announcement that non-Jews were now permitted to "take back" from the accursed Jews anything they wished—shoes, money, watches, jewelry, etc. Every people in the world has its criminal element and here too there were devotees of the easy life . . .

There were also some non-Jews, however, who cursed out the thieves in unmistakeable terms. As one of them said: "The Jews have enough trouble from the Germans without your help!" The thieves melted quickly into the mass of people.

The camp commandant came up with another refinement: Jews would now be permitted a drink of water only twice a day. It was early July. The temperature was in the 90's.

At one point a gang of the murderers roared up on their motorcycles and their leader made an announcement: Educated people were urgently needed for "light work." About 500 Jews stepped forward. With a roar of the motorcycles they were led into the nearby woods. A little while later came the dread clatter of machine guns.

Three days later the cyclists were back again with a new call—for craftsmen. Distrustful but desperate, some 600 workers stepped forward, among them the four Slonimer. To get to the railroad station the men had to run after the motorcycles. Those who couldn't keep up with this "motorcade" were released from the suffering of this world by a bullet. At the station, the "volunteers" were ordered to sit motionless on the ground until the train arrived. But the train didn't come. They were forced to run back to the camp the same way they came.

Late that afternoon the sky suddenly grew dark. Thick black clouds descended upon the camp. Thunder and lightning ushered in a tremendous downpour. The thousands of people in the open field were drenched. Every lightning-bolt seemed to be aimed directly at them. Even the guards were frightened and hid like mice in their holes. Their watchfulness grew soggy. Out in the field, whenever it thundered, some of the men slithered forward on their bellies toward the stream. When the lightning flashed, they lay still as death. Under this cover, they not only reached the stream but crossed it and vanished into the bushes. Among those men were the four courageous Slonimer.

All night long they slogged through the woods. Toward dawn the flood receded and they could see where they were. Straight ahead, where two forest paths crossed—a German patrol. Had they crawled from the frying pan into the fire? Then they noticed something peculiar and breathed a little easier. These Germans seemed polite. They hadn't even reached for their guns. Merely asked them for documents and examined their Soviet passports. One of them said—in Czech:

"You are Jews?"

If one knows Polish, it's not too difficult to understand Czech. In Polish, the Slonimer gave him an affirmative answer. After all, the Soviet document said "Yevrei." The Czechs exchanged glances, whispered something to one another, and then advised them not to continue in the direction they had been heading, because they would soon come to a town where Jewish blood was flowing. Their commander pointed them in another direction with his riding crop.

"Thank you very much, gentlemen!" said the Slonimer in Polish. Apparently not everyone who wears a German uniform is a German.

After this lucky break the four Slonimer realized that they could not travel in the daylight. They would have to march the rest of the way under cover of darkness.

Fate led them to an old forest hovel, where they spent the day in the attic. When night came, they marched. At dawn the next day they came upon a poor Byelorussian village. They knocked at the door of the first cottage and received a friendly welcome from the peasant, who offered them some of his freshly baked bread. Like the Czechs the day before, he advised them to stay away from the next village, "where there are no longer any Jews."

When they reached Polonka, which was also "Judenrein," they learned that "something" had also happened in Slonim, which meant that if they succeeded in getting there, they would immediately have to find a place to hide.

They arrived at Slonim soon after dawn. Each of them went directly to his own house. Pesach Alpert's family had already been moved from the Christian neighborhood in which they had lived. On Ruzany Street they found a place to sleep. The next thing the learned was that on the 17th of July the first massacre had taken place in Slonim—1200 Jewish men.

In the afternoon of June 24th, when many front-line German soldiers were already in Slonim and vicinity, Meir Iznaiden had tried to escape, despite the fact that he was over sixty and the father of a family. His plan consisted simply in outwitting the Nazi guards. Iznaiden was a minor official in the volunteer firefighters brigade. On the last day he hurriedly put together a small group of Jewish firefighters who also wanted to escape: his son Shmuel, Abraham Sherreizen, Reuben Ogushkevich, Jochanan Rubinovski, Zyama Ostrovkes and a few others.

They showed up at the garage where the firetrucks were kept and offered the Polish driver a chance to get out on one of the vehicles. The Pole was not too enthusiastic about this Jewish plan to follow the Red Army, which he had just gotten rid of that morning. Apparently he was waiting to turn over to the Germans the splendid fire-fighting equipment, for which he would be suitably rewarded.

In the meantime our guys kept an eye on him, so that he wouldn't slip out and bring the Germans. Meir Iznaiden started warming up the motor, and when he had checked everything, gave the order: "Let's go!" They all put on their fireman's hats and took their places on the truck. Four kilometers outside the city they came to a German checkpoint, where a guard ordered them to stop. Meir jumped out of the cabin and explained that they had just received an emergency call from the carton factory in Albertin—and he pointed to the hill in the distance.

Iznaiden played his role with such artistry that the German guards, after taking a long look at the "firemen," gave them the green light. When the truck had climbed up Albertin Hill they didn't turn left to the town but went straight ahead toward Baranovici. Iznaiden stepped on the gas and at Leszno they caught up with the Soviet military equipment that had retreated from Slonim. One hour after the firetruck left Slonim it flew into a Baranovici that was already in flames. Here they turned the vehicle over to the army and reported for mobilization.

Only some of them lived to see the day of victory.

The First "Good" Germans

Sowing destruction and death, the main force of the Hitlerite hordes appeared on the rim of the hill between the Catholic church and the Jewish cemetery, where the Bialystok and Brisk Roads join and then plunge downhill into the city through Ruzany Street.

First came their advance scouts on motorcycles. After them, in a cloud of smoke, came the heavy tanks. Simultaneously came a crushing cannonade from Poniatowska, where several of the tanks broke through. Then the tanks lumbered in with their hated swastika flags, a sign that the city must come out to greet the invaders. But the population stayed in their hiding-places and the streets were gapingly empty. Doors stayed locked, windows shuttered or curtained. People spent this time of fear in cellars, behind their own walls. A bit later, when they sensed a cease-fire, a few of the bolder men appeared in the street. The fluttering swastikas darkened and saddened our beautiful city, which lay wounded and bleeding beneath the metal-studded Nazi boots.

This was the advance army which handled "administrative" problems. It did not distinguish too much between Jews and non-Jews at first, but their visages bade us no good. They showed their wolfish teeth almost immediately. The city was jolted out of its stillness by the loud drumbeat of thousands of boots over Slonim's paved streets. These tried and tested Hitlerites, their helmets decorated with death's-heads, rounded up men of military age as one rounds up cattle. They beat the heads and backs of the confused victims with clubs and rifle-butts, to the accompaniment of frequent gunshots into the air, spreading terror among the population with their ferocious brutality. They dragged the men out of their homes and through the streets. In growing columns they chased them from all sides toward the cemeteries, to the courtyard of the Elementary School on Skrobive Street and to the stadium behind the barracks, where they had set up "camps." Anyone who tried to duck into a yard or hide behind a bush was shot on the spot. On Skrobive Street, Yosl Lidavski attempted to slip into his own building, but was stopped by a bullet. The same thing happened to the Polish carpenter, Druzbalski.

The camp on the Bialystok road was very quickly packed with more than 10,000 men, guarded by sadists who took special delight in shooting over the heads of the prisoners and occasionally *into* their heads. When their targets dove to the ground to avoid the bullets, the supermen would burst into ecstatic laughter. Thus entertaining themselves, they slaughtered scores of people, then ordered other prisoners to bury the dead in the bushes, after which they also "liquidated" the gravediggers.

All around this place of horrors lay colorfully blooming fields, and at the edges of both roads, the slender white birches gleamed against the blue of the over-arching sky and the green horizon of the forest. Here and there, ancient willow trees bowed low in the wind. Tall maples stretched heavenward in the dazzling sunlight, which innocently illuminated this latest murder technique.

Meanwhile the German tanks pressed hard upon the retreating Red Army, raising clouds of dust which settled on the camp and crept into the mouths of the hungry, thirsty and exhausted prisoners.

After holding the men for three days without food or water, the guards suddenly released their prisoners under a hail of blows. For the Jews they had a special "recommendation"—it would be better for them if they came here to sleep in the open, because any Jew caught sleeping in a house would be shot on the spot. In all the places where Jews were permitted to spend the night—Julian's Kino, the Great Synagogue, the two high schools, the city theater —the Nazis created such a hellish atmosphere that no one could sleep anyway. At the door stood a vicious guard. Bands of rampaging soldiers burst in during the night and ordered everyone to stand at attention. Early in the morning they would take groups of Jews out "to work," but those who went out with them never came back.

In one corner of the fenced-in yard of the Elementary School the Germans had already set up a small camp where they were starving a group of Red Army prisoners. Now they drove young civilians into this camp. At the gate stood a table where the black-uniformed field police searched the new prisoners for money, watches, rings, fountain pens and other valuables. Anyone whose hair was cut short was classified as an "escaped" Red Army soldier and immediately executed. The bodies of these "Red Army men" lay on the ground; some of them may have run away from our company at the Issa River.

After the robbery and shooting process, they forced the living to run the gauntlet between two rows of Nazi thugs armed with a variety of implements. The yard was surrounded by guards carrying automatics and machine guns, and at the gate stood a tank, just in case it might be needed.

Out of "mercy" for the starving men, the murderers brought out a "lunch" of watery soup and horsemeat. Hardly able to stand on their feet, the prisoners held out beneath the cook's ladle whatever they could put their hands on—a can, a hat, a cap—but most of them only their own cupped hands.

All of a sudden the "Aryans" noticed that the camp had not been "deStalinized"—outside the building stood a statue of the "great" Stalin. They selected about twenty Jews and ordered them to "smash this swine at once." Then, to make the work go faster, they beat the Jews around the head until only a pile of stones was left of the statue.

A perpetual, impassioned debate went on among the men about the war. They argued and interpreted and analyzed and always came to the same conclusion: they could not expect any mercy from this army of cut-throats. Most of the men believed that salvation would come from the east; the only force that could stop this diabolical machine was the Soviet Union.

June 27th was a beastly hot day, and with the night came a coolness that was a relief for the strained nerves of the prisoners. They fixed their eyes on the glistening stars. From the Szczara River the breeze brought the familiar croaking song of the frogs. But this peaceful reverie was suddenly shattered by the crackling of gunfire. From the excitement at the gate the prisoners on the ground could tell that the tank had left the camp and was rumbling toward the center of town. Had the Red Army returned?

All night long the sounds of battle reached their ears from several directions and the breeze brought a whiff of smoke.

June 28th, early in the morning, the air grew uncommonly still, but as soon as the camp rubbed its sleep-famished eyes, the guards herded in a small group of uniformed men and put them among the Soviet war prisoners. It turned out that they were Red Army tankists. Later that morning a new contingent of young Jewish prisoners was brought into the camp. From them the inmates learned that during the night Soviet army units had tried to break through to Slonim.

One unit, with two heavy K-V tanks, had tried to sneak across "Shaye's" Bridge under cover of darkness. The Germans fired mortars at them. The Soviet tanks soon put them out of business and started across the wooden bridge over the canal. But apparently the Poles who had built the bridge in the 1930s never imagined that two iron fortresses would cross it at the same time, at full speed. A few weeks later the tanks and their drivers were hauled up out of the water. A third tank got stuck in the middle of Skrobive Street. A fourth fought valiantly on Ruzany Street and burst into flame, burning down several houses.

In the meantime, Soviet infantrymen "knocked at the door" of the German Staff Headquarters, which had made itself at home in the dwelling of Dr. Efros, in Shereshevsky's building on Panesve Street. After cleaning out the "pure Aryans," the Red Army men sent the house up in smoke.

On "Crooked Street" near the Panesve synagogue the fascists buried a group of Jews and Red Army men in the same grave. Before they were shot the group proudly sang the Internationale together. (The Germans, accusing the Jews of hiding escaping Red Army soldiers in their homes, had rounded up young Jews and brought them to the camp.)

The German troop deployment tactics, together with the betrayal by Generals Pavlov and Novitski in Byelorussia and Vlasov in the Ukraine, temporarily splintered the Red Army. Various units that had lagged behind the quickly retreating front moved during the night, at great peril, and were forced to do battle with an overwhelmingly superior force. Some of the soldiers died in battle, others were taken prisoner, and the rest spread out through the forests and organized the partisan movement.

This explains why the Germans set up the camps during this uncertain transition period, as well as why they seized all the young men as hostages. They were deathly afraid of unexpected attacks by the splintered Soviet army units, who were supported by the local population. When the front raced forward and Slonim became more secure for them, the Germans liquidated the camps.

On June 28th the Germans decided to clean up the area that had been the "home" of several thousand prisoners for a few days. Selecting a group of better dressed Jews, they forced them to clean up the human excrement with their bare hands. During this "operation" they mocked the "clean-up squad" continuously with the refrain, *"Juden kaput! Juden kaput!"*

On June 29th the Germans opened a passageway to Zhireve Street and let everyone out, one person at a time. With the German officers stood representatives of the Jewish community—Itzkevitch and Jakimovski—and for the Poles, the priest from the Zamoshche church and several monks. This "committee" was supposed to identify those among the released prisoners who were Jews from Slonim. Thus ended the bullying of innocent people, but for the Jews it was only the beginning.

During the next few days the German army plastered the city with warnings in German and Russian: (1) For any display of hostility to the German army: death by shooting; (2) For hiding Soviet soldiers or weapons: death by shooting; (3) For not taking off one's hat to Germans: death by shooting.

They rousted Jews out of their homes for forced labor, or to wash their dusty trucks and tanks, etc. Cutting down a Jewish life was a daily occurrence for them and a matter of great enjoyment. These representatives of the *Herrenvolk* raped young women, not sparing even those who were pregnant. They turned out to be experts on stealing, too. They removed the locks from government stores and took out the most expensive items.

After they finished with the stores they turned to Jewish homes. Under the pretext of searching for weapons they stole clothing, gold, silver, jewelry. At the Shepetinkis on Panesve Street an officer and a guard piled up a heap of old clothes. When Shepetinki stammered that the German would get very little use out of them, the officer commented: "Very soon they won't be of use to you either." Apparently these "trophies" were of use to their relatives in Germany during the lean years of the war.

The "advance army" of the Germans was a little more human than the S.S., S.D. and Gestapo who came later. They still let the Jews move about "freely." But they spread such Jew-hating propaganda that it was better for Jews to stay indoors. Meanwhile, Hitler's minions steamed down into Slonim like lava, day and night, in their *Drang Nach Osten*. They raced through the streets and highways in their brand-new gleaming tanks and trucks, their uniforms still clean and fresh, their boots and helmets glossy. They exuded arrogance and a thirst for blood. But that was only in the meantime.

A characteristic episode took place on the afternoon of

June 28th. In the city hospital, most of whose staff were Jews, a messenger suddenly arrived from the Kommandant: they needed an interpreter who knew German and Russian. Dr. Ashkenazi, a surgeon from Lodz, volunteered. They took him to the camp where the Soviet tankists were interned. A German officer asked a Russian captain:

"You knew that you were in a hopeless situation—why did you fight so hard that night?"

Without a moment's hesitation the Russian officer replied: "As an officer yourself, you shouldn't even ask that kind of question."

Discomfited by this dignified response, the German grew red in the face and tried to extricate himself from the situation. "Don't you know that Stalin ran away from Moscow? Soon we'll take Moscow too."

The Soviet commander again replied bluntly: "Time will tell. We can retreat another thousand kilometers and you'll still be fighting us. When he was lured by Kutuzov all the way to Moscow, Napoleon soon realized that the Russian border is on the Kamchatka."

With a curt nod the German officer ordered him to rejoin the other prisoners.

The Polish Police

On June 23rd, having decided they must retreat from Slonim, the Soviets emptied the local jail. Among the prisoners released was Jan Chmeliewski of the Polish secret police, from whom the Soviets had obtained details about his anti-Communist work. On the recommendation of local Poles, the German Ostkommandant "anointed" this tried-and-true wolf as Chief of Police for Slonim and environs. This honor of working for the Germans was awarded to him mainly for his knowledge of the Slonim population and for his shrewdness in fighting the Byelorussian Jewish Communists.

In his new position he surrounded himself with a loyal retinue of well qualified murderers, cut-throats and hoodlums "of the higher classes," plus several former Russian White Guardists who had sniffed the wind and realized that the swastika now had need of their experience and their services.

The new police headquarters was in the former Hotel Krakowsky on Schloss Street. Chmeliewski (now Schwartz) had picked up the trail of Shiel Fisher, a well known Jewish Communist in the city. One day he caught up with him on the street and "interrogated" him as they walked. Was Fisher still working for the Party, what were the comrades of MOFR doing, etc. (MOFR is an acronym of "Organization to Help International Revolutionaries.")

Shiel, one of the "Old Guard" of the Jewish Communists, had
had many run-ins with this police informer before, so he knew only
too well that he was about to be arrested. He answered Schwartz's
questions bitingly:

"You and your gang are in for a big disappointment. Just because
the Germans are fighting Communism, as you did, doesn't mean
they are going to spare the Poles. As soon as they finish with the
Jews, they'll start on you."

Shiel's blunt reply struck home. Chmeliewski-Schwartz grabbed
him with both hands and signalled for help. Two Polish cops came
running up, dragged Shiel to the police station and beat him unmercifully. The following morning the "Chief of Police"—sitting
beneath a portrait of Der Fuehrer—interrogated him again. Shiel's
only reply was that it was unseemly for such a Polish patriot as
Chmeliewski to do the dirty work for an enemy that had occupied
Poland. Shiel could see that his words had hit the target, at least
with the other "bloodhounds" who were in the room. Trying to
save the situation, Schwartz accused Shiel of being a "dangerous
Bolshevik" and shouted at the top of his voice:

"I'm not afraid of you Jew-Communists, so I'll let you off now—
but we'll meet again!"

Shiel Fisher, his body full of bruises, walked out of the hotel
under his own power.

Schwartz's abilities were so useful to the German authorities
that they sent him to Berlin for special training, from which he
returned a full-fledged Nazi and was officially named Chief of the
Slonim police, many of whom were Byelorussians.

Chmeliewski, however, was nothing if not shrewd. He always
managed to know which way the political winds were blowing and
acted accordingly. He soon realized that the fanatic with the little
moustache would never defeat the Soviet Union. He also understood what the significance was of a Polish Division fighting alongside the Red Army. So at the end of 1943 he and several of his
trusted lieutenants began planning a way to save their own skins.
Through peasant activists they sent several notes to the partisans

in which Chmeliewski represented himself as a Polish engineer named Borkowski who had organized a Polish partisan "army" and that they wished to join forces with "the forest." Having cleaned all the former Communists out of Slonim and the surrounding villages, he was certain that no one would recognize him and that everything would go smoothly.

In the forest, however, they arranged for a meeting with "Borkowski" to which he was also supposed to bring weapons. The correspondence with "Borkowski" was conducted by the Byelorussian Communist Kavalievski, but neither of the two men knew each other. When Chmeliewski met with Kavalievski's people, they immediately recognized him and that's how they greeted him: "Good morning, Panye Chmeliewski!" And they very quickly settled accounts with him.

Anti-Jewish Decrees

———————•———————

Through the raging waves that inundated Slonim, there soon surfaced an *Ostkommandant* who moved into Rutkowski's building. Almost immediately the priest from Zamoshche was at his side, along with local Poles who, in September 1939, had swallowed the bitter pill of having their independence taken from them. With the Soviet defeat came the hope of regaining some of their power, even if it meant helping the Germans subjugate Poland. Out of these power-hungry Poles a sort of fictitious city council was formed, as well as a police force. They also made a gesture toward the Jews by inviting Hertz Itzkowitz, an attorney, and Moshe Jaki-mowsky, a former merchant, to join the council.

Despite the fact that the Germans and the Poles had been blood enemies "from time immemorial," there now arose between them a mutual understanding, a brotherhood of murderers who got drunk together and "sang together" on the basis of anti-Semitism and anti-Communism, a traitorous coupling of the Hitler sawstika and the white Polish eagle.

Imitating the Poles, a Jewish "initiating group"—Wolfe Berman, Zalman Ivansky and Moshe Jakimowsky—set up a Jewish As-sistance Committee, a *kehillah*-type organization that took over the empty building that had formerly belonged to the manufacturer

38

Jezersky on Bernardino Street. The Soviets had deported Jezersky
and his family to Siberia.

In accordance with Goebbel's infamous Nuremberg laws, a rain
of brutal decrees descended upon the Jews and darkened their
existence. Jews are forbidden to walk on the sidewalk—and when
they walk on the street, it must be only singly. Groups of Jews
going to work must be accompanied by a foreman. Jews are forbidden to appear in the marketplace, either to buy or to sell. Jews
are forbidden to enter municipal offices. Jews are forbidden to
smoke in public. Jews are forbidden to drive wagons. A Jew coming
face to face with a German officer on the street must remove his
hat. Then they forbade Jews to take off their hats to German
officers—they must do so only in the case of German civilians.
Jews who violated this confusing order were beaten.

Everywhere the familiar notice appeared: FOR GERMANS ONLY.
FOR ARYANS ONLY. The sign on Julian's Cinema said FOR GERMANS
ONLY. Certain barbershops said FOR GERMANS ONLY. All hospitals
now were FOR ARYANS ONLY. But almost all the doctors in the
hospitals were Jews.

The Jews in Slonim were particularly distressed by the decree
ordering them to wear the yellow patch on their chest and on their
back. With their usual precision, the Germans specificed the size
of the patch and how it must be sewn onto the clothing. Jewish
backs had known this shame in the Roman ghetto of the 15th century. The Nazis only emulated the Roman satraps.

Because the barbering trade had been in Jewish hands for generations, and the Hitlerites would therefore have to lay bare their
swinish throats to Jewish razors, they ordered the Jewish barbers to
teach their trade to "pure Aryans."

The purpose of all these decrees was to demean the Jews, make
them feel they had no right to live, to dehumanize them, so that it
would be easier to destroy them. They were intended to create a
chasm between Jews and "Aryans," to place Jews outside the law,
to make them easy prey to the bully and the cut-throat.

There were also general orders issued to the entire population,

Jews and non-Jews alike: radios must be turned in to the authorities, all marriages performed under Soviet law were annulled and had to be performed all over again by priest or rabbi. In the brief period of Soviet rule, the majority of Jews had become acclimated to the Soviet atmosphere, in which they had equal civil rights, something they had not achieved during the 21 years of the Polish fascist regime. The "ethnic Poles" and the wealthier farmers in the Byelorussian villages had therefore looked enviously upon the Jews as more privileged citizens. Public displays of anti-Semitism had been strictly forbidden, so the Jew-hatred went underground. Now, with the Nazis in control, many of the Gentile hoodlums freely washed their hands in Jewish blood. Poles with whom Jews had lived on friendly terms for years now took off their masks and became partners with the Nazis in their dirty work.

In order to make it easier to destroy the 25,000 Jews of Slonim, the Germans began concentrating them in one compact mass, expelling them from streets on the outskirts of the city, which were populated mostly by non-Jews, and forcing them into the neighborhoods along the riverbank. Jews who owned workshops and businesses that were important to the Germans were, for the time being, not touched.

Meanwhile, Schwartz and his minions had a field day. The Jewish cemetery was "busy" day and night. Graves were being dug constantly. The police would merely drive their victims to the edge of the grave and shoot them. Especially "active" was a young Pole from Albertin named Kishko, who was a fanatical "sharpshooter," particularly if his targets were Jews, Red Army men or "rebellious" Byelorussians.

These "watchdogs" were busy sniffing out left-wingers, radical intellectuals, people "from the east" who had not managed to escape, Jews who had worked for the Soviets as managers of small enterprises, artels, etc. In many instances, under cover of their witch-hunt, the police took advantage of the situation to settle personal scores. They had a blacklist of Jewish attorneys, Jewish teachers, Jewish intellectuals. Prominent on that list were Dr. Kowarski, a beloved pediatrician, and Leybl Bliacher, with whom Chmeliewski had a personal grudge to settle for his testimony to the N.K.V.D. When they came for him, Bliacher resisted the police with an ax, but they were all carrying guns. They locked him up and Schwartz himself "interrogated" him, then shot him—along with Dr. Grodzenski—at the edge of a grave in the Jewish cemetery.

Itche Jaffe, a Communist, had been hiding in Ruzany Street in the home of his wife's parents. The police, not finding him there, took his youngest brother, Israel, held him prisoner for a while, then led him out to the cemetery in one of the groups to be shot. Paula Zirinsky (Dr. Zirinsky's daughter), was known among the young people of Slonim for her beauty, her unpretentiousness and her talent as a ballet dancer. During the Soviet period she had often danced at the municipal theater. The police arrested her and her father and dragged them along Panesve Street to the outskirts of town. Along the entire way Paula called out anti-fascist slogans to the people on the street. Her captors tortured her in the presence of her father and, unable to witness her agony any longer, Dr. Zirinsky took his own life.

In those tense, nerve-wracking days a bizarre episode took place that almost cost 200 Jewish lives:

Two German soldiers suddenly "disappeared." After a 24-hour search that failed to turn them up, the occupation authorities accused the Jews of having murdered the two missing men and held the Jews collectively responsible for the "crime." The penalty: for each German soldier a hundred Jews would have to pay with their lives. On the third day, from eleven in the morning until evening, the fascists rounded up the required 200 Jews and locked them up in the Polish Teachers Seminary on Skrobive Street. The Jewish population was overwhelmed by helplessness and despair. The blade lay on 200 young Jewish throats and only a miracle could save them.

The prisoners were being herded out to the cemetery under a hail of blows and insults. But just at that moment, from a Polish house on Ruzany Street, the two drunken "heroes" suddenly emerged in the company of two prostitutes who were just as drunk. After a few unspoken signals between the two "pure Aryans" and their officers, a new volley of blows rained down upon the 200 captives, but this time they were permitted to "escape."

Registration of the "Easterners"

During the year and a half of Soviet power, many Communist Party people were sent from Minsk to Slonim to manage the various branches of political, economic and cultural life in the city. Simultaneously, leading cadres from the local population were also being trained. In Slonim they were called "the Vostotchniks" (Easterners). When the Soviets retreated from Western Byelorussia, the top officials went with them, using all kinds of government transport, or they simply fled on foot. Many, however, fell into German hands, especially members of their families.

From the beginning, the new German authorities tried to track them down. They captured a few "Easterners" in the Polish high school. A German with a goatee (his name was Mezner) talked to them in Russian, calling upon them to fight against "the Jews and Commissars." "We must free the world of the Jew-Communist yoke!" he bellowed.

Knowing that not all the "Easterners" had been caught, he registered the captives, interrogated them for a little while and then released some of them. Shortly afterward, he freed the rest of them. With this cunning approach he concealed his criminal intentions and won their trust, so that a few days later he was able to call them in again "for a talk and re-registration." Several hundred "Easterners" showed up . . . but none of them were ever seen again.

Bloody Thursday

Thursday, July 17, eight o'clock in the morning, the 24th day since the Soviet retreat from Slonim. The German jackal-howl *"Raus! Raus!"* echoes in the streets as Jews are brutally herded toward the municipal theater with their hands in the air. Like messengers of the devil, the police with death's-heads on their helmets chase Jewish men from their homes—only middle-age men—to the accompaniment of blows and insults. Group after group is driven toward the theater. For what purpose? "To work." Proof? They are taking only able-bodied men. First they ordered the men "to stand up against the wall," then they lined them up and marched them to the theater building. The day is suffocatingly hot. Blood and sweat mingle freely.

On Breger Street a German with the face of a bulldog is having a good time. With many Gentiles looking on, he commands the Jews to dance. *"Tanzen sie, verfluchte Juden!"* Then he orders them to sing, as the Gentiles standing around keep time with their hands—to show that they are on the side of the bulldog. Observing that the crowd likes this game, the bulldog orders the Jews to jump over sticks. What choice do they have?

Beaten, dirty, their clothes torn, the victims were driven into the theater yard, where bullies in uniform closely inspected their

45

pockets and tossed everything into a sack. Soviet and German money went into separate sacks. Valuables into a third sack. Soviet identity cards were torn up on the spot. After this robbery, they ordered each man to state his profession. This was supposed to be further "proof" that the Jews were being rounded up for work. When most of them answered that they were workers, the "interrogators" were beside themselves. "Where is the Jewish bourgeoisie?" It goes without saying that this entire procedure was punctuated by punches, blows with rifle butts and billyjacks.

As they were cleaning out Itche Michelewicz's pockets he noticed that one of the soldiers seemed more "humane" than the others; as he surrendered his 70 rubles, the German let him pass without hitting him. The head of the squad, however, noticed this "violation of the rules." His face growing redder by the second, he barked: "You don't like this? You must be one of them! We can give you the same treatment as we give the stinking Jews!" The "humane" inspector quickly corrected himself as he beat the shoemaker Vengrovski with such enthusiasm that he fell to the ground unconscious.

The news of this "episode" reached Rabbi Yehuda Leyb Fein, who immediately ran to the place, naively believing that he could influence the murderers and protect his "flock." The German guards, apparently affected by his saintly face, stopped him and advised him to go home, but the rabbi insisted on speaking with the "head man." Again they advised him to go home, unless he wished to join his flock in the yard. "If necessary, I'll go where my people are!" the rabbi protested.

The guards took him into headquarters and reported what he had said. The bulldog, drunk on whiskey and Jewish blood, scowled at this white-haired rabbit who had walked right into his paws. Before Rabbi Fein could say a word he grabbed his beautiful white beard.

"You have my permission! Go where your people are!" And with a few slashes of his dagger he cut off the old man's beard and threw it to the crowd with a gesture of disgust. He then tore off the rabbi's hat and with a wave of his hand ordered his "assistants" to welcome the holy man with their truncheons.

As the Jewish prisoners witnessed this degradation of the saintly rabbi they felt as if they themselves were being beaten. To ease his shame, Zerach Krupenia, a grain merchant from Lower Skrobive Street, put his own hat on the rabbi's head.

By mid-day the sun was beating down like hot metal and the Germans themselves were growing weary of this game. Krupenia, quickly sizing up the situation, proposed to the Germans that he could provide them with cold drinks. They realized that this was a "useful Jew." Under armed guard, Krupenia ran back and forth with the cold drinks as 1400 Jews, hungry and thirsty, pressed together so tightly they could hardly move, looked on. Finally the Germans divided them into groups of 21 and 30 and ordered them to sit down on the ground and sing Yiddish songs while they waited for the trucks that would take them "out to work . . ."

With the help of Zerach Krupenia and others, the rabbi climbed up on one of the trucks. Along the entire route he comforted and encouraged his flock, reminding them that from earliest times Jews have been tortured and burned for their Torah. His example raised the spirits of the men. After the crowded, suffocating yard, the green fields and the fresh air eased the pain a little.

The truck passed the Zamosche Lake. Beyond the village of Petralevici the "Red Tavern" appeared against the green wall of the forest. On a narrow road deeper into the woods, the trucks stopped. A slaughter-house. Five newly dug ditches were already piled high with the bodies of hundreds of Jews.

The rabbi stepped forward, spoke to his group: "We are about to fulfill the sacred commandment of *kiddush ha-shem*. We are living in Moshiach's time, which goes hand-in-hand with the most terrible suffering and bloodshed . . ."

Zerach Krupenia, however, had decided that for him it was too soon to fulfill that commandment. At an opportune moment he dove into the bushes, pursued by guards who emptied their weapons in his direction. But they missed. He was the only one to escape . . .

The guards ordered the Jews to undress. A burst of machine-gun fire put an end to the beating of thirty Jewish hearts.

Yehuda Leyb Fein, the last rabbi of Slonim, died in that first massacre. He had become rabbi in Slonim after the death of Rabbi Mordkhele Oshmener.

After four that afternoon no more trucks came to the yard. The remaining 200 Jews there now knew that they would never be "taken out to work." Instead, about fifty hoodlums, the cream of the Slonim underworld, showed up with appropriate weapons. Soon the air was filled with the choicest epithets in the Polish anti-Semitic lexicon. Vodka bottles passed from hand to hand. Suddenly the narrow door into the marketplace opened. On the other side of the door stood police with two snarling dogs. The armed hoodlums drove the 200 Jews through the door, where a fresh ditch had been dug. A mound of human bodies quickly filled it up—and then the dogs were let loose. The yells of the gangsters, the barking of the dogs, the screams of the dying, all echoed eerily through the marketplace like the caterwauling of demented witches.

From a distance the families of the victims watched as a few of the men who had "merely" been wounded clawed their way out of the ditch and ran the entire length of the marketplace under a hail of bullets. For days afterward these survivors lay in their beds with broken limbs and battered bodies.

Manya Ackerman, noticing that they had taken away her brother, made a note of the number on the truck. When it returned in a half-hour, she realized that they were not taking the men very far. Removing the patch from her clothing she went off in the direction of the "Red Tavern." Soon she heard the rattling of machine-guns. A few minutes later the shooting stopped and she noticed an empty truck speeding back toward the city. Soon afterward a truck filled with Jews passed her on the way into the forest and again came the dread sound of machine-guns.

The next morning several of the women went back to the same place. Some peasants showed them the direction from which they had heard terrible screams the day before. The closer the women came to the place of horror the more signs they saw of what had happened. And then they saw the pits—five ditches, each 50 meters long, filled with bodies. Hundreds of yellow patches on the ground told their own story—the murderers had taken the victims' clothing for themselves.

The first massacre had been organized with military precision. In an 8-hour work-day the German murder-squads had killed 1200 Jews. Up until then most of Slonim's Jews had lived with an illusory optimism: "They just won't shoot innocent people. Anyone can see they are only rounding up men for work." Now they began to think more realistically, to understand the consequences of Hitler's "race philosophy." After this massacre Jewish men no longer appeared in the streets. The idea of active resistance began to mature.

(The Germans who perpetrated the slaughter were from Einsatz-gruppe B, a special operations commando of S.S.-men, police and S.D. Following behind the front-line army, their job was to clear the newly occupied hinterland of Jews and other Soviet citizens.

The Judenrat and
The Regional Kommissariat

With the smell of the blood of the 1200 slaughtered Jews still in the air, the Ostkommandant ordered the leaders of the Jewish community to send him a 15-man delegation from which he would choose a Judenrat (Jewish Council). It was no easy task, because the Soviet government had previously deported to Siberia many Jewish leaders in Slonim, including Dr. Shmuel Weiss, Dr. Isaac Efros, Deputy Mayor Boris Piasecki, Itche Sweticki, Jezerski, Gurvich and Dapkowski.

At a meeting in Jezerski's empty house, some 20 elderly Jews discussed the problem for several hours. They did not even know what the functions of the Judenrat would be. The concept was familiar to them only from the horror-stories they had heard from Jewish refugees from Poland. For some of them the heavy responsibility of being a Judenrat member was a matter of fate or fear. Some withdrew from the task quietly and modestly. Others, whose Jewish soul overcame all their hesitation and placed the welfare of the Jewish community above all else, agreed to become part of the leadership upon whom the burden would be placed.

The next morning the following men stood in a semi-circle in the office of the chief German authority, which was located in Rut-

kowski's building: Wolfe Berman, Jacob Goldfarb, Zalman Ivi-
ansky, Gershon Berenstein, Jacob Luboschitz, Moshe Zackheim,
Moshe Jakimovski, Trachtenberg, Joseph Mordecai Ripp, Karpl
Ripp, Chomak, Noah Mitz, Paius, Jacob Rabinowicz.

With a revolver strapped to his right hip and a riding-crop in his
hand, he stared at his victims without saying a word. Diabolically
he "inspected" each man separately and with his crop and the
command *"Raus!"* he eliminated Ivianski, Berenstein and Luboschitz. With the same crop he poked the 80-year-old Berman in the
chest and announced in a tone saturated with hatred:

"Du virst der Elterste zein!"

For the "chosen" Judenrat it immediately became clear that the
relationship of the Judenrat to this beast would be as between a
sheep and a tiger. Having no alternative but to agree, they left the
Ostkommandant's office dejected and without hope.

Wolfe Berman was well known in the city as a devoted Jewish
leader. Before the war he was Director of the Merchants Bank and
gabbai of the Zionist synagogue. His building on Student Street
had served for years as a community center. Now, blind fate had
chosen him to defend his long-suffering people. Berman and the
other Judenrat members would have to maneuver uneasily between
Jewish troubles, on one side, and a death-dealing brutality on
the other.

The Judenrat now became the target at which the Kommandant
kept up a relentless fire. He was constantly inventing new ways to
put an end to the "Jewish plague in Slonim." His first shot was
designed to create an ever-ready pool of Jewish slave labor.

Gershon Quint, another well known public figure, was pressed
into service with the "Labor Office." The Judenrat was ordered to
create its own *Ordnungsdienst,* a kind of para-police armed with
rubber truncheons. Misha Lotz, who was not ill-suited to the work,
was appointed Commander of this police force. His deputy was
Max Rabinowicz, a bookkeeper. The force consisted of 30 men,
most of them recent refugees from Poland.

The first "good" Germans, who warned the Jews that their

"benevolence" would cease the moment the "Brownshirts" arrived, were telling the truth. When the Brownshirts appeared in Slonim in the latter half of July the Jews immediately felt their dark presence.

The Regional Kommissariat moved into "Rabmil's Palace" on Schloss Street. "Rabmil" was a firm of three lumber merchants— the two Rabinowicz brothers and Miłowski. The S.D. (Security Services) occupied Quint's two-story building on Ulan Street, across from the Polish high school. The police headquarters was in the home of the Shabbatai family of Jewish musicians across from Rabmil's. The Gestapo settled on Bridge Street in the home of Dr. Kremien.

The chief hangman, Regional Kommissar Gerhardt (Gerth) Erren, was in no hurry to move into Rabmil's Palace himself. He had a number of assistants working for him, notably the Junker Dietrich Hick, "Section Leader for Jewish Affairs," who had come to Slonim from Pomerania. Then there was the translator, Alfred Mezner. Both of these Nazis loved to get drunk on Jewish blood. Their carefully elegant appearance was a cover for sadism, cunning brutality, murderous coldbloodedness and wanton deceit. What they said, they didn't mean; what they meant, nobody knew. The Jews of Slonim shunned them like the plague. Their 18-month reign in Slonim is one long, horrendous account of Jewish degradation, of robbery, murder, torture, pogroms, of Jewish bloodbaths and oceans of tears.

Mezner, who was born in Kiev in 1895, knew Russian very well. Despite the fact that he had worked in Berlin for a Jew and himself had a half-Jewish wife and a son named Wolfe, his hatred of Jews was boundless.

In order to "get to the insides" of the 24,000 Jews in Slonim, the German leeches considered it extremely important to count the Jews and divide them into three categories. The Judenrat stalled for as long as they could before giving Hick the information he wanted. The first category consisted of Judenrat employees, the Jewish Police, the Jewish medical workers and all the handicraftsmen. The second category consisted of all the laborers; the third category were the elderly, the sick, the invalids, women unable to work, and a certain number of people with a higher education. To each of these categories Hick distributed different color "passes." By this means the Jews were divided into "useful, less useful and useless," which was tantamount to: those who were to remain alive temporarily and those who would be killed at the earliest opportunity.

A "good pass" immediately became a priceless item, a means to work and life. The passes, about the size of a postcard, were printed on postcard stock and contained the insignia of the Regional Kommissariat and the name of the "lucky" passholder and his family. It was signed by Kommissar Erren.

All this "legislation" made it quite plain that the Jews were now outside the protection of the law.

Various workshops were set up to employ the best craftsmen in the city. The manual laborers were put to work, for example, in the stone quarry in the village of Derewianczycy where they pushed and pulled heavy wheelbarrows loaded with rocks, or as loaders at the railroad station, or in the sawmills hauling wet pine-trees from the river.

For this kind of labor the groups would gather early in the morning outside the Judenrat office and the Jewish police would assign them to barracks. From the barracks, trucks would take them to various work-sites. The group leaders were usually Shimek Rachmielewicz, Judkowski, Issa Kolker, Sholem Glatzer, and even Lotz himself. In the evening the workers would be brought back to their homes.

These defenseless slave laborers were beaten continually with blackjacks and clubs, kicked and cursed. In order to strike terror in the hearts of the *zhids* the brutal guards would often shoot over the heads of the Jews as if it were a great sport. They would play this game precisely at the moment when their victims were pulling a heavy load, or dragging logs up a hill, or digging a roadway. Every guard had the "right" to beat a Jew to death, with or without a "reason." In this manner Israel Lichtenheim, foreman of a group of Jewish workers, was shot to death in the winter of 1942 in the village of Shilovici. Most of the guards there were Poles from Posen, in German uniforms.

The work-day was eight hours, with an hour for "lunch," which consisted of 250 grams of bread mixed with potatoes or beans. There were many men who were not accustomed to such hard physical labor and who had stocked up a food reserve. They would "hire" others in their place, men who were not working that day and who needed the extra slice of bread for their children. Mostly they were from among the refugees, who were more needy than the Slonimer. The Judenrat was not opposed to this trading of work-days.

More than a hundred Jews worked under easier conditions in the military camp across the railroad station. This work consisted of cleaning and repairing captured Russian weapons.

Kommandant Hick had to be very careful how he carried out his policy of making Slonim *Judenrein.* He had to do whatever possible to make life appear "normal," but the reality of the situation was that without the Jews he could not do it. With Jews more than 85% of the Slonim handiicraftsmen, there could be no talk of a functioning "Aryan" handicrafts industry. Meanwhile he could only dream about replacing the Jews with Byelorussians and Poles. He therefore expanded the existing workshops and created something similar to the Soviet artels, but under military supervision. And in order to enable the Slonim "Aryans" to take over, he organized trade schools for them where Jewish master craftsmen were forced to teach their skills to peasant apprentices.

Meanwhile, the only commerce going on was the provision of food stores and restaurants with food products for the Wehrmacht and for German employees. Bakeries and butcher-shops were turned over to private "Aryans." The tanneries, the sawmills and similar enterprises still functioned, but nowhere near their former capacity.

The Nazi authorities kept assuring the public that the 1200 Jews had not been killed but sent out in a labor transport. Some Jews even believed this. People did not want to admit even to themselves that such barbarity was possible. And the Germans let loose such a mighty stream of deceit and falsehood that their evidence was almost convincing. Why would they slaughter 1200 ablebodied men when they needed their labor? And hadn't they permitted a member of the Judenrat (Paius) to open a little textile mill where some Jewish workers were employed?

And as things quieted down and the German brutalities slackened off, the entrepreneurial spirit began to hope again, because after all, people must earn a living. It escaped their notice that a storm-cloud was suspended over their heads on spider-webs. Some people began repairing the roofs on their burned out houses. How long could they live under the open sky? The blacksmith Dubranski on Skrobive Street even rebuilt his smithy.

The Judenrat meanwhile had to worry about food and housing for the thousands of poor and hungry Jews and provide them at least with minimal sustenance.

When all the dispensaries and hospitals in Slonim were marked "For Aryans Only" the question of a Jewish hospital became urgent. It was a difficult problem for the newly appointed Judenrat. One day in August they invited Dr. Noah Kaplinsky to a meeting, where a decision was made to open a hospital and a dispensary. The hospital was to be located in the home of the baker Pintchuk on Skrobive Street and Michalowski Lane, the dispensary in the Jewish school on Opera Street. Head of the hospital was Dr. Gavarin. The dispensary manager was Dr. Blumovich of Lomze.

In order to equip both these institutions the Judenrat appealed to the Jewish population to give whatever it could. The response was generous and immediate. People brought beds, cots, mattresses, pillows, underclothing, chairs, curtains, dishes, utensils. The hospital and the dispensary began functioning and became a heart-warming meeting-place for Jewish medical personnel.

Around this time the German authorities issued a new decree: anyone with large food reserves must turn them over to the Judenrat. The Germans were anxious to set a quick example. They made sudden raids on Jewish homes and confiscated food supplies that exceeded the prescribed norms. The owners of these "illegal" provisions were shot.

Even this did not satisfy the Germans. The Regional Kommissariat hatched a brand new kind of intimidation: the Jews had to pay a tribute of two million rubles. This demand was so unexpected that the Judenrat was bewildered and didn't know what to do. First they tried the time-tested policy of *shtadlanut* and even made an attempt to bribe certain high-placed Germans to reduce the demand, but Kommandant Hick only smiled cynically and "explained" that he was only asking for the return of German possessions that were now temporarily in the hands of the Jews. As for "Jewish possessions," he told the Judenrat, no such thing existed any more.

Thus the Judenrat had to resort to a collection of money from the already impoverished Jewish population. A tax was placed upon every Jewish family in accordance with their ability to pay and the tribute was delivered to the blood-suckers within the allotted time. The Judenrat's hope that with this two million rubles they had satisfied the German greed was of course completely unfounded. Now that they had the money, the German satraps had to destroy the evidence that they had ever collected it.

One Friday evening all the Judenrat members and their families were invited to Hick's home. Not knowing his murderous intentions, they marched there in a kind of procession and we don't know exactly what happened there, because none of them ever returned . . .

The orphaned Jewish community of Slonim was shaken to its depths by this act of wanton banditry. It proved unmistakably that to be a member of the Judenrat was to live under a sentence of death.

Without even a lying "explanation" of what had happened to the first Judenrat, Hick ordered the creation of a second one. But who would now "volunteer" for that position?

Still, there were a few courageous souls who did. Hanaan Steinberg was the first to come forward. "I am an old man," he said, "and I don't have too much to lose." Following his example, a few others also volunteered: Gershon Berenstein, Jacob Lubowicz, Chaim Ruzhanski and Leon Smolinski (a refugee from Suwalki).

Camps for Soviet Prisoners of War

All during this time there were still two camps for Soviet war prisoners—one in the Elementary School on Skrobive Street, the other (on the same street) in the factory buildings near the highway bridge. The prisoners there were constantly subjected to all sorts of nightmarish tortures. They got very little to eat. Colds, fever, lice, filth, shootings, were their everyday fare.

The heart-rending cries from those camps, which could be heard in the surrounding neighborhood, depressed the spirits of the population, especially the Jews, who saw these prisoners as people who were even more unfortunate than they. Every morning the Germans would march the Jewish slave-laborers from their barracks past the barbed wire fence of the camp near the bridge. And every day hundreds of begging hands would be waiting for them; hundreds of pairs of eyes would be pleading with these Jews who themselves had been condemned to death by the same jailers. At the risk of their own lives these Jews would toss their last bits of food over the barbed wire and the skeletons on the other side would fall upon the crumbs like a flock of birds.

As a result of starvation and the unhygienic living-conditions, an epidemic of stomach-typhus raged throughout these camps. The prisoners died like flies. Instead of trying to cure the sick, the Nazis merely waited, and every day shot scores of infected Red Army men.

There were a small number of Jews also working in the camp, and several of them caught the disease. In the Jewish quarter it was well known that anyone infected with a contagious disease would be shot by the Germans. On Breger Street, Moshke Zinkin's house fell victim to the disease. His Jewish neighbors immediately "quaranteened" the house until the people inside it recovered . . .

Stars of David
and Yellow Patches

———————•———————

In accordance with the "legislation" of the German authorities, any non-Jew outside the city who wanted a Jew to work for him had to obtain a special permit from the Judenrat Labor Office. Thus, a Polish peasant from the village of Uginowici (on Ruzany Road), who needed a carpenter, hired Shiel Fisher to work for him. They went to see Quint, who gave them the permit. The Pole turned out to be a sympathetic person and Shiel worked for him under very good conditions.

A month passed and Shiel suddenly realized that his own work-pass had expired. He decided to go into town to get an extension on his pass and to learn what was going on in Slonim. It was a very risky business, however. The Pole offered to do it for him, since he could move about more freely, but Shiel had made up his mind to go himself.

It was a mistake. Shiel did not know that new regulations had been issued, including one that ordered Jews to wear yellow Stars of David (instead of plain patches) and that they had to be affixed to the left side of the body.

When he reached the cemetery at the city limits he put the yellow patch on his coat, walked down the hill and was immediately apprehended by the Polish policeman Tchernichowsky, who stared at him as if this Jew had lost his mind. He marched Shiel straight to the Ostkommandant's headquarters, where the Germans punished him on two counts: 25 blows with a rubber truncheon for not wearing the Star of David and 25 blows for not having a "legal" work-pass . . .

First Steps of the Partisans

The first random killings of Jews, the continual decrees which placed Jews outside the law and violated their national honor, aroused feelings of revenge against the brutal occupying power. Particularly oppressive was the first mass slaughter of 1200 men. This portent of total Jewish destruction chilled the blood of the surviving Jews in Slonim.

Hundreds of young people, of all political convictions, were moved by this reality to begin a feverish search for a way out, for a way to do something practical. Whenever people met, the same question would soon rise to the surface: "What is to be done?" There was almost no one who doubted the urgency of doing *something*. They also felt intuitively that they were not alone. They sensed the presence of partisans in the forest. There was also hopeful news from the battlefronts. Still lacking, however, was a force that could organize and move their search onto the path of effective resistance.

One thing was clear to everyone: without weapons there could be no resistance. There were isolated individuals who had armed themselves for defense, but that was not the way out. There were a few dozen hardened World War I veterans who had returned in the wake of the unsuccessful evacuation carried out by the retreating Red Army. From practical experience in World War I and the Russian civil war they knew that the first step was to set up a disciplined underground leadership capable of organizing a mass collection of weapons.

In the days of the first massacre, Anshl Delyaticki returned to Slonim and immediately began making plans to create such a movement. Among the many trade union activists from the "Polish period" then in the city were Anshl, Shiel Fisher, Shlomo-Chaim Alpert, Moshe Ogushevitch, Pesach Alpert, David Epstein and Yankel Pripstein.

Anshl was short and had a bit of a hunchback, with the broad shoulders and calloused hands of a cabinet-maker. Born in Warsaw, he had lived and worked in Slonim. When he came back to the city he did not report to work for the Germans, as all the others had done. For a few weeks he stayed home and studied the new situation that had been created by the occupation. During that time the old Byelorussian Bogdanchuk, from the village of Czemeri, came to visit him. He told Anshl that there were partisans in the forest from routed Soviet army units, that they had been encircled by German troops and were now battling to avoid being taken prisoner. So far, however, they were keeping their distance from the local population.

Bogdanchuk gave Anshl a realistic assessment of the situation and cautioned him: "It is possible to organize Jewish partisan groups in the city, but long before that is done and long before they can have any effect, the Germans will annihilate most of the Jews. The most you'll be able to do is lead small groups of fighters into the forest." That was the grim reality.

During the few weeks he was at home Anshl had another visitor—Moshe Byer. Byer told him that there was a German camp in the city where Jewish workers were cleaning captured Soviet weapons (Beuten camp). Excited by this news, Anshl decided on the spot that his place was there. He shared his feelings with Byer. Byer spoke with Sgt. Braun, head of the camp, who hired Anshl on as an upholsterer. Thus Anshl learned that it was possible to work *against* the Germans while working *for* them, but you had to be skilled at that if you wanted to stay alive.

Before long he was known among the Germans in the camp as a first-rate upholsterer and a "good" worker, which enabled him to move about the camp and observe where things were stored. The large number and variety of weapons intoxicated him. His head filled up with plans to "liberate" these weapons for future Jewish partisans.

Life in this camp was not too difficult. The Judenrat provided 400 grams of bread a day for each man and there was also a soup kitchen there. After the day's work you could go home to sleep. In addition to all these "benefits" the Germans even gave out special passes that entitled the bearer to live.

At lunch-time one day, sitting near a group of young fellows, Anshl caught snatches of conversation about "four rifles that were going out today." He got up and sat down next to the gossipers, among whom were Avreml Bubliatsky, Zyama Shusterovich, Itche Grachuk, Joseph Shuchatovich and Nonye Zirinski. Anshl informed them quietly but sternly that their loud talk could be overheard. The young folks objected naively that "there were only Jews here, so there was no one to be afraid of."

Anshl measured them with an icy, penetrating gaze and replied: "Jews come in all sizes and varieties."

The look in his eye dampened their lighthearted mood, but their unspoken agreement with what he was saying testified that they had recognized him as a leader. They immediately grew more serious about the necessity for conspiratorial behavior. He proposed that they meet with him after work in the attic of the carpenter shop.

Later the excited bunch of young men stole cautiously up the steps leading to the attic, careful that no strange eye (even a Jewish one) was observing them. Anshl arranged for a lookout at the attic window and the door was left ajar so they could hear an intruder's footsteps. These precautions sharpened their senses and helped to prepare the "greenhorns" for the dangerous underground work that now lay ahead of them.

In the semi-darkness they took seats on scattered blocks of wood. The air was electric with the idea of active resistance against the German murderers. In a whisper Anshl painted a picture for them of the Nazis' step-by-step annihilation of Europe's Jews. "Our duty," he pointed out, "is to organize armed groups that will join the partisans in the forest to fight our hated enemy to the death. We must be ready, should it become necessary, to go unafraid to our death, for the sake of the Jewish people." His voice rose a little through his barely open lips. "If we have to die, then let us die with weapons in hand, and make the Nazis pay a high price!

"But we are not organizing to die. We are organizing to sow death and destruction among the German cannibals. We've got to open another front against them to draw off large German forces. The only way we can do that is to turn their attention to us! In that way we'll help the Red Army in its long, hard struggle to reverse its temporary setback.

"Our first task is this: while we are still here in this camp, we've got to recruit more people into our ranks. They must be trustworthy, courageous and willing to fight. Never mind their former political affiliations. We are all Jews here—Hitler wants to kill us all. We need to set up cells of five, we've got to steal more and more weapons from Kommandant Braun. We need to learn to shoot straight. And the main thing: we've got to conduct a quiet, undramatic kind of sabotage—clean the guns, but not too thoroughly; oil them, but not too well. Here and there remove a little part—a screw, a spring. Get some water into the gunpowder. Anything to keep the weapons from working too accurately when they're in the hands of the executioners."

After this meeting, where the core of the future Jewish partisans was born, the fervent young men were further buoyed up by the idea that now they were an organized force with clearly thought out tasks and goals. Knowing Anshl from the old days, they now shook his calloused hand warmly and promised to carry out whatever orders he gave them.

"Little Anshl" was the first one to plant correctly the idea of armed resistance among the heavy-hearted young Jews. In them he saw the stuff of splendid fighters, even heroes. But they had a lot to learn. The thing that had to be done now was to weld the scattered forces into a disciplined conspiratorial undergound organization.

Anshl Delyaticki had all the requisite qualities of an organizer in these extraordinary conditions: wisdom, fearlessness, quick orientation in emergencies, a tough boldness and an endless supply of energy. At any given moment he saw clearly what had to be done. He was constantly weighing and measuring all the factors beforehand. This soon earned him the respect and trust of his men.

The very next day they began their work of collecting weapons and smuggling them out of the camp. The men had the permission of the Kommandant to take home sacks of kindling wood. Many a weapon was taken past the guards in these sacks. Smaller weapons were tied underneath their pants to their legs, or next to the body. Temporarily this "arsenal" was stored at Zyama Shusterovich's house on Michalovski Street. In a comparatively short time they smuggled out many gun parts that were later assembled into 12 rifles and 15 pistols, as well as two boxes of grenades and large quantities of cartridges.

Playing the role of loyal workers for their German masters, these new Jewish underground activists—doing conspiratorial work for the first time in their lives—quickly learned to outwit and take advantage of them.

Regional Kommissar Gerhardt Erren

Finally, on September 1, assigned by Rosenberg's staff, Regional Kommissar Gerhardt (Gerth) Erren "reported" to Slonim and took charge of his staff of mass murderers: Gunther Stelle, his personal aide and deputy; Dietrich Hick, Section Leader for Jewish Affairs; Ewald Kohler, regional inspector; Alfred Mezner, translator; Vitold Oslender, translator; Gerda Rogowski, stenotypist.

After his first inspection of the burned out city the new despot over the Slonim region concluded that the situation there was not too promising. He could not conceal his impatience with the apathy, neglect and uncleanliness, with the listless attitude and even dress of the population. Visibly agitated and upset, he spat out his opinion to his aides: *"Schmutz-schweinerei!"*

With one-third of all the buildings in the city in ruins, and with the steady stream of refugees coming from Poland, the problem of living-quarters had become catastrophic. In typical fascist manner, Erren began "Aryanizing" his "territory."

The unpromising outlook was sweetened for him by the former Director of the Soviet State Bank, who brought him a gift of 3,083,489.50 rubles. Erren happily accepted this tidy sum, and with one bank manager (the same Russian traitor), one bookkeeper, one cashier and one female janitor, he opened the Reichsbank on Bernadino Street.

Now at last the working people of Slonim understood why the Soviet bank, in the final months of the war, had not paid out wages in full, but only doled out small advances with the excuse that the bank was low in cash. Not understanding the Director's real intentions, everyone had put the blame on the Soviet government. The impoverished workers had tightened their belts and resigned themselves to waiting until the bank's cash reserves were replenished. Instead, they got Hitler, and it became obvious that Party member Niechayev, who occupied such a high position in the bank, was really a two-faced traitor who, on instructions from Berlin, had starved half the city and held on to the cash for his Nazi bosses. He didn't enjoy his reward for very long, however. In 1943 the people he had victimized settled their score with him . . .

Kommissar Erren took over Schloss Street, on which his headquarters were located, and turned it into a "retreat" for the German "community." Finding himself among hostile peoples, Erren decided that his "supermen" would be safer during their free time if they stayed closer together. Schloss Street became a place where they ate, drank, played cards and chess and listened to the radio— together. With the help of Berlin they even opened a German library for the few men who read books. Here they even held discussions on daily problems, etc. On that same street, Jewish workers built a "rest-home" for them. The construction job was headed by Wolfstein, a Jewish engineer from Lodz. For the Jewish workers, the job was a relief—no one harried them, no one beat them, and most important, they were close to home.

To help him keep the population in line, the Kommissar had to gather information concerning the peculiarities of the various ethnic groups in the region and what frictions existed among them. This was elementary tactics. First he carried out a census and came up with the following figures: Byelorussians, 165,128; Russians, 1704; Ukrainians, 501; Poles, 12,988; Jews, 14,461 (down from

25,000); Tatars, 321; others, 251. This distribution was a matter of great significance to him.

Leaving the Jews out of his calculations—since they were not going to be among the living for very much longer—he found that most of the educated class were Poles, who snatched up all the jobs in the German offices as "politically trustworthy." The Byelorussians, Ukrainians and Russians he considered potential Bolsheviks and Partisans. Only a few of them were given "employment" and even then they were always under the watchful eye and the ready fist of a German authority.

Constantly taking the Byelorussian pulse, he diagnosed that it would take many years before this lazy rabble could be retrained into diligent workers and farmers. He began their retraining with the young people.

As to the Poles, the Kommissar came to the "logical" conclusion that although they possessed a certain European intelligence, they were fanatical nationalists who were hopelessly infected with the seeds of betrayal and that they were therefore ripe for the gallows.

With typical Nazi "talent" Erren used these national antagonisms to his own purpose. Against Byelorussian Partisans he sent Poles. Against Polish rebels he sent Byelorussians. As village elders he appointed mostly Poles or younger Byelorussians.

All these Slavic groups were "apprenticed" to Jews to learn a trade or to learn the German language. The Kommissar hammered it into their heads that this was the only way they would get anything to eat. His best pupils were the Tatars. He bemoaned only that there were so few of them.

Of the four Polish doctors in the city, one was appointed Regional Physician; the others were divided among two regions. They were permitted to call upon the Jewish doctors for help only in an emergency.

The proximity of the "Third Reich" caused the Kommissar some concern—Jews frequently fled there from Slonim. The Russian political propaganda also played havoc with the Kommissar's brain.

His behavior was "modest" and foxy. As the chief architect of the carefully refined plans to make Slonim Judenrein, he directed the proceedings from behind the scenes. Giving orders to others, he stayed out of the limelight, studying the reports from his lieutenants, so that he, in turn, could report punctually to Berlin.

Pogrom in Zhireva

One day at the end of September 1941, news reached Slonim that the Jewish community in Zhireva, which had existed there for centuries, had been wiped out.

Again some Jews in Slonim refused to believe it, unable to comprehend how the Germans could have done such a thing. Unfortunately, we soon learned how they did it.

First they ordered the entire population of Zhireva to gather on the Church Square and to take with them small packages of food. This gave rise to various guesses about what was going to happen—maybe the Germans were going to resettle the population for military reasons, etc.

On the appointed day the Germans ordered the crowd to form two lines—one for citizens "of Jewish extraction," the other for Christians. Then the police made a show of taking a count of all the people in the square and writing the totals down in a book. Then they ordered the Christians to go home. It was a transparent trick to prevent Jews from going into hiding, but it worked.

The 162 Jews of Zhireva were then beaten and marched to the village of Gloiczevici. In a forest, which had formerly belonged to Count Fuslawski, the victims were ordered to undress . . . Only one family, a family of tailors, was allowed to live—temporarily.

Among the dead were Naznicki, Berniker, Jacob Kahn, Malkin, Haika Chomsky, Isur Peshkin and his wife.

From the "Third Reich"

During the first months of the occupation of Slonim, the Germans sliced off a large area of Byelorussia and annexed it to the Third Reich, which had already swallowed up all of Poland. The border of this artificially expanded Reich passed near Slonim and included Ruzany, Zelva, Jesarnice, Pruzany, Wolkowic and all the other towns and cities on that line.

Although the German tanks and the Brownshirts appeared here a little earlier than in Slonim, and although all the infamous anti-Jewish decrees were introduced, life was nonetheless a bit easier here for Jews until the winter of 1942. The Jews here were not terribly harassed, there were no random killings and no large-scale massacres. Occasionally the Germans would arrest a Jew for violating a law—like walking on the sidewalk. They did not lock the Jews up in a ghetto. The Jews moved around freely and were even able to engage in business.

Contrary to the experience in Slonim, the Jews in this new "Third Reich" were driven out of the center of towns and forced to live in the outlying areas. The Germans appointed Judenrate to act

73

as go-betweens between the Jewish community and the occupation authority.

All this was well known, so that many Jews, escaping from Slonim by various routes, settled in these areas. For many Slonimer Jews the "Third Reich" seemed like a dream, a place of refuge—until November 1942. Then the "good times" for the "Third Reich" Jews came to a tragic end.

Quint's Activities
on Behalf of
the Jews of Bitten

———————•———————

During the first week of November 1941 two gendarmes brought Gershon Quint to Bitten in an automobile. They also brought a new edict to the Judenrat there: they were to prepare, in the center of town, an eight or ten story building for a police headquarters. The building must be in good repair, it must be completely furnished, it must have a fully equipped kitchen with six female cooks. The building must be ready in ten days.

While the two gendarmes went out to explore Bitten, Quint met with the Judenrat and earnestly advised them to carry out the order precisely, because the lives of the Jews of Bitten depended on it.

On December 12, after the second massacre in Slonim, Hick "invited" the Bitten Judenrat to his office and demanded that they deliver to him, no later than the 20th, two kilos of gold, along with all the valuables that the Jews had in their possession, including manufactured goods, leather, rawhide—and 200,000 rubles. And to make sure the Jews fulfilled their "obligation," he took as hostage: Israel Judkovski, Chairman of the Judenrat, A. Karelitch and J. Rozanski. He sent Arbuz and Rabinowicz back to Bitten to collect the tribute.

Thanks to Quint's intervention, Hick freed Judkovski after three days. The other two were freed after the ransom was delivered.

What Is to Be Done?

Anshl Delyaticki's activity among the young people in the labor camp went even better than he had hoped. The militancy among the youth, regardless of previous party affiliation, was not to be denied. Every one of them was aware of the mortal danger that faced the Jewish people. In their new organization they saw an alternative to the helplessness that had existed up to now. The approaching armed struggle against the Nazis helped to dispel their previous apathy. The young people were no longer able to suppress their anger or to remain silent in face of all the decrees and killings; they thirsted for revenge.

In September, Anshl met with Shiel Fisher and confided to him that he had already organized six cells, with five people in each cell, and that these were carefully chosen, trustworthy and courageous young people ready to face whatever might come in actively resisting the oppressor. Shiel in turn, told Anshl of his work in the barracks among the young people, who were impatient to start doing something in the underground partisan movement. Anshl cautioned him to wait just a little while longer.

Around the same time, Anshl also met with Pesach Alpert, a metal worker who had been a trade union leader in Slonim. They too talked about "what must be done." Pesach told Anshl that many workers and intellectuals were in agreement on the necessity

77

for armed resistance and that they already had the beginnings of an underground organization. Anshl agreed to find a place where both groups could meet together.

Shortly afterward, Pesach arranged the meeting in the home of the brothers Avrom and Chaim Azef, old leather workers who lived in an old white frame-house at the end of Balione Street.

They took every precaution essential to an illegal meeting. The two small windows facing the canal were curtained and Avrom kept a lookout through a crack. Two of the "conspirators," disguised as lovers, "took a little walk" outside, examining all the passersby very closely before directing them into the house. Present that evening were Anshl, Pesach, Zyama Shusterovich, Braina Lunianski, her husband Shlomo-Chaim Alpert and David Epstein.

Braina stemmed from a well-to-do family of merchants in Slonim and had been a student before the war. Zyama was from a small town nearby. David, who worked in a bakery, read widely and was a powerful speaker, was unanimously elected chairman of the meeting.

The first item on the agenda was the name of the organization. Everyone at the meeting was opposed to adopting any Communist Party names. David proposed the creation of an underground, secret Jewish self-defense organization whose aim would be the defense of the ghetto against German attacks. His facial expression remained calm, but his intense eyes darted from one person to another, looking for disagreement. The others threw quizzical looks around the room, but listened to him attentively.

"We must not leave the ghetto and its Jews who are under sentence of death. We must always be with the people, defending them, and if it happens that way, die with them!"

Anshl opposed David's plan. He spoke about the senselessness of trying to defend the ghetto with a small number of untrained, poorly armed fighters, especially with a "hinterland" of three-and-a-half little streets. This could be only a heroic path to martyrdom, against an enemy that was armed to the teeth, who could even use tanks and artillery against the ghetto. The ghetto would be encircled by an iron hoop. His counter-proposal was: First we have to draw more and more people into our ranks regardless of previous political affiliation, so long as they are able to fight. We must, however, always be on guard against corrupt elements. His voice had grown louder with excitement, and Braina had to caution him that he could be heard out in the street.

Lowering his voice, Anshl continued: "We must make contact with a partisan unit as soon as possible. We must fight in the forest, where we have a chance of attacking the enemy and not always be waiting for him to attack us. The longer we wait, the fewer people we lead out of the ghetto into the forest, the weaker we get, because every day the enemy is taking people away from us who can fight." He gave examples from his "cells of five," where young people from various parties were accepting the responsibility of underground partisan work for the first time, preparing themselves for battle under partisan leadership. "In the last few months," Anshl said, wonderful young men and women have come forward who are ready to defend the honor of our people and, if necessary, to die with guns in their hands."

Thus two schools of thought emerged around these two positions. Zyama was on Anshl's side. Shlomo-Chaim was on David's side. Pesach and Braina vacillated. It was a serious controversy that gave both sides much to worry about. This first meeting disbanded with an agreement to meet again soon.

New Provocations

For about four months the Jews in their yellow patches slaved for the Germans without any mass bloodbaths, but everyone could hear the bomb ticking away.

Even after the first massacre, and after so many random killings of individuals, the large number of Jews in Slonim was still a thorn in the Regional Kommissar's eye. He kept weighing and measuring his forces against the 15,000 Jewish lives over which he had absolute power. To keep such a mass of Jews locked up in a ghetto, to house them and feed them, even on a starvation diet, was too heavy a burden for him to carry. But so long as these future corpses were still alive, he had to squeeze as much out of them as possible. The result of this new calculation was a second "assessment" of one million rubles plus five kilos of gold.

At the same time, he had to preserve the labor force necessary for his wellbeing as long as possible. So he created a new catagory of "useful Jews" and issued new yellow "life passes" at the work places. Every day, Jews were expelled from the side streets and pressed together more tightly into the neighborhood of the Sczara River and the canal, so that it would later be easier to find them.

The "lucky" holders of the new passes—about 500 handicraftsmen and their families—were squeezed into 50 houses on the island, from which the Germans had moved a few Polish fishermen and their families into vacated Jewish homes in other neighborhoods.

Eight kilometers from Albertin Hill, opposite the village of Czepelow, in a little woods, the Nazis found a "scenic" spot for their next massacre of Jews. First they did some "trial" shooting there to determine whether the noise would be heard in Zhireva, Albertin, Slonim and Czepelow. The *Aktion* was scheduled for Friday, November 14, 1941. The plan also called for the Jews to dig their own graves, the dimensions of which were carefully stipulated: 5 meters wide, 6 meters deep, 80 meters long. "Transport" would be on foot, except for the old, the sick and the children, who would be taken there on peasant wagons and trucks.

Upon Hick's order, Quint put out a call in the ghetto for sixty workers to do a special job. Not a single Jew volunteered. Everyone knew what the job would be.

The Germans and the Jewish auxiliary police then went through Jewish homes and "conscripted" sixty gravediggers. The next day the Judenrat was informed that the job would take several weeks. From peasants in the area it was learned that the gravediggers were living in a bunker near Czepelow. The Polish carpenter Dudek, who heard it from some Germans, warned Jewish acquaintances that the ditches were being prepared for a Jewish massacre.

As soon as the sixty Jews finished digging the graves, they became the first victims. Kommissar Erren did not want the Jews of Slonim to know about the graves until he was ready.

In order to inflame this whole murder enterprise, the Police Kommissar wrote an "essay" in a Baranovici newspaper "proving" that the Jews were responsible for the war and therefore the deaths of millions of "pure Aryans." He also "proved" that if the plans of international Jewish capital had been carried out the whole world would have been destroyed. Therefore, he concluded, "after Germany's total victory over the Jews and the Communists, the Jews would be deported to special labor camps and their capital would be used to rebuild Europe."

At the same time as the Jews were being moved from one area of the city to another, the Judenrat was busy collecting the second tax. People turned in their last bit of money. "Better to live with nothing than be buried in a mass grave."

Precisely at the appointed time the five exhausted Judenrat members, their hearts pounding as if they were entering the cage of a wild beast, reported to the Regional Kommissar. Also present in his office at the time was Dietrich Hick. And, of course, the photograph of Adolph Hitler scowled down at them from the wall.

Hanan Steinberg laid the ransom money on the desk. The jackals counted and weighed their loot and discovered a new Jewish machination—the weight of the gold was 20 grams short.

"You're trying to cheat the Regional Kommissar?" Hick exploded, pulling out his pistol. "If you don't produce the other twenty grams within an hour, I'll fire this gun right into your yellow patches!" The Judenrat members knew this was not merely a figure of speech.

When they returned at ten that evening with the twenty grams of gold, the Kommissar piously assured them that "no further harm would befall the Jews of Slonim." Shortly afterward, during the second massacre, this Judenrat too was liquidated, in order to destroy the evidence of the Kommissar's personal "tax collection."

Among the unfortunate Jews of Slonim there were also a few debased souls who let themselves be used as rumor-mongers and informers. In their own way they helped the murderers cover up the truth and confuse the people, spreading rumors, for example, that the ditches in Czepalow were anti-tank trenches "to protect the German retreat."

Meanwhile a more and more menacing cloud of oncoming disaster moved closer and closer to every Jewish street and every Jewish home. Still grieving over the recent killings, Jews went about their daily lives in a kind of daze, not knowing what to do in face of the calamity they sensed was about to descend upon them. People stood around in clusters, speaking in whispers about the freshly dug ditches, about the truckloads of Lithuanian police that were coming into the city, and tried to fathom the purpose of all these things, but found no reassurance in anything that was happening. But most Jews only shrugged helplessly: "Whatever God has in store for us . . ."

There were also some sympathetic Germans who warned Jewish friends to be on guard. One German who had ordered something from Shmaya Berkowitz, a stitcher on Bridge Street, came running on the 13th to take his leather back and advised Berkowitz to hide the next day. On November 13th a German officer hid his Jewish sweetheart and her mother in his own quarters.

There was also an opinion current that the forthcoming *"Aktion"* would "only" be a roundup of men for forced labor in Germany. The rumor mill had diligently spread the word that the "Third Reich needed workers."

The Second Massacre

On the evening of November 13th the German authorities ordered a tenfold increase in the number of guards around the planned ghetto in the canal and the Breger area. They also posted guards throughout the neighborhoods where there was still a Jewish population. At dawn they sealed off all the roads around Slonim and permitted no one to enter the city. In the morning, as the Jewish workers were going out to work, the police ordered everyone back—"*Nach Hause!*"

For the Jews this was a warning. Jewish men burrowed deeper into their hiding-places.

At 8 a.m. the jackals began their murderous work. They broke into Jewish homes with a maniacal screaming. They went from room to room, searching every corner. They dragged women out by the hair. They used their fists and their feet, their clubs and their rifle-butts. At intervals they fired warning shots. The cries of the children were heart-breaking.

The handicraftsmen on the "island," with their yellow passes, looked on hopelessly, in fear.

Rounding up large groups of Jews, the guards drove them, hands held high, from the tangle of smaller streets to the marketplace. Similar streams of Jews were also coming from Jurdzitka, Panesve, Skrobive, Ruzany, and from the streets around the synagogue.

The Nazi "psychologists" confused the minds of the Jews, who had expected a repetition of the first massacre, when only men were taken. So the women, children and older people felt "safe" inside their homes. The Germans, however, were now intent on filling their "quotas"—more and more yellow patches—regardless of who was wearing them. But they still went to great lengths to continue their tactic of deception: they advised the Jews to take along small packages of "valuables." So some of the victims put on two or three dresses, one over the other, and went that way to their death. Older people were put into cars or peasant wagons, because it would be "too difficult for them to walk all the way."

At the same time, infants were torn away from their mothers and piled onto trucks like logs. The half-crazed women were kept away from the trucks with clubs and dogs.

A car rolled into the marketplace and stopped. The driver got out and stood stiffly at attention while the chief hangman Hick stepped out. A murmur went through the crowd. Hick! The name alone struck terror into their hearts. His uniform freshly pressed, his cheeks rosy, his little eyes darting over his prey, a smile of pleasure spread over his face.

He strolled amidst the Jews with his entourage, swinging his riding-whip against his gleaming boots. He stopped, pursed his lips and began his "explanation": "You are all going to Leszno!" And as evidence that he was telling the truth, he reminded them that he had permitted them to take along small packages of valuables and even extra clothing.

The *Aktion* was ready; they had only been waiting for Hick to come and give the order. In columns of six, with 500 in each group, they marched through Skrobive Street toward the Baranovici Road. Under heavy guard the cclumns moved slowly, casting a pall over the city. The streets were empty, the windows curtained. Here and there a Gentile who had lived for decades among Jews followed the fearful procession with his eyes and sorrowfully crossed himself. Many of the onlookers offered a word of farewell or a wave of the hand to Jewish friends and then ran and hid in their homes.

On Zhabinke Street, amidst shouts of *Raus! Raus!* a motorcycle roared to a stop and an S.S. officer leaped off, ordering the Jews to stand at attention, to be quiet. He assured them: "We are putting you into a camp where everyone will work and be fed. This neighborhood will be only for Aryans." One elderly Jew tried to ask him a question. A gunshot was his only reply. "Any other questions?" he sneered. Mothers quickly covered the mouths of their children.

From here the Jews were marched to the right, around the prison, toward Baranovici Road. At the juncture of the two roads the guards ordered the Zhabinke column to sit down on the ground, so that the Skrobive column could pass. On the highway bridge the guards leading the Skrobive column tore babies out of their mothers' arms and threw them into the Szczara River below. A moment later there was nothing on the surface of the water but little children's caps and flecks of blood. On the bridge above, there were smothered screams . . .

Thus, silently, with heads bowed, the bewildered Jews of Slonim took their last slow steps, as if they were deliberately prolonging their lives . . .

The ancient luxuriant avenue of willows, with its dense, unbroken line of trees from Skrobive to the Albertin pine forest, creates a magnificent, shaded, pleasant road that one recalls from childhood. Now the trees are the last mute witnesses of the living shadows that move in an agonizingly slow procession toward a ghastly end. Climbing up the high Albertin hill they can already hear the machine-guns.

Before the executions each group is ordered to "sit down and rest." From the marketplace to the ditches it had been a long way . . . When the shooting in the woods stops, the order comes: "On your feet!" Armed guards lead the group to the edge of an open ditch. For "humane" reasons there are separate mass graves for men and women. Those closest to the ditches step back instinctively, but the *Einsatz-Kommissar* fires his revolver and drives them back to the ditch between two rows of wild beasts.

"Undress!" A guard picks up the "best clothing" that people were advised to bring along and places it on a pile that has been growing all morning. Valuables are placed in another pile. With their eyes the victims bid farewell to each other . . .

At four in the afternoon the shooting stops. The plan of the Regional Kommissar has been fulfilled. 9400 yellow patches have been added to the total.

Afterward, certain Germans told Jewish acquaintances that if they had not "delivered" those 9400 victims the Kommissar would have started on the "island."

The execution teams were Latvian volunteers handpicked by the SS. Group leader who was Untersturmfuehrer Ameling. Metzner, brandishing his revolver, supervised the transport of old people and children on the trucks and wagons.

"Details"

At Guzanski's building on Skrobive Street they "invited" Moshe Gankowski to come to the assembly point. He protested that he had only one leg. They pushed him out of the second-floor window.

With the knowledge of the priest, many Jews in the Breger neighborhood hid in the Bernardino Church, but a Polish informer told the Germans about it and they were discovered. Among them were: Beyla Rabinowicz, Frumka Kravchuk and her two daughters, Chernikov and his wife and son, Slutchak the carpenter's daughter, Kastrawitsky the parchment maker and his wife and two daughters, Chavin the hatmaker, and Eshke Karlitsky.

Shmaya Berkowitz hid in the water-closet in the yard. It had a double wall. Many Nazis used this place, but they never found him.

Zelig Fein and his son Leybke continued to operate their blacksmith shop on Kosava Road because the Germans had need of the workmen there. They gave them special passes, which also included their families. A few days before the massacre a Polish neighbor,

Sudnik, advised Leybke to run and hide with some friendly peasants in the village. Leybke didn't think it was necessary, because "the Germans need our work and we have these passes." On the day of the massacre they all hid in the smithy, but the Germans found them. Living out there in the village, the news had not reached them that the Germans had rescinded their "special passes."

The wife of Zelig Pashenitsky, the baker, said to one of the German guards at the marketplace: "I want to go across the street to our bakery and get my husband and my son, so they can go with me." The Germans let her go.

During the roundup my sister Zlatke and her family were in hiding. When the situation calmed down a little, her three children —Mirele, Judith and Meir—unnoticed by their parents, went out to play with the neighbor's children on the first floor. They were picked up by the Germans. Their parents, frantic, lost all desire to live. Zlatke could not stop crying.

•

Mira Isaacowitz, a teacher in the Jewish elementary school, who was loved and revered by all (she had educated several generations of students), had been seized for forced labor. People would weep as they watched her marching to work barefoot and with a shovel on her shoulder. Standing at the edge of the ditch, she cursed her murderers—and they let her speak for a moment. "You are heroes at shooting defenseless women and children, but you'll never defeat the Soviet Union! You are supposed to be a superior, cultured people, but your army is nothing but a gang of depraved killers! The Red Army will wipe you out like a plague!"

With a hysterical cry of "old whore" the Nazis tortured her until she took her last breath.

•

As thousands of despairing Jews took their last steps on earth, Meir Iznaidin's daughter Elka kept fighting. Along the entire line of march she shouted anti-Nazi slogans in Yiddish, Russian, Polish and German. "Long live the Red Army! Death to the German murderers! Stalin will avenge us!" Her courage raised the spirits of the despairing. Along Skrobive Street several Polish underworld characters screamed at her: "Damn Jews—you won't suck our blood any more!" Elka was not intimidated. "You're celebrating too soon," she shouted back at them. "Today it's the Jews—tomorrow it will be the honorable Poles!"

Fanya Katzenelnbogen did the same, slapping and scratching the face of a German officer before she was killed.

•

Avrom Moyshe Melamed, *shammes* of the Great Synagogue, standing at the edge of the mass grave, shook the air with his powerful *El Mole Rakhmim*—and the executioners did not stop him. The "Amen" of the condemned congregation served as a release from their pain.

•

Moyshele Fuchsman, a *hasid,* who used to announce the advent of the Sabbath every Friday afternoon to the shopkeepers in the marketplace, had been sitting in his home with a group of Jews, reciting Psalms. When someone proposed that they hide, he said, "You cannot hide from God!" When the Nazi guards broke down the door, he cried out, "God of Israel! Where are You?" In that moment between life and death, he pleaded with his fellow worshippers:

"Remember! We must die as Jews! For our people and our God!"

•

Twenty Jewish barbers, who had been cutting the hair of German soldiers in their barracks, were rounded up and taken to the ditch.

The soldiers ran after them, released them and started back toward town. A spark of hope arose in the hearts of the barbers, but on the way, Hick and his squad appeared and ordered them taken back to their executioners. Among those barbers were Kodesh, Bora, Januszkewicz (a Lithuanian apostate) and Ravich.

•

My cousin Chemke Alpert was an expert tailor and the Germans hadn't bothered him. But his wife and children were rounded up and put on a truck. Chemke, enraged, pushed past the guards and joined his frightened family. The Nazis refused to allow him this "luxury." They shoved him off the truck. Chemke, refusing to be separated from his family, again forced his way on to the vehicle and went with them to their death.

•

On Ruzany Street, Chernichowski tried to run away from a Polish policeman, who shot and killed him on the spot. As he shot him, the Pole was heard to cry out: "I've waited for this moment more than twenty years!"

•

Sasha and Nonye Zirinski and their mother were hiding behind a double wall in their own house. Several times the police had broken in, shouting in Polish, Russian and even Yiddish that they were now free to come out. Nonye had been going out occasionally for water, but having been isolated in the darkness for such a long time, they became disoriented and lost track of the number of days that had passed since the roundup began. Finally Vovke Abramson (who knew where their bunker was) came and led them out of their imprisonment.

•

Avrom Moyshe the *shammes* and his family were already settled in the planned ghetto area. When the Germans came banging on their door, his daughter hid her child Yankl in the woodshed and then, certain that the Nazis would not be taking women and children, she opened the door. The Germans entered, flailing wildly with their sticks and breaking everything in sight. When things quieted down, the son-in-law came cautiously into the house and amidst the debris found Avrom Moyshe's hat on the floor. They had taken him away bareheaded. Of the 36 people who had been in the house, not one survived.

•

The Kunitzes lived on the corner of Panesve and Senkevich Street. Lithuanian police broke into their house and drove out the grandmother, Rachel, her daughter Fita, their daughter-in-law Lyuba, her two-year-old daughter and Lyuba's mother. Mr. Gubar and Lyuba's husband Hershl Kunitze, were hiding in the attic. Lyuba managed to save herself and the child by hiding in the cellar. When the child began crying, Lyuba crept up into the house for food, but the police unexpectedly entered the house again and caught her. Again they were lucky. At the ditch they were not hit by the bullets and fell into the grave unhurt. Afraid that she and her child would be buried alive, she begged the Germans for "mercy." The murderers shot them both. Again Lyuba was "lucky." She was only wounded. Her child was killed.

•

There were Christians in that jungle who saved their own skins by revealing Jewish hiding-places to the Nazis. But there were also Poles, Byelorussians and Germans whose humanity Hitlerism had not extinguished. Risking their own lives, they saved the lives of Jews.

A group of twelve Jews were locked inside Wulkan's shoe store by a Pole. The bar across the door indicated that the store was closed, but a Byelorussian policeman grew suspicious and arrested the Pole, who was rounded up along with the twelve Jews.

A German guard, on duty at a post near the corner of Ruzany and Jurdzitka Street, used the roundup as a "cover" to chase a score of Jews into the cellar of a yeshiva in the Shulgass. When the roundup was over, he let them out one by one.

In one Jewish home a German found a Jew hiding under a bed, but did not report this to the local police. When they found the Jew under the bed, the German blamed his "nearsightedness" and under his breath swore at the *"verfluchte Schwein."*

Several German soldiers, "escorting" Jews into the forest in a truck, not only let the Jews "escape" but showed them where to hide until the massacre was over.

Aftermath

———•———

After this massacre the German guards vanished from the streets of Slonim. Jews could again move about the city without risk of life.

On the evening following the *Aktion* the leaders of the Nazi death squads gathered in the Regional Kommissariat's office—Ritermeyer, Hick, Stelle, Banke, Schultz, Hertz, Heckert, Mezner and Ameling. They reviewed the day's work, criticized its short-comings, promised to correct them in the future. Erren was pleased; he had gotten rid of 10,000 superfluous mouths to feed. The yellow patches that remained could now be driven more efficiently into the ghetto, where they could be more easily handled. Erren had not taken part in the massacre personally but he had planned all the details and given all the orders to the Judenrat in a way that concealed his real intentions.

In the two mass graves, a few of the "lucky" Jews returned from the dead. Groping their way blindly, walking on the tips of their toes, they rummaged in the pile of clothing that remained after the executioners had taken the best for themselves. Since all the guards had left the scene, they were able to make their way into the dense darkeness of the Albertin woods.

Izzy Bonetski, a boy of 16, ran half-naked from the ditch to a farmhouse, where they gave him some clothing and directions to the city. In the "women's ditch" there were about ten survivors, among them Lyuba Kunitz. Several managed to get help from peasants in the area. The ten-year-old daughter of Shlomo the barber, crawling across a layer of dead bodies, came upon a younger girl whom the Nazi bullets had also missed. The younger child could not stand on her frostbitten feet and the ten-year-old could not help her. She herself could not reach to the rim of the ditch. But the will to live is stronger than iron. Pushing a few of the corpses together, she made a sort of pyramid, and with great effort climbed out of the ditch, grabbed a few articles of clothing and ran into the woods. She knocked at the door of the first cottage she came to. The peasants fed her and warmed her and put her on the road to Slonim. On the 15th of September she came to the home of Israel Yudelevitch, with whose daughter she had been friends.

On the day of the massacre, Doctors Noah Kaplinsky, Slonimski, Paretzky and Czeslaw Orlinski were working their normal shift at the city hospital. They knew, however, that something horrible was happening. Not until late that night, however, did they get the story from the frightened, bleeding survivors. For the first time the horrified doctors heard the blood-chilling truth about the massacre of the Jews of Slonim. Esther Fuchsman (herself a nurse), in a quiet monotone, gave them detail after detail of the destruction. She and her younger sister, half-naked in the cold, had been standing at the edge of the ditch. A bullet had gone through her hand and into her sister's head. Both of them fell into the ditch. Still in possession of her faculties, she had struggled to keep her head high enough to breathe, but her moving body out of sight of the guards. Her sister had died instantly.

In the morning, when the hospital administrator, Ivan Gasiuk (a Ukrainian) came to work, he called the police, who "reregistered" the wounded.

Meanwhile, the astounded guards who reported for duty at the ditches, found traces of blood going from the graves to the woods and concluded that during the night some of the corpses had escaped. The news of this "revolt of the dead" soon reached the

Regional Kommissar, who reprimanded the guards for being so drunk they couldn't shoot straight.

The Jewish doctors tried to save the situation by discharging all the wounded, some to their homes, some to the Jewish hospital. A few days later a police squad entered the Jewish hospital, took the wounded Jews back to the ditches and executed them a second time.

This grisly "affair" created even more panic among the surviving Jewish population and it eventually reached the ears of the higher authorities in Baranovici. Gerth Erren, who had been crowned by the Germans themselves as "The Bloody Regional Kommissar," was an angel of death who "couldn't take a joke."

After the massacre the Germans rounded up some Byelorussian peasants to cover up the ditches. The pile of clothing was carted off to the Regional Kommissariat, where they put some Jewish women to work sorting and cleaning it.

Several days later a German newspaper reported that Poles and Byelorussians, in their hatred of the Jews in Slonim, had attacked and killed a great many of them, and that benevolent Germans had intervened to stop the pogrom, to calm the over-excited nationalist emotions and to place the suffering Jews under their protection, saving thousands of them from certain death . . .

News of the second massacre did not reach the Jews of Bitten until late Friday afternoon, when Sasha Savitsky, a non-Jew, had come to Slonim on business but been turned back. Sunday morning the Judenrat in Bitten sent a young Christian named Surzhansky to Slonim with a letter to Lifschitz. He returned the same evening with a reply: Forty percent of Slonim's 23,000 Jews had perished on Friday, including the brothers Zelig and Chaim Glazer, of Bitten, who happened to be in Slonim that day.

This news bewildered the Jews of Bitten. How could 9000 people be wiped out in a few hours—and for what reason?

In Slonim, however, the sudden "disappearance" of ten thousand Jews was a source of great satisfaction to the Jew-haters. Together with the Germans they descended like locusts on the homes and possessions of the murdered Jews, many of them former neighbors. The most valuable things went, of course, to the Germans; others got the leftovers. They carried off their loot on foot and in carts. Feverishly they smashed walls and ripped up floors, expecting to find gold. For three days and nights this looting continued, until Jewish homes lay ransacked, violated, empty. The raped Jewish homes were then sold to peasants from the villages for a pittance. On Shepetinski Street, Matliye Band's home was bought from the Germans for a kilo of butter.

The Jews who remained in Slonim after all this terror and killing and degradation were left without hope and without the will to live. The Germans tried to calm their spirits with lying promises that this would never occur again, not even omitting cynical plans for a revival of their previous life. One of their methods of dulling Jewish watchfulness was to employ a large number of Jews in the construction of a "rest-home" for the German executioners . . .

Next the Germans attempted to set up a third Judenrat. But there was no one now from whom to choose such a council, so they agreed to settle for one man whom they could hold responsible for all the impossibilities they demanded of the Jews. Finally one volunteer appeared, one sacrificial lamb. His name was Yelishevich. Having lost his entire family in the massacres, he felt he had nothing else to lose. Perhaps, he thought, he could make life a little easier for the remnants of Slonim's Jewry.

But the occupation authorities immediately ordered him to carry out a new registration of all the Jews left in the city. The next order reduced the food rations. Any Jew who received more than his ration was supposed to return it, under penalty of death . . .

In the Barracks

———————•———————

After the second massacre Shiel Fisher came to work in the barracks for military engineer Schmertz. Many young Jews were employed here. On Anshl's suggestion, Shiel organized cells of five among them. Choosing those who were most trustworthy and most politically aware, he began training them to collect weapons, money and articles that would be useful to the partisans. In this group were Berl Belski, Nonye Bunimov, Gedaliah Agulnik, Zavel Chomak, Moyshe Sefer, Meir Volkomirski and others, including refugees from Poland. They went from house to house, explaining the aims of the partisan movement. Most of the Jews had come to believe that their situation could be changed for the better only by the partisans.

The overriding question among the Jews in the barracks was: "When will the Red Army finally come to liberate us?" The members in the cells had to explain that the Jews would have to liberate themselves; they might have to wait a long time before the Red Army reached Slonim.

Something happened with Zavel Chomak one day that not only could have cost him his life but brought disaster to the whole underground movement. Engineer Schmertz found several grenades that Zavel had hidden on his person. Fortunately Schmertz had no idea what was going on—he thought Zavel was just "playing around" with the grenades. He slapped him a couple of times and called him stupid, but that was the end of it.

It was in the barracks that the young fellows learned how various weapons were made and how to handle them. They even organized a kind of "target practice," with Schmertz's permission and even his participation. It gave him an opportunity to show what a sharpshooter he was . . .

The Ghetto

———•———

Immediately following the massacres Gerhardt Erren reported gleefully to Berlin: "The *Juden-Aktion* of November 14, 1941 has greatly ameliorated the housing problem and also rid us of 10,000 unecessary mouths to feed."

At last his plan of imprisoning the remaining Jews inside a ghetto could be carried out. Actually there had been a ghetto even before the second massacre. All the handicraftsmen had been moved to the island. The rest of the Jewish population was crowded together on both sides of the canal. The massacre had freed many side streets for "Aryans"—the entire city area, Jurdzike Street and the densely populated hill area.

Early in December Hick gave the Judenrat a precise diagram of the ghetto boundaries. The Jews themselves, at their own expense, were to put up the barbed wire without any further delay. Quint's labor office went out on the dams to set up the designated boundary.

Under Engineer Wolfstein's instructions they stretched a rope along the length of the dam. Wolfstein then measured off intervals where the posts were to be sunk. Behind him came a worker who tapped a wooden marker into the ground. Jews with pick and shovel dug deep holes into the frozen earth. The posts were carried up on the shoulders of the men and placed into the waiting holes.

Then rocks were brought up on wheelbarrows and set around each hole as supports.

Wolfstein marked off about fifty of these holes and then turned that job over to an assistant. Quint had supervised the hauling of the logs and the delivery of the barbed wire. When the workers had set up about twenty poles, Wolfstein showed them how to attach the wire.

In this manner the Jews of Slonim constructed their own cage.

In the midst of this "operation" Hick suddenly made a dramatic appearance and the Jews instinctively quickened the pace of the work. Quint and Wolfstein immediately gave him a "progress report." As they were doing so, his stare measured them coldly from head to toe. Then he turned and strode toward the Balione Bridge, pointing out to them where they must extend the wall to Zhabinke and Balione Street. From there he marched them back to the main gate at Ulan Street, where he lectured them on the importance of that particular gate.

Hick's ghetto boundary began at Michalowski and Skrobive Streets, at the fence of the Polish Teachers Seminary. Facing the center of the city, on your left is the right-hand side of Skrobive; on your right, the canal, Balione Island, up to the bank of the Szczara River. Then, left of the canal, Breger Street and all the smaller streets that go uphill to Bernardino Street, which now became the main street of the ghetto, with the Judenrat office in Jezerski's house. On Bernardino the government offices, the Bernardino Church, the bank and the municipal theater were reserved for "Aryans." Where Barnardino runs into the marketplace, only the right-hand side of the street was included in the ghetto, since it connects with Ulan. Only the right-hand side of Ulan was included in the ghetto, except for the Polish high school.

Where Breger intersects with Opera, and on both sides of Ulan, the main ghetto gate was erected. From Ulan the boundary continued along Opera. Where Opera intersects with Bridge Street, the boundary stops at the left-hand side of the canal, and on the right side, across the bridge at Zhabinka.

All windows, doors, gates and passageways from one side street to another must be walled up so that no one can get in or out. The boundary was a high barbed-wire fence.

For the "Aryan" population the Balione Bridge would serve as the only transitway through the ghetto. Any other route was *verboten*.

A smaller gate was erected on Bernardino, where it runs into the marketplace near Ulan.

All the canal dams were cut off from the ghetto. Erren's intent here was two-fold: to prevent the Jews from engaging in any contraband business with the outside world by boat, and to make it impossible for them to enjoy the canal and its environs during the hot summer months.

When all this construction was finished, Hick made a "tour of inspection" and on December 24th issued his long-expected order to the Judenrat: within two days the rest of the Jews living on the side streets were to be "resettled" into the Breger streets.

The Jews residing outside the new ghetto boundaries began packing whatever they could carry or move on a pushcart—except furniture, which was forbidden. On the way to the ghetto the police inspected packages and removed the best things by force, beating or shooting anyone who resisted. Mrs. Itzkowicz, Dr. and Mrs. Zackheim, Mordecai Kunitza, Weisenberg, and many others, were killed by the police during this "operation."

The unsanitary conditions, the starvation ration, the lack of medical care, resulted in cases of typhoid fever which threatened to reach epidemic proportions. But the Regional Kommissar was prepared for such an eventuality. He permitted several of his "Aryan" physicians to conscript their Jewish professional colleagues and the danger of an epidemic was averted, an accomplishment which he hastened to report to Berlin with a great deal of self-glorification.

Thus he finally succeeded in concentrating all the Jews of Slonim into one place and under 24 hour a day guard. Now it would be easier for him to carry out his murderous plans. But first he had to degrade his victims a little more, to demoralize them psychologically. He prohibited the Jews in the Breger area, under penalty of death, from visiting their "more privileged" brothers on the island. The handicraftsmen on the island, however, were permitted to visit the left side of the canal. But their safety there was not guaranteed in case of a roundup.

Leaving the ghetto was permitted only to columns of workers and only under supervision of a foreman. After six in the evening any Jew found outside the ghetto was subject to the death penalty. On the inside, the gates were always guarded by the Jewish Police; on the outside, by Aryan police. The barbed wire and the gates were the dividing line between two worlds, one "free" and one a death-camp for the temporarily living dead.

The second massacre convinced the Jews that the first order of the day was passive resistance—which meant hiding during the roundups. Everyone was busy building hiding-places. They used every method they could think of—attics, cellars, double walls camouflaged so that the Nazis would not discover them. They made use of all the technical skills of carpenters, locksmiths, masons. The main problem was insufficient air to breathe, so they built concealed air-ducts. Everyone burrowed underground like moles. The most effective hiding-places turned out to be the double-walls and the rooftops. The hangmen never imagined that Jews would hide between walls . . .

Help from the Aryan Side

One day, while she was in Dereczin, Anshl's wife met Fanya Feigen-baum, an amiable young woman in whom she confided the news about the partisan organization in the Slonim ghetto. The very next day Fanya appeared at Itche Gratchuk's house, where Anshl's group happened to be meeting. She waited until the meeting was over and then introduced herself to Anshl as a former Communist from Lodz. She couldn't wait, she said, to become involved in their sacred work, for which she had been preparing all her life.

Although she came recommended by his wife, Anshl nonetheless approached her—properly—with reservations and even mistrust. First he tried to stall her. When she persisted, he gave her some minor tasks to do. From the way she carried these out he finally became convinced that she possessed considerable organizational ability. Thanks to her Aryan appearance she later was able to set up contacts between the ghetto and the "Aryan side."

Fanya was bold and resourceful. She had a great deal of experience in the Polish underground. On the surface, she looked like an average Jewish girl with a "Gentile face," but her limitless energy, her alertness, her temperament, made her eminently suited for the work. Very soon Anshl entrusted to her the leadership of some of the cells.

Walking through the city one day without her yellow patch, she bumped into a Polish Communist named Walczak whom she had known in Lodz. She invited him to meet with Anshl. They had a long, serious session. The Pole was pleased to hear that the Jews were not asleep, that they were almost ready for practical deeds. Walczak explained to them that he would gladly participate in the struggle with them, but that he was now too old and physically unable to do very much. He promised to help in any way that he could.

His first helpful act was to make contact with a wonderful young Pole named Wacek Wilczinski, who turned out to be of great assistance to the Jewish partisans. Among other things, he often supplied them with food.

The Second Meeting

Early in the winter of 1942, on Pesach Alpert's initiative, a second meeting was arranged in the home of Braina Lunianska on Balione Street. Present were representatives of both groups, which by that time were widely rooted among the ghetto population. Anshl's group was the much larger one. In its "jurisdiction" was the Beuten camp, from which they had organized a steady flow of weapons.

David's group still stuck to its position that they must stay and fight in the ghetto. After lengthy debates, Anshl had not succeeded in winning them over. Braina often sided with Anshl but she still clung to her feeling of "staying with the people." Anshl then gave them an ultimatum: Either they make contact immediately with "the forest" and begin taking the young fighters there, or he would act on his own, because he bore no responsibility for David's group. His parting shot was : "I will not permit my organized people to fight here and be slaughtered; to try to defend the ghetto is an act of insanity." Then he and Zyama Shusterovich left the meeting.

Anshl was politically schooled and had a keen eye for future developments. He approached life-and-death problems with cold logic, but he sometimes took great risks. From the very beginning he had decided that the only effective thing they could do was to attack the enemy from behind. David Epstein, on the other hand, insisted that it would be a betrayal and an act of cowardice to send fighters into the forest and leave the Jews in the city defenseless.

Anshl's Practical Work

Anshl continued even more resolutely to recruit more and more young people into the underground. Zelik Milikowski, a quiet, honest young cabinet-maker, had had some military training in the Polish army. On Anshl's instructions he would have gone through fire and water. Yankl Pripstein was a trade unionist who had worked for many years in Pajewska's tannery on Highway Street. He quickly grasped the importance of building an anti-Nazi underground. Aba Yudelevich, a strong, husky youth with military training, was aching to fight the Germans.

The brothers Matus and Shimon Pinowski, bold and fearless, were expert locksmiths. The Regional Kommissar had ordered them to keep their workshop in Panesve open. Matis didn't "believe" in the laws of the occupation. Without his yellow patch he would walk around the city—and on the sidewalks with everyone else.

Archik and Avreml Band, from the village of Skoizici, both grew up in the hard life of the countryside. Archik was more impulsive and inventive in "liberating" weapons from the German storehouses. David Guskin, Karpl Shevchik, Avreml Bubliatski, Yoske Shuchatowicz, Shiel Fisher—all of them were tested and enthusiastic workers in the partisan movement. Zerach Kremien and

Nonye Zirinski, dedicated and fearless, were two of Anshl's best assistants.

The brother Kunitz, blacksmiths from Opera Street, also had been ordered by the Kommissar to keep their smithy operating. Honest men, hardened by their life, they too were eager to join the fight against Hitler. Whatever they owned, whatever they knew, was available to Anshl. Jacob Khatskelevich, who worked in their smithy, was also active in the underground.

Doktorchik and his wife, refugees from Poland, both highly educated young people, were devoted to the partisan movement. Rivka Mashkowski, energetic and full of enthusiasm, was a leader of her cell, which consisted of Itzik Klebanski, Haikl Kokoszitzki, Yosl Shelyubski and Yisroel Rabinowicz.

Isaac Alpert, age 15 (Pesach's son) and Meirke Slovaticki, were Anshl's "runners." His briefest orders were enough—they knew what he wanted them to do almost before he told them. Without hesitation they would steal out of the ghetto, carrying medicine from the pharmacies or the hospitals to the partisans. Later they helped to load weapons into wagons for the forest.

In one of the massacres, Lyuba Abramowicz lost her husband Lazar Volkovitski and their only son, along with her entire family. This nightmare left her in such a depressed state that she prayed for death to release her from the pain. The partisan activity in the ghetto threw her together with Nonye Zirinski, who was able to find the right words to reach her. "We are still young and strong," he told her, "so not only must we take the lead ourselves in the underground, but we must encourage others. Vengeance for our loved ones is the only thing that can give meaning to our lives now. We must not allow ourselves to succumb to despair or helplessness!"

"What do you want me to do, Nonye?"

He gave her an address and a password to Wacek Wilczinka's house on Krenti Lane. Wacek put her in touch with the Snowski brothers. Matus gave her a task to fulfill and then recommended that she apply for work in the police barracks where Jewish women were cleaning and sorting captured weapons. Before long, Lyuba had learned how to smuggle weapons out to the locksmith work-shop. She became a member of a cell. Through her hands passed bullets, pistols, grenades and gun-parts for the partisans.

After a while she was joined by Vova Abramson, who had come to Slonim from Minsk with his younger brother Leon. (They were related to Slonim's Rabbi Yehuda Leyb Fein.) As a young Soviet citizen brought up in the spirit of "the October Revolution" Vova immediately joined the underground. Around the same time, Jascha Shepetinski was drawn into the movement by his younger brother Hertzl. They were both sent by the underground to work in the Beuten camp. Not having previously known each other, they were very cautious and circumspect at first.

One day Jascha hid a pistol, intending to smuggle it out of the camp at the end of the day. He went to lunch and when he returned he couldn't find the pistol. It was an extremely dangerous situation. He decided to take a risk. He asked Vova, "Did you see the pistol that I was cleaning here before?" Vova smiled and reassured him, "Don't worry. It's already on the way to the ghetto." Thus they learned that they were comrades in the same cause.

And thus, Communists, Bundists, Shomrim, Halutzim, General Zionists, together with "unaffiliated" Jews who saw in the newly created underground movement a way out of their desperate situation, joined together to fight against their hated common enemy.

With his tireless work, Anshl Delyaticki breathed into the souls of the new partisans the lesson that they were all connected by the bitter fate facing the Jews. As a result, he now had about ten secret "cells of five" around him, all working feverishly on the dangerous mission of moving weapons from the German arsenals into the hands of the partisans in the forest.

Anshl is "Fired"

Some time after that second meeting, Anshl carefully packed a few automatics inside a box of soap and "transported" them into the carpenter shop while two of his men kept a lookout for any stray Germans. Unfortunately he was spotted by a known Jewish informer, a refugee from Poland, who said nothing to him at the time, but only stood and watched. Anshl noticed him and guessed that the man probably thought he was stealing the soap. He expected him to try and get something out of this for himself.

The next day the informer came into the carpenter shop, confronted Anshl and demanded a thousand rubles. Not wishing to cause a scene, lest it jeopardize the collection of weapons, Anshl offered him 500 rubles which he had prepared for just such an eventuality. The parasite, however, grew highly indignant and waved his fist in Anshl's face, insisting on the thousand. This made Anshl so furious that he refused to give him anything at all.

"We'll see about that!" the man hissed menacingly.

The following day, at lunchtime, Sgt. Braun summoned Anshl and accused him of stealing soap. He slapped him a couple of times, took away his work pass and ordered him to leave the camp.

For Anshl this was a blessing in disguise. At that particular moment he had a new grenade in his pocket. If Braun had searched him, one of them would not have come out of that confrontation alive and the underground movement would have suffered a death-blow.

As a result of this narrow escape, Anshl also came to realize that he had been naive not to understand that in this life-and-death struggle between the Jewish people and German fascism there would inevitably be some Jews who would betray their own brothers to save their own skin, even when they knew full well that it would be only for a short time.

•

Around the same time, David Epstein gradually began to see the incorrectness of his opposition to Anshl's plan, but he did not give up the idea of an uprising in the ghetto itself. It was understood, however, that without a connection with the partisans in the forest, and without help from the Byelorussians in the villages, they would not even be able to begin that uprising.

In a word, they began slowly to accept Anshl's position, but they didn't completely give up their dreams. David himself began searching for a contact with the forest. Perhaps he planned to join forces with Anshl only after he had made that contact.

One day Pesach Alpert met Anshl accidentally on the street. In general it was very difficult to meet someone by prearrangement in the separated ghetto areas, and one always had to be extremely careful about informers. Pesach told Anshl about the change in his group's thinking and that they themselves were attempting to es-tablish contact with the forest. They hoped to accomplish this soon through a certain Sasha who was working in a sawmill and had already asked them for 2000 rubles "to buy medical supplies."

Anshl wanted to know what they were doing about acquiring weapons. Pesach's reply was:

"They are being armed by Moscow."

Anshl couldn't help laughing at the naiveté of such old experienced political activists. He warned Pesach that they would be fleeced by this clever swindler.

Regrettably, that's how it turned out.

Behind the Barbed Wire

The Jews of Slonim, who had finally been locked up inside a ghetto, continued to work at the various places in the city. Many of the shops were still being run by their Jewish owners, but after work all the Jews had to return to the ghetto for the night.

Life gradually returned to its now much narrower framework and the Jews were forced to make peace with the idea that they were imprisoned. Some even tried to joke about it: "We're living like the bourgeoisie!"

Although death was always imminent they lived with hope and faith in their eventual liberation. Some were waiting for a divine miracle; most were looking hopefully toward the east, whence good news kept coming about heavy German losses. It was easier to endure their bitter lot because they were certain that many of them would survive to see the total defeat of their hated Nazi enemy.

There were also a small number who were so terrorized and so defeated that they had lost all capacity to hope. Overwhelmed by the unexpected privation and misery in which they had to live, they could not "adjust" to the ghetto life. They slunk around in the narrow streets like gloomy shadows, their heads down, devoid of any feelings of human or national dignity.

The dreaded Slonim winter arrived and froze the canal. But this made communication easier between both parts of the ghetto. People risked their lives and crossed the ice. Hunger drove the Jews to disregard the German decrees in order to obtain food. A barter "commerce" with the Aryan side was carried on through the barbed wire—food products for finished goods, or for cash.

Near the Breger synagogue an illegal marketplace emerged, doing a pitiful "business" in rags, old clothes, even some wretched food products—everything was "merchandise." People sold their last undershirt to get through the day. The sudden appearance of the police would send the "tradesmen" running like mice into their holes. As soon as the police left, the business transactions would begin again.

There were also a few more substantial merchants who, through secret channels, brought necessary goods into the ghetto—leather, soap, saccharin, cigarettes, cocoa and other prohibited "luxuries." In their language, dollars were "the green ones" or "the soft ones." Gold rubles were "the yellow ones" or "the hard ones." Early every morning they would study the currency rates and you could hear conversations like this: "Where does the green one stand? The soft one has fallen to 120."

Certain lower-rank German officers trusted Quint, Max Rabino-wicz or Mischa Lutz more than they did non-Jews and did business with them. Sergeants Mutz and Braun from the Beuten camp would drive right into the courtyard of the Labor Office with a truck and unload goods and products that the ghetto so desperately needed. They conducted their business directly with Gershon Quint, who often used the money to ransom Jews who had fallen into German hands.

Part of the ghetto population still had a little cash. Many collected the remaining property of relatives who had perished in the last massacre and exchanged it with "Aryans" for food products. With these people there was a marked tendency to overeat, like condemned prisoners. This was a direct result of having the Angel of Death always before your eyes.

With their organizational and entrepreneurial abilities, Jews did not throw up their hands helplessly even amidst the ghetto horrors. In addition to all the "business" they also maintained an illegal "restaurant" and a "bakery" where they could sometimes satisfy their hunger. Some families had kerosene stoves on which they could prepare a quick meal. In general, Jews thumbed their noses at the blood-thirsty Kommissar and his decrees.

In Meltzer's former candy factory on Ulan Street, Yerishevetz set up a soup kitchen. The room was partially below street level. The floor was dirty, the walls were discolored by dampness, and there were no tables or chairs. The place was always filled with hungry people, cripples, recently orphaned children, homeless refugees, professional beggars. They stood around with vacant stares, as if they had been drugged. Unkempt women with feathers in their hair mumbled unintelligibly through parched lips. The smell of human sweat was oppressive. For hours at a time they stood there waiting for "lunch." When the food was finally brought out of the kitchen in the iron kettle, they all moved toward it together like a wave. The "lucky" ones who received a portion of the soup then stepped to one side, swallowing it down in one gulp.

The Judenrat undoubtedly had more important problems to solve, so they didn't concern themselves too much with these few-score people. The growing partisan movement, however, did make this its concern. One day Anshl, Lyuba Abramowicz and Nathan Licker walked into the soup kitchen, took one look around, went straight to the Judenrat office and talked to Quint, Yelishevitz and Rabinowicz. After this visit, conditions in the soup kitchen improved greatly. They painted the walls, scrubbed the floor and put in some wooden tables and chairs.

The religious Jews engaged a new rabbi who had come to Slonim from Ostrow-Mazowiecka with his large family along with the stream of refugees in 1939/40. Rabbi Singer reinstituted the services in the ghetto synagogue and the congregants poured out their hearts in prayer, which helped sustain them.

The ghetto also had a small "old-age home" on Skrobive Street, in Guzanki's building. From this building it was possible to get across the border (through the narrow street opposite the Hasidic court). Here, for a few rubles slipped into the hand of the attendant, you could take a bath.

At the beginning of March this "calm" was suddenly shattered by what were perceived to be preparations for a third massacre. In the ensuing panic people again disappeared into hiding-places. There were even some Jews who reported that their German friends had advised them to "stay on guard." Large contingents of police kept coming into the city, which was enough to spread panic and hopelessness among the Jews.

But this time there was a reprieve. It turned out that a policeman had been shot by partisans and the preparations were for his funeral . . .

Soon after the ghetto was set up, the Germans ferreted out—in Slonim, in nearby towns, in villages, in churches and monasteries —all the apostate Jews they could find, brought them into the ghetto and settled them in the old-age home. Among them were even some priests and monks. Many of these people had totally rejected their Jewishness. Some of them had even become anti-Semites. Some had been apostates for many years—one of them had been ringing the church bells in the famous Zhireve monastery for 26 years.

The Jews in the ghetto did not treat these apostates very kindly. And the apostates continued to act as if they were somehow different from and superior to the Jews.

News from the Front

The winter was a severe one and the Russians were inflicting one defeat after another upon the Germans outside of Moscow. The notorious "Grandfather Frost" was also helping. Columns of frost-bitten and wounded German troops rode through Slonim every day. It became clearer and clearer that the Germans had suffered worse defeats than they had the previous year.

The Regional Kommissar announced a "voluntary" contribution from the population in Slonim on behalf of the German army. These contributions were to consist of gloves, fur coats, blankets, warm clothing of all kinds. The Jews were also expected to contribute—under direction of the Judenrat. In response, the partisans organized a "counter-collection." The Jews understood this tactic—they knew quite well who was in greater need of the warm clothing.

In the fascist newspapers one could read about the real situation on the front—if you read between the lines. The retreating columns of wounded and bedraggled German soldiers told the story even more graphically.

For the first time, the Jews had reason to feel a little more hopeful. Smiles appeared on lips that hadn't smiled for a long time. And the news helped the partisan movement grow too.

Rabbi Singer's energetic work received the support of a large section of Slonim's Jewish population. Through his religious approach he raised their spirits. His message: God had turned His face away from us because we had sined and therefore we must pray for God's mercy.

Many weddings took place. Widowers and widows married, as well as younger people. One winter evening Rabbi Singer married ten couples. Meir Yoresh even received a dowry of 20,000 rubles. A few days later he had second thoughts and chased his wife out of the house, creating a scandal that even had people laughing.

News from the front about German defeats outside Moscow kept reaching the ghetto over the "illegal" radio, but so did the lying propaganda of the Nazis, who had put up a loudspeaker at the border of the ghetto. Their "newspapers" reported that Stalin and his son had been killed in a bombing raid on Moscow. In the Beuten camp an officer who had been wounded at the Moscow front regaled some of his fellow Germans with stories about the drubbing the Russians had administered to the Reichswehr. He didn't even seem to mind that Jews were within earshot and that his story gave the lie to the braggadocio of the German radio.

The same loudspeaker also transmitted—in the Byelorussian language—vile descriptions of Jews as Communist parasites who headed the Soviet government. In the show-windows in the market-place they hung caricatures of Jews along with the screaming slogan: BEI ZHIDOVSKEY NADINU! (beat the Jewish serpent).

News also reached the ghetto, however, of anti-Hitler pacts between the Soviet Union, England and the United States. Jewish hot-heads were already fantasizing about a quick defeat of Germany and the imminent arrival of British and American troops who would liberate the enslaved Jews. These hopes, fantastic as they might have been, did help to create a sort of Jewish solidarity which made it a little easier to endure the harsh ghetto winter.

In the spring, people even began planting vegetable gardens in all the open spaces in the ghetto . . .

Expulsion from Ivacevici

Ivacevici, a small Polessian town and railroad station between Kossovo and Bitten, with 600 Jews, was under jurisdiction of the Slonim Regional Kommissariat. At the end of February 1942 the German authorities decided that the town should be made Judenrein, not by a massacre this time but by expulsion. Early in March Erren's deputy, Gunther Stelle, ordered the Jews of Ivacevici to leave the town and go wherever they wished.

Messengers from the Jewish community immediately went to Slonim and asked Quint for help. His first efforts to have the decree rescinded failed.

The desperate Jews of Ivacevici could do nothing now but wait for a miracle, because where could they go? They knew very well that eventually the Germans would expel them by force, but no one imagined that Stelle would choose the morning of March 14, in a freezing snowstorm, for the expulsion. The police drove people out of their beds and into the street, half-dressed and only half awake, and would not even allow them to take along any clothing. They herded them along the Bitten Road for three kilometers and then left them there, exposed to the icy winds. People fell and were covered by the snow. Parents carried their small children under their clothing.

Two of the younger Jews arrived at Bitten first with the terrible news. The Jews there sent wagons and warm clothing to bring the people on the road into Bitten. In that expulsion 21 Jews froze to death. Many others suffered wounds and frostbite.

Dr. Wodnik, a refugee from Lodz, treated all the patients. Some of the more serious cases were taken to the Jewish hospital in Slonim. For a few of them it was too late.

Joseph Pajewski and Joseph Jezerski collected a sum of money from the tannery workers in Slonim to help the Jews of Ivacevici. The Judenrat sent two wagonloads of food and clothing.

Serving "The Fatherland"

In accordance with an order from Slonim, the Bitten Judenrat, from February 24 to March 9, had to supply 150 young workers "to serve the Fatherland." The Judenrat appealed to Quint to do something to avert this decree. Through his intercession, the 150 was reduced to 80, with the other 70 to be supplied later.

Also sent to Slonim under that decree were Jews from Derecin, Kossova, Kazloishchina and other places to make up a "labor army" of 500 men. They were quartered in the small prison opposite the railroad station, formerly called "Monopolke." The Slonim Judenrat also "negotiated" with the police for a weekly food delivery to the 80 men, among whom were Matus Slonimski, Bomme Didkowski, Nisl Minkowicz and Mulye Mendelewicz (all from Bitten).

This "labor army" did the heaviest, dirtiest work, such as cleaning the debris of the war from the streets, particularly Ruzany Street which, on June 27, was set ablaze by a burning Soviet tank near the home of Shcherb the carpenter.

The Monopolke, which was now outside the Slonim ghetto, got its orders directly from the Regional Kommissar. The foremen were not sparing of insults, blows and even shootings. The head of this work group was the German engineer Krieger, assisted by Engineer Wolfstein. At the end of each week Krieger, Wolfstein and Hick himself evaluated the "Jewish labor efficiency." If they were satisfied, the men might get the following day off. Very often they did not.

Saturday, April 20, Hitler's birthday, Hick and Krieger appeared in a drunken state and began terrorizing the men, beating them and shooting over their heads.

Monday, April 22, seventy of the group, all craftsmen, were separated out; the rest were sent to Puzevici, among them Shmuel Ostrovetski, Yisroel-Osher Berenstein, Moyshe Zackheim, Yisroel Slonimski and Nonye Mendelewicz.

One morning at the end of April the Germans suddenly rounded up 60-70 middle-aged men and ordered them to line up in two rows outside the synagogue. From the Judenrat office, through Jezerska Street, a German officer and Gershon Quint came running down the hill.

The officer, in great good spirits, chose forty of the men and explained to them in an extremely pleasant manner that the Jews too must serve the Fatherland by hard and diligent work. He illustrated what he meant by using himself as an example. "Here I am, a German officer, and I've been away from home three years, stuck here with you Jews. I am doing it for the Fatherland." And he signalled to Quint to say something "inspirational" to the men, who didn't appear all that eager to "serve the Fatherland."

The officer warned the 40 Jews who were chosen that their families were now hostages, just in case someone had any idea of running away. Meanwhile, he said, they could all go home, pack up enough food for several days and report back in 15 minutes.

At the appointed time they assembled at the synagogue with their packages and baskets. Another ten men joined them—construction workers for the Regional Kommissariat. At the ghetto gate their names were checked against a list and, led by a foreman, they marched to "the long bridge," where they were met by representatives of the Regional Kommissariat, who again checked the list and gave Quint his instructions. Then, under police guard, they were marched toward the Zamoshch lake.

The first signs of spring were appearing. But the bright green grass, the newly sprouting blossoms, the cheerful magic of the birdsongs, these were not for the Jewish prisoners of Slonim, marching in double-time, their heads bowed in pain and longing, longing for their lost freedom, for their loved ones whom they might never see again.

All day long they were driven without rest. That night they slept in a dark hut in the middle of the woods. They chewed the food they had brought with them and drank it down with cold water from a spring. By mid-afternoon the next day they had reached a camp where Jews were laying a wide military road near Puzevici, a village some 20 kilometers from Slonim. With not a moment's rest they were put right to work, using pick and shovel and wheelbarrows. Jewish muscles here did the work of modern machines— pulling and pushing wheelbarrows loaded with rocks. Jews here were the diggers and carters of sand from one place to another. Most of the foremen were Poles from Slonim with white armbands on their sleeves.

The camp into which the 500 men were crowded consisted of four large, windowless stables. Nearby was a small cottage that served as a "clinic." It was run by Ilyusha Rabinowicz, a young doctor from Slonim, who could do very little for his patients because there were practically no medicaments.

Five days after they arrived, Quint managed to have all the craftsmen "transferred" back to Slonim, among them Shiel Fisher, Yudel Ribatski and two of the Shepitinski brothers. The youngest Shepitinski remained in the camp, but a few days later he escaped in a haywagon belonging to a Jewish driver. On the ninth day Quint got permission from the police to have a supply of food products sent to the camp from the hometowns of the prisoners.

One Saturday morning Hick rode up to the camp and ordered all the workers to line up and listen carefully. "I sent you from Slonim to Puzevici to build a road," he began. "Starting today your ration will be increased to 250 grams of bread and 30 grams of cereal a day and 100 grams of meat a week. Naturally, since we are giving you more to eat, we expect you to do more work. Is there anyone here who still wants to go back to Slonim?" No one "volunteered."

"Dismissed!" he shouted, and got back into his car.

Shortly afterward, the Regional Kommissar dispatched a new order to Bitten: A hundred more men for the camp. Quint got the number reduced to 60, with an increase in the food allowance. All this, of course, he did with the help of gold rubles.

In mid-May the partisans became more active in the area. There were rumors of partisan bands having attacked Germans on the roads. The rumors boasted of "hundreds" of heavily armed partisans against whom the Germans were helpless.

On the evening of June 20th all the dogs in the village started barking and rifle shots were heard. After a while the Jews in the camp realized that the Byelorussian guards had run away. Later that night real-life partisans appeared at the camp, flung open the gates and liberated the Jewish prisoners. One of them spoke to the men:

"You Jews are suffering so much at the hands of these lousy fascists. Yet you go on building roads for them. Why don't you join our ranks and fight them?"

One man agreed to go with them. The others explained that the Germans were holding their families hostage. If they joined the partisans, the Germans would kill their wives and children.

The partisans destroyed all the engineer's building plans, cut the telephone lines and threatened to shoot him if he continued to work on the road.

The Jews waited two days, but the authorities did not return to the camp. On June 22, 1942, early in the morning, they all went back to their home towns.

A Real Contact

Having lived for many years in the village of Zaverze (between Bitten and Zirovici), the Shepetinski family had connections with the Byelorussian peasants in the area, especially with their neighbors, the Fidriks. Hannah Shepetinski herself and grown up in the village; her three sons—Jascha, Herzl and Reuben—were active in the Slonim ghetto underground.

When the problem of making contact with "the forest" became urgent, Herzl, a bold and enterprising young man, utilized his familiarity with the Byelorussian countryside to carry out this mission. Very often he disappeared from the house for several days at a time. In March 1942 he finally succeeded in meeting a Soviet Commissar named Dudko Grigory and winning his trust. Herzl brought him up to date on the activities of the underground and told him there were many Jews who were waiting eagerly to fight the Nazis.

Dudko's eyes opened wide when Herzl told him about the rich supply of weapons, leather, soap and medicaments that they were stealing from the Germans. He sent comradely greetings to the Slonim ghetto partisans, congratulated them for not sitting by with folded hands and advised them to stay in the ghetto as long as possible and to continue "liberating" all those supplies that were so important to the partisans in the forest. He also set a date for a meeting with Pronyagin, a message which Herzl delivered immediately to the underground leaders Anshl, Zerach, Nonye, Blumovich and Wacek Wilczinski.

In early spring 1942 Pavel Pronyagin and Michail Pashchenkov met with two veterans of the war with Poland—Misko and Wacek Wilczinski. One dark evening they walked to Zirovici and went to a cottage where they met Herzl Shepetinski. The three of them then walked a little further toward the city and were admitted to the home of Ivan Khilko, who had been assigned to meet with them, but even before the meeting began they realized they were in trouble.

Attackers were breaking down the door. The windows were being smashed by machine-gun bullets. They returned the fire and, under cover of grenades and rifle fire, they crawled out a back window and vanished into the night. Later they learned that the house had been staked out by the Germans as a meeting-place for partisans.

Zerach was then given the task of making another contact. Hannah Shepetinski mapped out a route to Zaverze. Fidrik promised to arrange the contact because the Shchors detachment was ready and very much interested in establishing contact with the Slonim ghetto. He set a meeting for the following Sunday.

When Zerach came to the edge of the Rafalovka Forest he found the leaders of the detachment waiting for him. They discussed ways of getting the weapons into the forest. Two days later Zerach returned with favorable results: He had established a password connection with the Shchors detachment and had gotten to know some of the forest partisans, who had sent greetings to the Jewish ghetto partisans and were pleased to have them come and fight side by side with them against the common enemy. At this time, however, because the detachment was still weak, they could only accept doctors, nurses and radio technicians, plus certain individuals whom the Germans had marked for "special attention."

They also requested soap, weapons and medicaments and they gave Zerach 500 marks for tobacco. Thus was a real connection finally established with the partisans of the Bulina Forest or the *wolczi nori,* the "wolf-caves."

After this, Fidrik would periodically deliver a wagon-load of "potatoes" to the Snovskis, which was actually a cover for weapons.

Unification at Last

After contact had been established between the ghetto and the forest, another meeting was held of the two ghetto resistance organizations. Because of this new situation, a spontaneous movement toward unity had already begun "below," but officially, steps had to be taken to clarify the roles of the leadership. The final act of unification was due in large measure to the tireless efforts of Pesach Alpert, who was already a man past middle-age. His particular talent lay in mediation. Both sides respected his knowledge, his judgment and his organizational ability.

To Itche Gratchuk's empty attic, with its crumbling chimney and cobwebs in every corner, came David Epstein, Pesach Alpert, Shlomo-Chaim Alpert and Anshl Delyaticki. On guard outside were the "lovers" Fanya Feigenbaum and Itche Gratchuk, who, arm in arm, were "promenading" in front of the house. When everyone had arrived, they removed the ladder leading to the attic.

Pesach opened the meeting with a warning to both sides: "We can no longer have two separate sets of leaders here. We must find a middle way, and come to a meeting of the minds."

Anshl asked David: "What is your position today?" Again David vacillated. In principle he was still in favor of defending the ghetto, but he was no longer so adamant about it.

Again Anshl laid down his ultimatum: "Either we all agree to do something concrete about sending Jewish fighters into the forest or I no longer have anything to do with your plan—which only results in doing nothing." He leaped to his feet, his face flushed. "Salon communists who spend all their time in pilpulistic discussions never do any practical work!"

The others tried to calm him down. They sat him down again on the overturned wooden crate by the attic window. No one said a word.

After a brief period of silence, David reproached Anshl for being "in such a big hurry" in this life-and-death matter. Shlomo-Chaim offered a compromise: "In view of the fact that we now have contact with Shchors detachment, we need to do two things—take fighters into the forest and at the same time collect weapons and get them into the homes of all the resistance fighters who are still in the ghetto, so they can put up a fight if the Germans try to stage another one of their roundups."

Anshl thought about this for a moment and agreed. It was also agreed that David would serve as commander of the united partisan organization in the ghetto. Anshl was assigned to organize the collection of weapons. They agreed to meet again in a week to report on their work and to discuss methods of collecting medicaments, underwear, money and weapons, and of getting the finished leather products into the hands of the partisans. And thus Anshl, the hunchback with the bald head, eventually came to train scores of young Jews to be courageous fighters against the Nazis.

Dietrich Hick

———•———

As a young boy in Goebbel's youth movement, Dietrich Hick received his training in terrorizing Jews and stealing their gold. His face always wore a cynical expression and his eyes had the look of a bloodthirsty jackal perpetually on the alert for a victim. He was always accompanied on his "tours" of the ghetto by his "Aryan" she-dog whom he called *"Jude."* His right hand always held a riding-whip that he kept slapping against the leg of his boot. After the dog gave birth to a litter of two puppies, all three animals accompanied him. The moment the ghetto caught wind of these visits, the streets emptied out. Accidentally, a car from the Beuten camp once ran over his yellow bitch while they were in the ghetto. Hick ordered the Jews to give the dog a proper burial.

Eight o'clock one morning in the spring of 1942 Hick ordered an inspection of all the ghetto workers as they were being marched out to their work sites. He lined them up on the Balione bridge and began checking their work passes. At that moment a Jew appeared on the dam, walking leisurely to work and even smoking a cigarette. Enraged, Hick ordered a Jewish policeman to give the sinner 25 lashes, while everyone watched. The policeman administered the punishment, but not to Hick's satisfaction, so Hick ordered a German policeman to give the same number of lashes to the Jewish policeman.

Some time later Hick's superiors in Berlin decided he needed a vacation. Hick used the opportunity to dispose of some of the gold he had robbed from the Jews. Using only Jewish workmen, he had them hide the contraband in various part of his car, quite certain they would keep mum about it.

This was the exemplary "Aryan" officer who lorded it over the Jews of Slonim. His deputy, Stelle, was the same breed of gangster, except that his face was a little redder and a little fuller.

"Exile" in Mohilev

In mid-May the Regional Kommisariat ordered the Judenrat to supply 800 workers, including some handicraftsmen, to do a "special job" in Mohilev for a period of three months. For Quint this was the last straw. Who would volunteer to go away for three months of slave labor? His reply to the Kommisariat was: "Do whatever you wish with me, but I cannot supply 800 workers." He tried the usual methods (including money) to get the number reduced, but the authorities refused to listen. After a while, they agreed to cut the number in half.

From a previously prepared list the Kommisariat sent orders to 400 men: Report on May 26 at the assembly point near the Breger synagogue and bring along food for three days. Since no one believed these "official" documents any longer, no "volunteers" showed up at the appointed place. Whereupon a number of S.S. squads, assisted by Ukrainian police, set out to round up the designated Jews. The Jewish police were also ordered to assist. Soon the ghetto streets were filled with shouts and gunfire.

Meir Khavin, a hat maker, fought free of a Ukrainian guard and jumped over a fence, but a bullet cut him down. Moshe Mishkin hid in his cellar. When the guards came to his house, his sister Basia stood on the cellar door and told them that all the men in the house had gone to the assembly point. Kasriel Eilender, a refugee

132

from Suwalki, climed up to the attic of his workshop and watched the roundup of Jews through a window. Many Poles stood nearby, enjoying the spectacle. One of them caught sight of him at the window and began yelling *Zhid! Zhid!* Two Ukrainian police burst into the house. One charged up to the attic and ordered Eilender to follow him down to the street. Eilender picked up an iron bar and hit him over the head, knocking him off the ladder. Eilender leaped over him and ran out into the street, where he was stopped by two other policemen who ordered him to lie down on the ground.

When they had rounded up about twenty men they loaded them onto a truck and drove them over to the railroad station, where some 300 Jews were already waiting with their packages of food.

These roundups for forced labor gangs resulted in conflicts between the German authorities and the owners of the various workshops. Many had posted armed guards in front of their shops to protect the workers, but despite this a large number of specialists were seized. Before the departure, various Nazi overlords appeared at the assembly point, as well as Reichswehr officers, who also got into the dispute over workers who "belonged" to them. After they selected a large number of men for themselves, other Jews were rounded up in their stead.

During all this tumult, Matus Snovski was in his workshop repairing a machine-gun for Hick, when an S.S.-man and two policemen burst in and started dragging him out. He protested that he was working for the Regional Kommissar and tried to show them his special pass, but the S.S.-man didn't ever deign to look at it. When they had rounded up 50 able-bodied Jews, they marched them all to the railroad station.

Sarah Snovski ran to tell her parents what had happened to her husband. She removed the yellow patch from her clothing and told them she was going over to see Hick. Her mother and father were opposed, afraid she would be shot. Sarah insisted that without Matus their lives would be worth nothing anyway. She ran all the way to the Regional Kommissariat.

At Rabmil's building a guard stopped her and asked her what her business was. She explained that she had to see Hick on an urgent matter. The guard replied sympathetically that the Regional Kommissar was not there at the moment, but that she could tell him what the problem was. Impressed by his humane manner, she asked him to report to Hick as soon as possible that Matus was being sent to Mohilev by mistake. He promised to do so.

She then returned to her post at the window. A few hours later Matus appeared and told her that two gendarmes had come to the assembly point with a list of 25 craftsmen, his name among them, and they were released.

The 400 slave-laborers lay on the hard ground all day outside the station. One young man, who stood up to adjust the knapsack on his back, was shot on the spot by Karl Ziegel, in charge of the transport. Late in the afternoon ten freight cars pulled into the station and the men were shoved into the train, forty men to a car. The three Jewish policemen, who had helped to round up these Jews, started back to the ghetto, but Ziegel stopped them and ordered them to get into the trains along with all the others.

Under Ukrainian guard the train crept along for a day and a night, through Baranovici and Minsk, stopped at Orsha and then proceeded even more slowly to Mohilev. Here the Jews were taken to a labor camp located in a bombed out military installation called "Dimitrov." Jews from other Byelorussian communities were also there, but no matter how hard the Slonimer tried to start a conversation with them, they got no response. On the towers surrounding the installation stood S.S. guards with rifles, keeping a close eye on the prisoners below.

Before they had been given food or water, or even allowed to relieve themselves, the Slonimer were put to work moving heavy slabs of iron from one place to another under a hail of billyjacks wielded by S.S.-men. After this introduction to the camp they were herded into a barracks where S.S. officers were strategically sitting at tables, their revolvers lying ready. Camp chief was Übergruppe-fuehrer Von Den Bak Zilienski, an Austrian "Aryan" with murderous blue eyes.

The S.S. officers ordered each man to state his occupation and lined up 60 craftsmen. The remaining 343 were sent to labor gangs that were building the "Government House."

The 60 craftsmen worked under somewhat better conditions than the common laborers. They were not harried or beaten. Their food ration was also a little better. The laborers were driven to work every morning in trucks. They suffered not only from continuous beatings by the guards, but were given so little to eat that they were slowly starving to death.

Israel Yudelevich worked as a shoemaker, Kasriel Eilender as a soap-maker.

Every Sunday morning there was a selection of the weaker laborers, a kind of "physical check-up." In this way the number of slave laborers decreased week by week, until October 8, 1942, when those who remained of the 343 were all liquidated. The 60 craftsmen were unable to help them in any way.

The soap production was run by Lipa Rosenthal, a German Jew, who "did business" with the personal belongings of murdered Jews, sending things out to the city to be bartered for various products that he needed for his own use. Sensing a potential competitor in Eilender, Rosenthal kept an eye on him and finally accused him—to the camp authorities—of telling lies. Eilender was then assigned to sawing wood for the camp, then to cleaning the bedbugs out of the barracks and the S.S. houses. Later he drove a wagon and transported provisions for the Germans by sleigh.

Among the Soviet army officers who had been taken prisoner, there was an underground partisan organization. One of them, a Jewish colonel, wanted the partisans to know what was going on in the world. When they discovered that Eilender could read German, they collected, from the tailors and shoemakers, old newspapers in which the German officers used to wrap the things they brought in to be repaired. From these newspapers, Eilender used to read and interpret the war news for them.

On February 17 this underground organization executed two German guards, allowing twelve prisoners to escape into the street, where a truck was waiting for them. That same night the S.S. lined up the entire camp outside the barracks and ordered all the "swine" shot. It was to their interest, however, to keep the camp operating, otherwise they themselves would have been sent to the front. So they selected "only" sixty men to be shot.

As the battle-front moved closer to Mohilev, they liquidated the camp. After 18 months of slave-labor the surviving craftsmen—29 of the original 403—were transferred to a camp in Minsk. Here they met Menachem Mendelevich, a foreman, who helped them in whatever way he could.

On their 13th day in Minsk, with the front lines again closer, the Nazis moved the inmates westward. At one of the railroad stations the Slonimer learned—for the first time—about the burning of the ghetto in their hometown.

With the front moving westward, the camps were gradually evacuated to Lublin and Radom, where there was an outbreak of typhus. Here most of the remaining Slonimer perished.

With Soviet troops on the outskirts of Krakow, the slave-laborers hoped for imminent liberation, but the Nazi beast would not let go of its prey. Retreating to Lower Silesia, the Germans left Kasriel Eilender behind in a camp near Wroclaw. On May 8 he was liberated by the Soviet Army. The other surviving Slonimers were taken to the camp at Matthausen and given camp clothing. Here they met prisoners from France, Germany and other European countries. The camp was so crowded that people slept sitting up.

After nine days the few survivors had the opportunity to see the death camp at Ebensee, where the helpless inmates, dying of starvation, were falling like flies. When the American army entered the camp, only Israel Yudelevich and the son of Weinstein (the painter) were still alive.

Underneath the Earth

After establishing contact with the Shchors detachment and after the unification of the two partisan groups, the work went more smoothly, spread out through the ghetto and became a force to be reckoned with. People began to sense that something important was happening. It gave them hope for the future. The number of German weapons "liberated" grew from day to day. At great risk, every gun-part, every rifle, every automatic, every grenade and every pistol was delivered to the ghetto underground and then, with extreme caution, to the Russian partisans in the forest.

In this situation the question arose of setting up workshops to clean, assemble and repair the weapons. To this end David Guskin thought up a plan: they would dig an underground shop which could also serve as a corridor leading to the forest. Yankev Pripstein proposed that they use the the cellar in the two-story building on Bernardino Street (across from the Judenrat) where he lived with his parents. Near the building there was a little street that led to the marketplace and to Vorobiovski's building outside the ghetto. This underground corridor led to the trash bin in Vorobiovski's courtyard.

The plan was that in this workshop they would prepare the weapons and, if need be, it could also be used for arming people at night, or for crossing the marketplace to Klebanski Street (Apothe-

137

cary Street), from there to the highway and the Jewish cemetery in the Ruzany heights, a stone's throw from the forest.

With utmost caution (because of the neighbors) they dug, during the night, a corridor 8-10 meters long. The earth that was dug out they spread evenly over the floor of the big cellar. They camouflaged the door and ran an electric line into the corridor. After setting up the workshop they needed to bring in the cache of weapons and get to work, but just at the moment when everything was ready, they ran into trouble. One of the neighbors noticed the shadow of a man disappearing into the cellar. Suspecting that it was a thief, he enlisted a few other neighbors and together they went into the cellar with flashlights.

Noticing that the cellar floor seemed to have risen, they started examining the walls and came upon the new door. The men inside the workshop heard the neighbors talking and turned out the lights, but it was too late. The neighbors pushed open the door and surprised the three men with weapons in their hands. David Guskin tried telling them a story about building a hiding-place, but they started a hullaballoo about the Jews asking for trouble and that the partisans would kill them all. It soon became clear what was at stake here. After a brief meeting the ghetto partisans decided that the first thing they had to do was save the few weapons that were already in the workshop. The nearest place they could take them to was Jachvidovitch's on Breger Street. Feverishly, they did so.

Another hiding-place for weapons had been set up in Kunitz' smithy on Opera Street. The weapons were hidden under chunks of scrap metal. Then Fidrik, who was a permanent contact between the Jews and the Russian partisans, would come in from the village and they would hide the weapons, medicaments and warm clothing in his hay wagon. Anshl himself ran the operation because he worked nearby at the Office of Water Transportation, across from the blacksmith shop.

Later the weapons cache was hidden with the Archik brothers and with Abraham Band on Michalovski Street. From there the weapons went straight to the partisans through the dam.

The unified committee also decided to set up a radio in a house on Breger Street near the synagogue. For this purpose they dug a passageway under the floor, with an entrance through a metal door, which Pesach Alpert installed. The radio receiver, built by Nathan Licker from Lomze, helped a great deal in getting war news from Moscow, so that they didn't have to live with the German lies.

Itche Gratchuk,
Nonye Zirinski and Eric Stein

Itche Gratchuk worked in the kitchen of the German watch in the Beuten camp, keeping a fire going under the kettles and also tending the pigpens. At the same time, he was also smuggling weapons out of the camp. Over his arm he always carried the canvas case of a gas-mask—which frequently held grenades. Sometimes he would hang his gas-mask on the kitchen wall while he did his work at the kettles and the pigpens.

This naive carelessness once caused a mishap that almost ended in tragedy. Working in the kitchen with him was a Polish woman who spoke German and who was friendly with the Germans. One day her curiosity got the best of her and she looked inside Itche's gas-mask . . . She immediately took it to a German officer named Mutz, who was eating breakfast nearby. At that moment Itche stepped into the kitchen and heard the unusual uproar. Without stopping to inquire about the cause of the excitement he beat a retreat and got as far away from there as he could. For a few weeks he stayed hidden in the homes of his friends in the resistance.

After this accident Sergeant Braun and Officer Mutz kept count of the weapons that were handed out each morning to the Jewish workers for repair. As a consequence it became more and more difficult for the partisans to obtain gun parts. For a while this activity ceased entirely. They began looking for new sources. In desperation they decided to make an effort to enlist the help of Eric Stein, a German Jew who was in charge of the weapons store-house and carried the keys in his pocket. It was common knowledge that up until Hitler came to power, Stein had been a captain in the German armed forces. He had come to the camp together with the Germans and lived in the same quarters with them, not far from the pigpens and the locksmith shop. The Germans had great con-fidence in him as a weapons specialist and excused him from wearing the yellow patch. As a result, the local Jews mistrusted him and he kept his distance from them. The people in the Jewish underground, however, wanted to reach him somehow, and Nonye Zirinski was chosen to "feel him out."

Nonye struck up a friendship with him and waited for a day when he found him alone just as he was unlocking a weapons bin. Admiring the large number of machine-guns and automatics, he remarked off-handedly: "If only some of these weapons could end up in the hands of our Jewish partisans . . ." He watched Stein's face. What he saw was an expression of joy and surprise. Nonye looked around and decided to take a risk:

"They are carrying out their plan of wiping out all the Jews," he continued, "so we Jewish partisans must take revenge on them right here in Byelorussia." Sensing a favorable response from Stein, Nonye aimed closer to the target. "We're prepared to accept you and your wife into our partisan detachment where we shall all fight together against the damned Hitler plague . . ."

"I've been waiting a long time for this!" Stein said. "You can count on my full cooperation. I'm ready to go out and kill some of these murdering Nazis, even if it means giving up my own life to do so!"

The Judenrat and
the Ghetto Partisans

———————•———————

Although the partisan movement in the ghetto was necessarily secretive, it had broad contacts among the Jews. Like similar organizations, it was built on units of only a few people, in this case, five. These cells were led by commanders who reported to a chief, in this case Anshl Delyaticki. Even the Judenrat yielded to the partisans and, in whatever way they could, met their needs.

The partisans knew full well that they would soon be moving into the forests. They therefore prepared themselves systematically and, in addition to guns, laid up stores of clothing, shoes, boots, medicaments and money. Some of these things were sent ahead to the Shchors brigade, whose ranks they were supposed to join.

It is known that on several occasions Max Rabinowicz wrote out Judenrat orders for partisans to go to Bitten on some invented errand. More than once he warned Anshl when the Gestapo was hot on his trail.

David Epstein was once caught bringing a loaf of bread into the ghetto, which was *verboten*. Something had to be done quickly. Pesach Alpert rushed over to Quint's office and pleaded with him to intervene. Quint merely asked him: "Is he important to you?" Pesach nodded: "Irreplaceable." Quint agreed to do something.

142

Watching from a distance, Anshl saw Quint take out a handkerchief, unfold it and remove several gold coins. When Rabinowicz later handed the guard at the gate a bottle of whisky and Epstein walked away from there with the loaf of bread still in his hand, Anshl was so moved that he wept . . .

A Jewish Agent for the Sicherheitsdienst

The German S.D. (security services) kept installing agents among the Jewish population in the ghetto. Their numbers were insignificant, but they were enough to hamper the work of the partisans and bedevil the lives of the Jews.

One such traitor was a refugee from Warsaw named Mariampol. Officially he was a foreman on a construction job, but there came a moment when he unmasked himself. Leading a group of workers who were cleaning out trash bins on Opera Street, it dawned on him one day that the workers were trying to hide several bins from him. When he reported this to the S.D. he added that he had "uncovered a partisan arsenal." From that moment the Jews avoided him like the plague.

Working with Anshl on the dam was a group of Jewish children that the Germans had rounded up from surrounding towns—starving, tattered orphans whose parents had been murdered by the Nazis. The Regional Kommissariat used them to do hard labor such as carrying lumber or pulling rusty nails out of old boards. Instead of food they were given whippings. One day these children found some potatoes in a ditch. Lighting a fire, they started baking their lucky find, but Mariampol came running up in a rage and began beating them for "leaving the job." He stamped out the fire and trampled their precious potatoes.

It happened that on that particular day Anshl was working nearby and witnessed this scene. Unable to contain himself, despite his role in the underground which made it dangerous for him to tangle with this informer, he ran over and dealt Mariampol a few well-deserved punches along with a few well-deserved epithets. One of the Kunitz brothers ran out of his smithy to help Anshl. A few Jewish wagon-drivers appeared and tried to "separate" the combatants, but actually they kept a tight grip on Mariampol, who by that time was frothing at the mouth.

Quite by accident, a Byelorussian policeman arrived at that moment. Mariampol instructed him to arrest Anshl and take him to the S.D. On the way, the three of them—Mariampol, the policeman and Anshl—stopped at the accounting office of the German Lumber and Forestry Department where Mariampol had some business to take care of. One of the bookkeepers there (Kaplan) who was a good friend of Anshl's, asked Anshl why he was being arrested. Anshl obliged him by telling everyone within earshot the whole story. Mariampol threatened to report "the whole gang" to the S.D.

Some of the Jews in the place pleaded with him not to deliver a fellow Jew into the hands of the enemy, but this informer and provocateur could not make peace with the idea of releasing his victim. Finally Kaplan, with the help of several other refugees from Poland, managed to lock Mariampol in another room while they "negotiated" with the policeman and sent him on his way . . .

There is no question that they saved Anshl's life.

The Great Synagogue: a Channel for Weapons

At the end of May a branch of OST, a German farm equipment company, was opened in Slonim in the foyer of the Great Synagogue. Most of this machinery went to large farms that supplied produce to the German occupier. The director was an ill-tempered old German named Rick. Working for him as a bookkeeper was a Byelorussian named Sosnowski. The manager of the warehouse was a Tatar named Baritonchik.

Through Sosnowski, Nonye Zirinski, a locksmith, got a job there assembling the machine parts for the customers. He did not have very much to do, however, because it was more convenient for the farmer to take the parts home separately and there assemble the machine himself. Thus Zirinski mostly assembled models of each type of machine displayed in the "showroom"—the foyer of the synagogue.

Nonye's yellow armband, which read "Locksmith for the Regional Kommissariat," gave him the privilege of walking through

146

the city alone on his way to and from work. This was a very desirable situation for the partisans because Nonye now had the opportunity to contact people outside the ghetto and in the busy center of town. From there it was easier to send the weapons right to the forest.

During the war years, paper currency was practically worthless. The peasants employed a barter system instead—exchanging their farm products for salt, matches, soda, soap, kerosene, candles, etc. And since the Germans often made sudden raids on the marketplace and confiscated these products, the peasants kept them in sacks on their backs and went from door to door to do the bartering. Frequently they came into the "showroom" to admire or to buy pieces of farm equipment.

The partisans decided to take advantage of this situation. Zirinski was often alone in the synagogue. Baritonchik, who trusted him and sympathized with the plight of the Jews, was "away on business" for long periods of time. The partisans brought some of the small arms from the Beuten camp into the synagogue and Nonye hid them away in various drawers in the walls, including the Ark which had once housed the Torah scrolls. In addition to weapons, he also hid radio parts, medicaments and printing type.

The weapons "transporters" would come to the "showroom" in groups. Those who wore the same kind of yellow armband as Nonye entered one at a time and unloaded their "merchandise." Often Nonye himself took a walk to the Beuten camp and brought back a weapon or two. The synagogue was so crowded with machines and machine parts that no one but Nonye could find his way around the place. He would pack up the weapons in a sack and, at an appointed time, a courier would come from the village with a sack of farm products on his back. If he spoke the right password, the sacks were exchanged. This "operation" never aroused any suspicion.

The partisan Nikolai Filenchik (from the village of Zalesia) would come into the showroom to look at the equipment. If Baritonchik were present, Nonye would make the exchange behind a large crate while tne "customer" discussed prices ana quality with the Tatar. Then he would leave the synagogue with the sack of weapons, heave it on the back of his wagon, cover it with straw and crack his whip over the horse's flanks . . .

The Conference

The partisan underground kept growing, sinking roots everywhere and enlisting the help of everyone and everything that would serve its cause.

The time was ripe for a conference with representatives of various enterprises where Jews were working for the occupying power. Such a conference took place on June 10th in the home of the tannery worker Chaim Azef on Balione Street. Represented were mainly the tanneries, the tailor shops, the carpenter shops and the shoemaker shops. Present, among others, were David, Pesach, Anshl, Shlomo-Chaim, Yankl Pripstein, the brothers Chaim and Avreml Azef and Noah Abramowski (all of whom we have met before on these pages.)

David Epstein was the main speaker. Knowing the Jewish handicraftsmen well—having grown up in their milieu himself—he understood how to speak to them so they would understand him. In his long and interesting report he described the new situation in detail and explained that until the Red Army crushed the German fascists the killing of Jews would continue and that therefore it was the duty of the partisans themselves to hasten this defeat. Listing concrete tasks for the future he proposed that self-defense units be formed in every German camp and enterprise to resist the Nazis in the event they started a new massacre. This proposal was adopted unanimously.

In the discussion that followed, the leather workers asked: "All the leather we have been liberating—where is it going?" The leadership explained that it was all going to the partisan bases in the ghetto and to the Shchors detachment, which the first groups of ghetto partisans would join in the very near future.

All the participants in the conference praised the work of the leadership and everyone left feeling inspired and hopeful for the future.

First Ghetto
Partisans in the Forest

With the growing influence of the partisan movement in the ghetto, the popularity of its leaders grew correspondingly, despite the conspiratorial nature of the organization. The identity of the leaders was well known. Anshl, Pesach and David were often called upon to answer questions and interpret events. Usually this took place at meetings in homes. It should not be forgotten that among the ghetto population there was an element of unknown and uncontrolled individuals who could not be trusted and whom one had to guard against all the time.

During this period it was Anshl who became especially well known. The Jews held him in great honor as one of the partisan organizers. He was therefore forced to go underground. A place was found for him in David Guskin's barn on Michalowski Street and it became his "headquarters."

On June 12th instructions finally arrived from the Shchors detachment: send us a few of your people. Four partisans were chosen: Itche Gratchuk, Fanye Feigenbaum and two refugees from Poland (one of them was named David Appelboym). Well armed, they were led out to the "Wolf Caves" outside of Bitten by Archik Bank and Zerach Kremien.

The spreading partisan fever in the ghetto and the exit of the first four partisans into the forest soon was made known to the German authorities. Apparently they were being kept informed by their Jewish agents. A few days after the partisans went into the forest, Anshl received a message from Max Rabinowicz: "Urgent we meet at once."

With extreme caution Anshl and David Guskin stole out of Michalowski Street one night and made their way stealthily to the home of the teacher Yachvidowicz on Breger Street. Max Rabinowicz was already there.

In a little room, by candlelight, Max and Anshl sat across from each other, their shadows large and bent on the wall behind them. Max's face seemed more gaunt than ever. Anshl's bald head, with the gray hair around his ears, was pulled down deep between his shoulders, as he listened to Max's whispered report:

"Yesterday the Jewish Police received an order from the Gestapo: Arrest Anshl Delyaticki and bring him to us. Therefore Misha Lotz and I decided we had to talk with you. What shall we do now?"

Anshl had not expected this development. He took a deep breath and his answer came slowly, one word at a time. "I thank you both for your unselfish concern. What you have done is very important not only for me personally but for our whole movement. You know that I'm deeply involved in all of its activities. I've got to choose a suitable representative and turn over all the strings to him so he can tie them together and continue the work. Give me three days. Tell the Nazi bastards that you're looking for me and haven't found me yet. During those three days I'll try to get to our detachment in the forest."

As they shook hands emotionally, Anshl added: "Our underground will remember your brave deed and will repay you for it at the earliest opportunity. Be aware that time is now on *our* side."

During the next three days Anshl set up the continuity of the partisan affairs. He was especially concerned that the procurement of weapons go on just as it had in the past. As his replacement he chose the young and energetic Vove Abramson, from Minsk.

Vove immediately arranged for a "triangular" delivery system for the weapons: from Beuten camp to Nonye Zarinski in the Great Synagogue, where Filenchik would pick up the "merchandise" and deliver it straight to the detachment in the forest.

On June 22nd, the first anniversary of Hitler's invasion of the Soviet Union, Anshl too went into the forest. With him went Dr. Blumovich, to work as a physician for the Shchors detachment.

The Wannsee Conference

From 1933, when Hitler came to power, to 1942, eleven million Jews fell into his hands. His "wealth of Jews" multiplied tremendously after he seized Poland, Ukrainia, Byelorussia, Lithuania, Latvia, Moldavia, the Crimea and many large Russian cities.

For the Nazis the Jewish problem had matured sufficiently for them to decide on a "final solution," and for that purpose they called a special meeting.

On June 20, 1942 this conference was opened in an isolated little palace in Wannsee, a suburb of Berlin. In attendance were fourteen high Nazi criminals, mostly military rulers over various countries, along with several political and legal experts from the Nazi Party.

To open the meeting the Chairman, Reinhard Heydrich, Deputy Protector of Bohemia and Moravia, reported that the Fuehrer was greatly concerned about the over ten million Jews in his "jurisdiction." Up until then, Heydrich told the conference, the Fuehrer had expected an attempt by the western countries to get those Jews out, to buy them in exchange for certain agreements with the Reich, but they had disappointed him. No one was interested in his great treasure of "Jewish merchandise." And now that America had entered the war, there was nothing further to expect from them.

Heydrich also reported that just to hold on to so many Jews and do nothing with them made no sense. He therefore proposed that they now give serious consideration to the final solution of the Jewish problem.

Eichmann then put forward some practical, technical suggestions as to how large numbers of Jews could be liquidated. He knew from memory how many and in what regions or city they were to be found, pointing out the best rail lines available to do the transporting and where trucks would be necessary to move Jews to the gas chambers. At the same time, he regretted that there were still minor gaps in the efficient operation of the death camps.

When a representative of the German justice system, an older Party member, tried to save the "half German" offspring of mixed marriages, many at the conference ridiculed him. Jewish blood is always stronger than German blood, they argued, so the half Germans were actually whole Jews. If they were left alive, the pure Aryans would demean themselves by greeting them with the Heil Hitler salute. The jurist explained that he was too old for this sort of thing.

The Wannsee Conference lasted only 85 minutes, but it decided the fate of European Jewry.

Four months after this collection of murderers met in Wannsee, Czech partisans executed the "blond beast," Reinhard Heydrich, who was Hitler's favorite, and whom everyone regarded as the most suitable candidate to take the Fuehrer's place.

Eichmann's inglorious end is well known to everyone . . .

Preparations for
a New Bloodbath

At the end of May the Regional Kommissar received an order from Berlin to liquidate the rest of the Jews in Slonim—in accordance with his own judgment.

Again dark clouds hung heavy over the ghetto. Gerth Erren and his bloodthirsty helpers began preparing for the "big day." The first thing he did was to step up the anti-Semitic propaganda among the non-Jewish population. At the work-sites, beatings and other punishments were intensified to the point of murder.

A Byelorussian newspaper in Baranovici spread the Nazi lies about "Jews taking over the world," about "Jewish responsibility for the war." "When the National Socialists have made the whole world Judenrein, the only place to see a Jew will be on movie screens or in museums."

Rumors about a new massacre spread through the ghetto. Some people even "knew" the exact date—"Monday, the 29th of June." How did they know? German acquaintances had warned them to be ready. Jews who worked for the Regional Kommissariat passed on the news about the telegram from Berlin. There were even people who had seen the telegram "with their own eyes."

Every day the signs were studied anew. But no one had any premonition of the horror that was advancing upon them. No one really felt that each passing day was bringing them a step closer to death.

Around the 15th of June the Germans sent in a new executioner: *Stabsleiter* Ritmeyer, who was short and potbellied but with the cold face of a hangman. He had been sent from Baranovici as a "specialist" to regulate the Final Solution of the Jewish Question in Slonim and he immediately made it clear to the "rebellious Jews" that he meant business. For attempting to smuggle a bottle of milk or a loaf of bread into the ghetto the penalty was death, with no questions asked. Compared to him, Hick was an angel.

It was at this time that a "black cat" ran between the Poles and the Germans, casting a shadow on their previous cooperation in killing Jews. The Regional Kommissar began a "clean-up" of the Polish intelligentsia, burying eighty of them on Petralevici Hill. This miniature German "Aktion" caused real confusion among the Poles. There were even cases of Poles "escaping" to the ghetto and asking Jewish acquaintances to hide them from the Nazis.

Many Jews believed that after this episode the attitude of the Poles toward the Germans would change, that now they would sympathize with the Jews in the ghetto and even help them. In the cynical strategy of the Regional Kommissar, however, this anti-Polish enterprise—which was organized immediately prior to the Jewish massacre—was intended as a smokescreen to dull the watchfulness of the Jews and to mislead them, because preparations for the massacre were becoming noticeable. From Bernardino Street, people in the ghetto could see dozens of trucks parked in the marketplace and surrounded by squads of police. At the same time, arrests of Poles were continuing.

The Jews soon came to the conclusion that it was time to get their hiding-places ready. Judging by the previous German "Aktions," they expected this new massacre to last a single day. They would stay hidden for 24 hours until things quieted down and then they would surface again.

The Nazis, on their part, had one last card to play in this "game"—they delivered a larger quantity of flour than usual to the Judenrat, along with newly printed ration cards giving every Jew, without exception, 300 grams of bread. This trick worked. If the Germans were giving out special ration cards, then the rumors of a massacre must be unfounded or just another means of spreading panic. Even some of the partisan leaders misinterpreted the signs.

On June 27th the Germans rounded up several hundred Poles. On the 28th the Jews in the ghetto saw what looked like a terror campaign against Poles. For example, Sluzewski was fishing along the canal near the Balione Bridge when three S.S.-men suddenly came up and arrested him. Sluzewski showed them his pass. The S.S.-men looked at it, tore it up, threw it into the water and marched Sluzewski off to jail. That same day a truck filled with Poles rode noisily through the ghetto on the way to the prison.

But on the same day, also, about 40 new trucks and 200 S.S. troops drove into the marketplace. Apparently Ritmeyer suspected the Germans in Slonim of being too "familiar" with the Jews in the ghetto, so he replaced them with S.S.-men from Baranovici, as well as with police from the Ukraine, Lithuania, Latvia and Estonia.

There were Jews in the ghetto who insisted that all these tricks were intended as a cover for German preparations for a third massacre, but Quint laughed at their suspicions.

Like a regimental commander planning an attack on enemy forces, Ritmeyer surveyed the ghetto borders, calculating how many troops he would need at each section of the "battlefront." Then he surveyed the battle positions from another angle: from Michalowski Street to Shaya's Bridge he calmly rowed a canoe along the canal, mapping out the ghetto positions on either shore.

That evening the ghetto's nerves had reached the breaking-point. Dr. Noah Kaplinski met with Quint, who explained the new situation to him: "Police in trucks have surrounded the ghetto. Tomorrow morning there will be a roundup of all known partisans." It never occurred to him that he himself had only a few more hours to live.

When the sun disappeared behind the Ruznoy heights, all the shadows merged into a dark, cool blanket over the lower city. From the calm waters of the Szczara River and the canal rose a light mist which veiled the willows, the maples, the lindens and the wooden bridges. The meadow around Fein's sawmill turned dark green, enveloped the vari-colored cows and became a smooth, velvet carpet.

The right bank of the river, overgrown with tall waterplants, is a breeding-ground for frogs. Along the shores the imperceptibly flowing water is covered with families of white lily pads that emanate an intoxicating fragrance. The birds, singing a farewell to the receding day, have nested down for the short summer night and ceased their chattering. Here and there a last birdcall is heard from their hiding-places among the trees and bushes.

Louder and louder grows the frog chorus. No wonder the Jews named the street between the Szczara and the canal "Zhabinke" — Frog Alley.

An evening breeze, light as a butterfly, caresses the grass around the quiet waters. Its whispering refreshes the clean air. Everything breathes with quiet, cheerful calm.

The ghetto Jews stare through the barbed wire with envy and with feelings for all these beauties of nature. Gradually the chaos of the day is stilled.

But in accordance with instructions from the partisans, sentries have been posted outside the houses to warn the sleeping Jews at the first sign of German "activity."

The Signal

June 29th, at dawn, the German hangmen completed their feverish preparations for the slaughter of Slonim's surviving 12,000 Jews. Trucks roared to and from the area around the ghetto, discharging hundreds of heavily armed thugs. An "international" army of Jew-haters, carrying machine-guns, hand-grenades, revolvers and daggers took up positions at all the exits from the ghetto, tightening an iron hoop around its rim. This time they did not differentiate between the handicraftsmen on the island and the rest of the Jews, as they had done during the second massacre.

People moved like shadows along the ghetto streets, trying to comprehend the terror that had suddenly encircled them. Reuben Abramowicz asked a Latvian guard through the barbed wire: "What's going on?" The guard replied: "It's none of your business!" Another guard told him: "Partisans have gathered in the ghetto here and we're going to drive them out."

By six o'clock that morning Gershon Quint himself was trying to digest the frightful truth. As the "boss" of the ghetto he ran around, advising Jews to get down into their hiding-places immediately. With the daylight came the panic.

As they did every morning, columns of workers marched to the ghetto gates. They were turned back with a curt "No work today!"

Quint, Max Rabinowicz and Misha Latz stood at the main gate on Ulan Street and waited, their faces pale and troubled. From their own experience they were deathly afraid of Ritmeyer. His order on June 29th, sending the German officers Bonke, Schultz, Reinert, Braun and others out of the ghetto to other "assignments" was extremely ominous.

As Ritmeyer's car drove up, Quint stepped forward out of line. Ritmeyer stepped out of the car. Quint removed his hat, bowed and said politely, "How is the Herr Stabsleiter?" Ritmeyer's reply came from his revolver. Quint fell backward to the ground. His hat rolled off his head and stopped near his limp, outstretched hand. Mimicking a Yiddish accent Ritmeyer repeated, *"Vos machn zi, Herr Stabsleiter?"* Quint was still shuddering convulsively as Ritmeyer barked: "Don't you have anything else to say to me?"

Another officer came up and shot Quint again, bent down over him and took a handful of gold coins out of his trouser pocket. Apparently Quint had promised it to him in return for certain "favors."

The bullet that killed Quint made it absolutely clear to everyone that the last act of the Slonim tragedy was about to begin. The Jewish police who, all this time, were standing at their posts, now fled in all directions. Seeing this, the Jews disappeared into their hiding-places.

For the waiting murder squads, Ritmeyer's shot was a signal to begin their day's work. With cries of *"Raus! Raus!"* they burst into the ghetto, firing their automatic weapons in all directions. The Jews of Slonim, however, had vanished, except for three of the partisan leaders—Vove Abramson (Anshl's deputy), Yoske Shuchatowicz and one of the Kunitze brothers. Having set up a machine-gun in a window of Moyshe Zinkin's house on Breger Street, they waited . . .

The first wave of Germans to come within range was met by a fusillade of bullets. Startled by this unexpected "Jewish rebellion," they retreated in panic, leaving their dead and wounded behind on the ghetto street.

Yoske and Kunitze, however, had been badly wounded, giving the attackers time to regroup and begin their counterattack—much more slowly and cautiously now. Alone at the machine-gun, Vove was ready for them. Again the Germans retreated—until Vove ran out of bullets. His helpless comrades were bleeding to death. He used his grenades, but his supply of these was limited too.

In the ensuing pause, the Germans ordered Vove to surrender. Vove did so, holding his last grenade in his hand. As they surrounded him, he pulled the pin. Several enemy soldiers died with him . . .

When the shooting and the turmoil stopped, the Germans realized that they had rounded up only about thirty Jews. It was time for another one of Ritmeyer's tricks. He sent the German factory supervisors to "negotiate" with their Jewish workers. This time the trick did not work. The bullets that felled Quint had finally opened Jewish eyes.

Stabsleiter Neudorf then persuaded Engineer Fitchkarnik, from Vilna, to talk to his tannery workers. Stabsleiter Winger did the same with Joseph Starobinetz and his sawmill workers. If the workers would come out on the dam, nothing would happen to them except a review of their work passes.

On the dam at the Hanging Bridge, Eliezer Gandler, Moyshe Volye, Hirsh Futrisky, Joseph Fayevsky, Reuben Weiner and a few other leather and sawmill workers appeared with their families. As the last person appeared, they were all herded together, with a machine-gun trained on them, and marched to the church in Zamoshtche. Neudorf was waiting for them there with a list of names. Calling out several of the names, he ordered the men to step out of line. They were beaten and taken to the church courtyard. Here another guard, revolver in hand, ordered them to line up facing the wall and wait there until their families were marched by them. Anyone who turned around would be shot on the spot.

As the women, children and old people were being herded toward the "Red Tavern," Osher Wolpe shoved a German guard aside and ran into the courtyard. The guard chased him and killed him with his bayonet.

The Third Massacre

Realizing that his "humanitarian" tactics would no longer deceive many Jews, Ritmeyer, cigar in mouth, said to one of his aides: "When we set fire to their homes, the bedbugs will come running out by themselves."

His order to do this came at ten o'clock. Fire-bombs flew into Jewish windows and doors. In only a few minutes the whole working-class neighborhood of Balione was ablaze.

The island is separated from the ghetto by a natural water boundary; in addition, the Germans surrounding it attacked with gasoline and grenades. It was impossible to escape. At the same time, in full battle-dress, the firefighters Kommando prevented the flames from spreading to the "Aryan" side.

In their hiding-places the Jews were now literally caught between two fires. The bunkers were not built to withstand flame and smoke. Half-crazed mothers and fathers, as they ran out of the buildings, were forced to watch as the Nazis hurled children back into the blaze. Jewish blood flowed as in a slaughter-house. Caught

164

and driven to the gathering-place on the dam, Jews had to pass Quint's body, still lying on the ground in a pool of blood. During all this, the organizers of the butchery did not forget to serve whiskey from a barrel on a handcart to every man engaged in the "operation."

Meanwhile the flames were consuming Jewish homes, leaving only blackened embers. Over all of Slonim, but especially over the ghetto, hung a fiery odor that burned the eyes. The stink of death was everywhere. The deafening gunfire and the exploding grenades assailed the ears. The yells of an army of criminals in German uniform curdled the blood.

In the midst of the slaughter the German factory managers went looking for their skilled craftsmen. When they found them they gave new yellow passes to the "lucky ones." The rest went to prison, or to the Beuten camp, to wait until a bullet would release them from their agony.

The next day, Tuesday, the S.S. and their helpers went through the houses that the fire had spared, looking for Jews in hiding-places. Those who fell into their hands were first beaten unmercifully. Then the skilled workers were selected out and permitted to take along their wives and *one* child. The rest were taken away to be imprisoned or shot. Unbearable scenes took place when parents had to make a choice of which child to take with them. Many parents refused to do this and chose death with their families.

Max Silverman, at the very beginning of the massacre, was ordered by Neudorf to go to the churchyard. He refused and went to his death with his wife. There were cases where those Jews who chose to die rather than work for the enemy had to fight with their tormentors for the right to die.

During this massacre the Germans dug three mass graves in which they buried the Jews who were shot or burned to death.

The terrible news about the burning of the Slonim ghetto was brought to the Jews of Bitten by the Byelorussian, P. Gritchik, of the village of Kazino. He described in detail how the burning ghetto was surrounded by a cordon of heavily armed soldiers, how they used guard dogs to ferret out people in underground hiding-places, how the Nazis were setting fire to those hiding-places and shooting the victims as they emerged with the clothing on their backs in flames.

Days of Life and Death

For three consecutive days the Germans ruthlessly set fire to house after house in the ghetto, trying to flush the Jews out of their hiding-places. Day and night the ghetto was heavily guarded by an inflamed pack of howling beasts that killed, burned Jews alive, drowned Jews in the canal, in the river, raped and plundered. Each day the number of the dead grew larger and the number of the living smaller, but still the executioners fell behind in their schedule.

Ritmeyer, Erren and Hick refined their strategy. On Wednesday they selected a hundred men from the jail, issued them yellow passes, brought them back to the burning ghetto and ordered them to call out to their friends that if they surrendered, they too would be given new work passes. The men carried out the instructions. That evening a truck from the Beuten camp rode through the ghetto announcing through a loudspeaker that every worker in the camp who had survived must come out and get into the truck, which would take Jews back to their jobs.

Many of the Beuten camp workers came out, plus other Jews, hoping that this would be their salvation too. The German guards from the camp used their rifle butts to keep these people away from the truck.

This trick proved successful. Wednesday and Thursday hundreds of middle-aged men came out of the hiding-places. They were

167

given passes and taken to the Beuten camp. On Friday, Saturday and Sunday, groups of men who had stayed in their bunkers because they didn't believe the German promises came out and were taken not to the camp but to the prison. In the prison, the Jews were crowded more than a hundred men to a cell. They were not given any food; water only once a day. Many of the men had not eaten since they had gone into hiding. Under such conditions, ordinary human beings become apathetic, indifferent to their fate.

About 800 craftsmen were moved to a new, smaller ghetto. Most of the Jewish doctors in Slonim were also moved to that ghetto and given permission to take their families with them. At the same time, Erren issued an order that only a hundred Jewish women were to be allowed to live. The physicians were organized into "sanitation brigades" with special Red Cross armbands that permitted them to move about freely over the burned out ghetto. Their job was to collect the corpses and whatever usable food products they could find.

After the Jews had been ground down in prison for a few days, a Nazi named Hertz would line them up in the courtyard and, waving his hands like a conductor, would make a selection: *"Rechts!"* Further down the line he would select another man, barking out *"Rechts!"* Everyone knew that one row of men would go to their death and another row would go somewhere else—for a little while. This "musical exercise" of Hertz's resulted in heartwrenching tragedies, because he deliberately separated families. When anyone tried to step into the wrong line he would slowly pull out his revolver, calmly shoot him and go on with his selection, *"Rechts!"* The few people he selected would be taken to the Beuten camp, the rest went to Petralevici, where they were shot.

The Polish prison warden had only one thing to say to those Jews going to their death. "Remember, Jews, walk slowly and quietly. Don't resist. Don't try to escape. If you take my advice, you'll die an honorable death and get a decent burial. If you don't, they'll throw your body to the dogs."

Seven brave young Jews did not heed his advice. They climbed over the high prison wall and disappeared.

At that time over 3000 men were crowded into the Beuten camp, where the same kind of selections were carried out, except that the Jews were lined up in two rows around the long barracks. During the selections the Jews were "assured" that in prison they would receive the long-awaited passes. But the trucks took them Petralewicz.

On one such occasion an old carpenter pulled a pass out of his pocket and said, "I already have one." Corporal Mutz shot him on the spot, without even looking at the pass.

A few hours later Mutz was instructed to send five more Jews to be shot. On the way to Petralewicz, Yakov Vaksmen jumped out of the truck and vanished. Mutz returned to the Beuten camp and issued an ultimatum: He needed one volunteer to take Vaksmen's place, otherwise he would take ten Jews instead. As he said this he looked at his watch. "I'll wait five minutes and no longer!"

After a few minutes one volunteer came forward. His name was Katz. A refugee from Lodz, he had served Mutz so well that the other Jews considered him to be an informer. What impelled him to do this? Perhaps it was his way of atoning for the wrongs he had committed against his fellow Jews. Mutz had no compunction about obliging him.

For two weeks the Nazis did not let the Jews catch their breath or even lick their wounds. They did not know which way to turn. Everywhere lay death—burning houses, prison, labor camp, mass graves. All this time the non-Jews in Slonim stood behind their shuttered windows and looked out. Others stood in the streets at a distance and observed the Jewish catastrophe. Most of them were not disturbed by what they saw; they were not angry with the Nazis for what they were doing to the Jews. Many were infected by Hitler's propaganda. Some fanatical Christians believed that God had "turned his face away" from the Jews and was punishing them through the Germans.

There were, however, a small number of non-Jews whose sympathies were with the suffering Jewish people, who helped them in every way they could, often at the risk of their own lives, because they understood that Hitler was the common enemy of Jews, Poles and Russians alike.

The fires razed the densely populated Jewish neighborhoods in Slonim: Breger and its many narrow side-streets, the island, Opera Street, both Michalowski Streets, many buildings on Skrobive Street, all the houses on both dams, a section of Bridge Street and several housed on Bernardino Street. Thousands perished in the hiding-places. When the "Aryan" population of the city was given permission to use the Balione Bridge and Ulan Street again, their eyes were met by a fearful sight. Burned out skeletons of buildings. Household goods strewn over the streets. Corpses. Limbs separated from bodies. Pools of blood that had not yet dried. The carnage and the chaos shook the entire population of Slonim to its depths.

Thus, in July 1942, the Jewish community of Slonim was finally annihilated by the "supermen" of the Third Reich.

Every Jew who survived the third massacre had a different story to tell—and there are hundreds of them . . .

The Ghetto in Flames

The first building the Nazis demolished in the ghetto was the Jewish hospital on Michalowski Street which the Judenrat had opened with so much effort and in the face of many obstacles. A few grenades blew the little hospital to bits, along with its patients. The medical personnel was taken to the ditches at Petralewicz and shot.

•

In the hiding-place of the Band family on Michalowski Street they soon began to suffer from lack of air. A refugee from Suwalki demanded that they let him out before he died of suffocation. They waited until all was quiet in the house above and then they let him out. Avreml Band, who was waiting to close the trap-door immediately, heard police chasing the man, who had ducked into another cellar. But Avreml was not able to close the door all the way and soon the police dogs discovered the hiding-place. Ordering everyone to come out, the police poked around through the opening with their gun-barrels, barely missing Avreml's face. While the people in the cellar held their breath, the police apparently decided that there had been only one person there and finally left.

171

•

In accordance with instructions from the partisans, Hertz Shepe-tinski stood guard outside their house at the end of Michalowski Street. Around five in the morning he noticed armed Germans and Latvians encircling the area and blocking all the exits. He called into the house, "Wake up! Wake up! It's beginning!" Before going down into their hiding-place, which was well camouflaged beneath the floor, they deliberately made a mess of the rooms in the house, hoping this would convince the thugs that their "colleagues" had already been there.

The women and children went down into the cellar first, then the men. Around one in the afternoon the Nazis broke into the house, searched briefly through the things that lay around in great disorder, decided that the Jews had already been taken away, and left. The people in the cellar breathed a little easier, but later that afternoon they were forced to start digging new holes in the earth, with their bare hands, in the direction of the garden, because the air in the bunker was becoming insufficient.

In the yard, hiding behind a stack of logs in the barn, were Hertz and Jascha Shepetinski, Artchik Band, Zerach Kremien, Leyba, Grisha, Jacob and a few others. They were armed with one machine-gun, several rifles and a few hand-grenades. Through the crevices in the wall of the barn they could see Ritmeyer, ac-companied by several officers and a German woman, leading the "battle" against the Jewish underground. With his ever-present cigar in his mouth, he made mocking comments about his soldiers who were "playing around" too long with these damned Jews. He kept urging them to get on with the job. His minions ran around screaming at the top of their lungs, "Come out or we'll set fire to the place!"

In the evening they attacked in larger numbers. Soon the Jews below heard gunshots and children screaming. Then silence again. In the barn, with their fingers on the triggers of their weapons and their hearts pounding, the Jewish partisans stood pressed together, shoulder to shoulder. A heart-rending shriek broke the silence, then a series of shots from automatics. They heard one soldier urging another to set fire to the barn, but an officer rejected the idea because no one was in the barn anyway and it was a pity to burn up all that good wood.

Later they returned and sprayed the house with gasoline. In a few moments the flames were devouring the wooden framework. Soon the smoke penetrated the cellar and began to burn the eyes of everyone down there. Under cover of a pile of potatoes they dug their way feverishly into the barn. But Reuben Shepetinski's clothing had caught fire. He ran toward the river, German bullets all around him.

Before darkness fell, the people in the barn assessed their position. Only a miracle could save them now and they didn't expect one to happen. There was only thing left to do: wait till dark, make a break for it and try to get to the forest. Leybe Shepetinski, his wife Rachel, their daughter and Grandmother Shepetinski decided to stay in the barn.

Luckily, the night watch, "worn out" from their day's work, sat over their whiskey glasses half asleep. One at a time, the Jews in the barn crept into the darkness and made their way to Band's hiding-place. It was only a short distance, but every step was perilous. The bodies of Jews who had been shot or burned to death lay all along the way. About a hundred people from the two Michalowski Streets had joined forces at this point prior to going into the forest. Many of them were armed.

Artchik Band crawled through a window and reached the fence of the Polish Teachers Seminary. One at a time the others followed. Moving as silently as they could, they reached Skrobive Street and waited a few minutes for the German guards to pass. Then, armed partisans took up positions at the street corners, in case of an enemy attack, until all the women and children and old people crossed Skrobive. When they were passing the stadium they did the same, and also when they were crossing the Bialystok Road to get to the brick factory that was adjacent to the Derewianczycy forest.

From the heights, this ragged remnant, plucked at the last moment from the claws of the raving Nazi beast, took a last look back at the ghetto. The dark blue sky was being cut to ribbons by a vast fireworks of flame and explosions. Faint echoes of gunfire reached their ears. The forest air was fresh and clean. Escaping from certain death, they knew they might be going forth to meet it another guise. Among them were young children who quickly grew old. Patiently they walked alongside their mothers, their faces unsmiling. The adults took turns carrying the youngest.

The guides were Artchik Band and Zerach Kremien. Protecting the rear were Avreml Band, Jascha Shepetinski and Mietyk. Slowly the mysterious column made its way to the Kossova highway, which led to the partisans.

The short summer night turned quickly to the dawn of June 30th. Worried that the Germans might pursue them or that unfriendly eyes would notice them, they camouflaged their positions and hid in the forest to wait until nightfall, when they would resume their march.

Artchik and Zerach went ahead first to make contact with the partisn unit, promising to be back by evening. In the village of Rafalovka they met the Shchors detachment and were astounded when Reuben Shepetinski, with tears in his eyes, came out to greet them. He told them that when he ran from the burning house, the Nazis had shot at him but missed, and that he got to the river in time to put out the flames. Swimming across the Szczara River, he had hidden behind a stack of lumber in Fein's sawmill. During the night he walked to the village of Zavercze, where the partisans had fed him, but could not understand what he was saying, because the experience had left him with such a bad stutter that he could hardly speak intelligibly.

In the forest, the Jews waited for the return of Artchik and Zerach not one night but two, growing more and more concerned by the minute. At dawn on Wednesday, the two finally returned with Brigade Commander Pronyagin and two other partisans, who were not particularly overjoyed with the "human material" that was waiting for them: too many women, children and old folks; only yesterday saved from fire and death, they looked quite bedraggled. And most important, only a few of them had weapons.

On the way back, Pronyagin sent out a scouting party. Not far from Rafalovka they stopped and "recruited" 70 young Jewish fighters into the ranks of the 51st Group of the detachment. One week later a family camp was organized as part of the brigade. The entire Shepetinski family was in this 51st Group—even Mama Shepetinski, who became a "company cook."

•

In the house on Bernardino Street (across from the Judenrat) lived five families. When the massacre started, more than 20 people —Dr. Kaplinsky's relatives and Abraham Orlinski and his wife—immediately went down into the hiding-place. Because the Kaplinskys had a very young daughter, who might start crying in the cramped quarters, Dr. Kaplinsky, the child and two other young girls stayed in the house.

Around eight in the morning they heard the heavy footsteps of soldiers and the frightening cries of *"Raus! Raus!"* as inflamed Latvians broke into the house. After a perfunctory search they drove the four people into the street to join other Jews being herded toward Breger Street. On the dam at Balione Bridge a group was already assembled. Before them, Ritmeyer paced restlessly back and forth, automatic in hand. Back and forth across the bridge went military trucks, soldiers, S.S.-men, police, all concentrating on one objective: to bring as many Jews as possible to the assembly point.

From one of the groups a young man came up to Ritmeyer with a passport in his hand and explained that he was an "Aryan" who had brought a Jewish delegation from Kossovo the day before and spent the night in the ghetto. Ritmeyer replied coldly: "Anyone found in the ghetto with Jews goes wherever they go!" As he turned away, the young man dived into the river. Ritmeyer, hearing the splash, turned quickly, waited for the man to surface, fired, missed, and kept running along the bank and firing until the young man did not come up again.

Ritmeyer then drew an imaginary line with his weapon and shouted at the Jews that anyone who stepped over that line would be "immediately extinguished." Suddenly a barefoot woman carrying a child stepped forward and spoke to him in Yiddish: "Sir, my husband went off to work in Mohilev and left me here alone with the baby." Ritmeyer's face flushed as he warned her to get back to the group. Not understanding him, she continued to register her complaint. Like a raging tiger he roared at her again, but she still did not understand. "I am here all alone—just me and my baby . . ." Ritmeyer fired his gun, first at the child, then at the woman, and continued his pacing.

Some time later a German medical student named Hans Zeifel came running up to Ritmeyer and urged him to release Dr. Kaplinsky so that he could treat the patients in the city hospital who were gravely ill. After a heated consultaiton, Ritmeyer gave in. Dr. Kaplinsky and the three women with him were separated from the group of Jews and placed under the protection of one of the soldiers. They were even permitted to go to a nearby Jewish home for a drink of water.

The rest of the Jews were herded into the churchyard.

•

Around seven that evening a squad of S.S.-men entered the churchyard and their leader gave them their orders in a whisper. He then lined up the Jews in fours and ordered them to pay close attention to what he was about to say. "If you want to stay among the living, run after this motorcycle!" Corporal Mutz then took off on his Rover, with the 150 men and two women trying to keep up with him through Koshchelne to Dluga Street.

It happened to be the Catholic holy day of "Pyotr and Pawel." All along the sidewalks stood festively attired Poles, staring at these Jews who were being rounded up to the Krasny Stolvar (Red Carpenter) artel, where it always smelled of carpenter's glue and dry rot.

This was the first night after a day so bloody that death was a welcome release. In the carpenter shop the Jews seemed to congeal into a frozen silence, choking back their tears and their sobs. Many of them stood looking out the windows at the burning ghetto that had only yesterday been their home.

In the morning they were all driven into the big yard. As they waited for new orders from their masters they tried to make sense of what had happened and why they had acted as they did. Why had they accepted the murderer's gift of "life" while their families were going to their death? Joseph Liemkin, half-crazed with regret, recalled sending his young daughter to stand with her mother in the ranks of those chosen for death, while he stood among those permitted to live. He compared himself to Max Liberman, who had chosen to stand with his wife and go with her to the grave.

Abraham Doktorchik and a young man named Nisn characterized Liberman's behavior as "despair," not heroism, and insisted that the only thing to do now was to stay alive and take revenge. No one tried to console himself. The grief was etched in their souls forever.

They did not have much time to think about these things. Soon Metzner came roaring into the yard with his trucks and a new set of instructions: "You are all going to work now—to clean up the ghetto! Into the trucks!" He even rolled up his sleeves himself, but his "work" consisted of herding the Jews into the trucks with a long club.

The trucks drove slowly, almost cautiously, through the Aryan streets as sleepy faces peered out the windows. The Balione Bridge was in flames. Sparks and embers flew into the canal and hissed. The dense rows of trees on both sides of the dams rustled mysteriously. The burning ghetto was reflected in the water upside down. With a screech the trucks stopped at the ghetto gate on Bernardino Street, where Stelle handed out new work passes. Dr. Kaplinsky was given card number one, which gave him permission, as Stelle told him, to "move about freely wherever he wished."

Not far from the Judenrat, Rabbi Singer (from Ostrow-Mazowiecka) stood under guard with his family and prayed to God for deliverance. Trying to comfort them, he said that a divine miracle could still save them at the last moment. Shortly afterward, as the guards started rounding them up, he noticed something that aroused his suspicions and he called out, "Children, save yourselves!" Like startled birds they scattered in all directions, but Nazi bullets found each one of them.

Suddenly the Regional Kommissar appeared and began a "selection" of his own. With blue chalk he marked the "useful Jews" on the back and chest, a sign to the hangmen that they must spare these lives for a while longer. These "useful Jews" were then led through the burning streets of the Breger neighborhood, where armed executioners swarmed among the ruins of houses, driving people out of their hiding-places. Many of the victims were covered with soot; only the whites of their eyes gleamed eerily. The dead lay everywhere, in pools of blood. The living dragged corpses on wagons from which hung legs, arms, leads, dripping blood onto the cobblestones.

From the Balione Bridge to Guzanke Street the dam was covered with the crushed bodies of old people, women, babies. Faint with hunger and pain themselves, filled with horror and despair, the "blue-chalk" Jews carried bodies and parts of bodies to a mass grave in a garden on Guzanke Street. Then they were ordered to drag the dead out of houses, courtyards and streets. Meanwhile, the police and the guards were stuffing their pockets with Jewish valuables.

The Jewish hospital, which the Nazis had blown up the day before, along with all its patients, now stood bareheaded, without a roof. The walls and the holes where the windows had been were black. Ash and embers still smoldered everywhere. Patients still miraculously alive lay on the ground in a state of shock. The stench of burning flesh assailed the nostrils.

Hick, his loaded revolver in hand, stepped like a hunting-dog through the skeletons of houses, sniffing in all the corners for hidden Jewish treasure. In Guzanke's building he uncovered a hiding-place and promptly shot all the Jews inside it except for one crying baby, which he turned over to a Byelorussian policeman, who tossed the baby into the ditch and fired a bullet into its brain.

Carefully and reverently the "blue-chalk" Jews buried the dead. Slonimski the carpenter bade them farewell in a halting, choking voice: "We are burying you in accordance with Jewish law, but who will bury us and who knows where our bones will end up?"

In the evening they covered the fresh grave on Guzanke Street. Slonimski recited the Kaddish as the other Jews tearfully answered Amen . . .

•

In Itche Mishelevich's bunker there were twelve people. Three harrowing days passed before they knew that the ghetto was burning. They had no idea what was happening outside. They did hear Reinert (Itche's German boss) calling him by name, but Itche did not answer, afraid he might endanger the others. They also heard the searches going on in the house. After three days and nights of darkness, hunger, and thirst and lack of air, one of the young women there went mad.

On the fourth day Itche heard the voice of his friend Hendzl the shoemaker. After a brief discussion, everyone in the hiding-place agreed that Itche should go out to learn what was going on. The sudden brightness blinded him temporarily and he stumbled. When he recovered he asked Hendzl to tell him what had happened "up there." The only thing Hendzl said was, "You'll find it all out for yourself soon enough." As he looked around more carefully, Itche became aware that Reinert was standing nearby and that he was looking for shoemakers. Itche informed him that Abraham Azef was also in the bunker. Reinert agreed to take him.

Itche then went to the place where his parents had been hiding, but all he found was two pools of blood. Later the son of the Polish owner of the house boasted to Itche that it was he, a policeman, who had shot his parents.

As Itche and Azef walked toward the Balione Bridge amidst the terrible destruction, Joshua Shilovitski stopped Itche and told him he had been pulling bodies out of burning buildings. He had just buried Itche's parents. At the bridge, Reinert turned Azef over to other Germans who were taking Jews to prison for "selection."

●

Twenty-five people were hiding in Motl Kletzkin's bunker. One afternoon Feyga Peshkin's child began crying uncontrollably. As the tension in the bunker became unbearable, Sarah Peshkin, the child's grandmother, was left with no choice but to silence the baby. Feyga almost went out of her mind.

Later that same day the hiding-place was discovered anyway. Eight of the men surrendered to the Germans. "Is this everybody?" the Nazis insisted. "Ja," said Jacob Peshkin, but they didn't believe him and fired their guns into the bunker. All the others came out except Motl. As punishment for his lie, the Germans split Peshkin's head open. To make sure there was no one left, they tossed a grenade into the cellar. Motl was buried under the debris, but survived, and after the initial shock, was able to dig himself out . . . and wait.

After a while he heard his sister-in-law Feyga's voice. She had escaped by hiding under a bed. Together they found their way to a neighbor's bunker, where Esther Rachelevski and the Hasid Yosl Pripstein were lying wounded. For six days they stayed there without food or water. On the seventh day a neighbor's dog got their scent and refused to budge from the spot. This animal-love for its master betrayed them to two Polish policemen who, in exchange for a sum of money, spared their lives, but took them to the assembly point on Breger Street. From there they were sent to prison, where Motl was selected to resettle in the new ghetto as an expert tailor.

•

In a warehouse on Breger Street there was a bunker where 23 members of the Moshkowski and Freedman families were hiding. For two weeks they stayed hidden behind old boards and cast-off furniture. Before the massacre the Moshkowski family had been subsisting on biscuits. During the night they drew water from a washtub in the courtyard.

One night some ghouls tore the lock off the outside door, broke into the building and began searching for ghetto trophies. The Jews in the hiding-place prepared themselves for the worst, but luckily the thieves were distracted by a box of expensive leather gloves. Every day new raiding parties would appear. One day the Jews heard someone calling in Yiddish: "Rivka, come out!" Recognizing the voices of Jacob Gibur and Hanan Shulkowicz, Rivka came out of the bunker. Jacob and Hanan, whose families had been taken away, led the group into the new ghetto on Bridge Street, where they were issued new passes. They found an empty attic and "moved in." Later, Rivka's sister Yocheved joined them.

•

The following were hiding in a bunker on Balione Street: Braine Lunianski and her new baby boy, her husband Shlomo-Chaim Alpert, her brother Itche, Yudel Abramowicz, his mother and his brother Nonye, and Jacob Konofka. One day, smelling smoke, they opened the cellar door and realized that the house was on fire. They scattered among the other burning houses. At the Balione Bridge the Alpert family was decimated by the Germans. Yudel and Jacob managed to crawl into Shklierman's house, but not before they were spotted by a Ukrainian policeman. They hid behind a pile of clothes, but this house too caught fire. Jumping out a window, they were confronted by the policeman, who chased them into the street. They ran to Zhabinke, where, through a gauntlet of German clubs and rifle butts, they escaped to Bridge Street.

At Shaya's Bridge Yudel found his mother and brothers among the Jews rounded up there. From this place the Germans were sending Jews to their death, fifty at a time. When their turn came, the Abramoviczes went to their death with their arms around each other.

At the Zamoshche Church stood the German "economic managers," sifting out the "useful Jews." The postmaster called Yudel's name; the guard, annoyed, pushed him out of line and sent him to join the others waiting in the churchyard. Whenever a group of Jews were being led to their execution, these "chosen ones" were forced to turn and face the wall. Thus, 150 men stood on their feet all day long until the Gestapo came and took them to the tailor workshop of the Regional Kommissariat. The next morning they were sent to the Beuten camp and given yellow passes marked with their craft. Then a new selection was made and the lucky ones were given passes. The rest ended up in the camp at Puzevici, among them Yudel Abramowicz. Later Yudel escaped from the camp in the village of Shostaki, near Kozloishchine, where he worked for the villagers as a shepherd and survived until liberation.

•

Without food and without any news from the ghetto, some 30 Polish refugees spent seven days and nights in an attic in Guzanski's building on Skrobive Street. Several times the Nazis tapped all the walls but failed to discover the hiding-place. On the seventh day the people in the bunker heard an unmistakable Yiddish voice. Taking every precaution, they convinced themselves that it was Dr. Kremien and his "sanitation group." Dr. Kremien led the Jews out one at a time as members of his work-group. Providing them with false passes, he moved them all into the new ghetto. (Among them was Manya Ackerman from Lodz.)

These "sanitation brigades" found many Jews still alive in the burned out ghetto and helped them in whatever way they could. More often, however, they found entire families burned to death.

•

The Germans appointed Mendl Shelyubsky "director" of his own carpenter workshop on the hill, where many Jews from the ghetto were working. On the night of June 29 he happened to sleep in the workshop and in the morning he went to his sister Feygl's in the ghetto, which was already under heavy guard. People were permitted to enter the ghetto, but no one was allowed to leave. A half hour after Mendl entered the ghetto Ritmeyer shot Quint and the last act of the Jewish tragedy in Slonim began. When Mendl's sister's house fell victim to the flames, he and Feygl and her husband Leybe Sokolovski ran out to the dam. They were among the first to be killed.

•

Gute Meyerson (from Augustov) hid in a bunker on Breger Street and for two days knew nothing about what was happening in the ghetto except that someone was rummaging through the house upstairs. On the third day Noah Servianski came and informed them that the ghetto was being wiped out and that the Germans were killing all the Jews except for a few hundred able-bodied men.

Gute put on a man's hat and as one of a group of men went to the Beuten camp, where they were given passes and sent to Panesve Street. Near the orchard Ritmeyer stopped them and checked their passes. All the men—except one—took off their hats in his presence, according to the "regulations." As he stalked angrily toward her, Gute panicked and snatched off her hat. Without a word, Ritmeyer returned the passes to the men and let them go, but detained Gute. Where was she working, he wanted to know. At Mendl Shelyubsky's, she replied. Take me there, he said.

When they got there, it was closed. Gute explained that the "Director" was probably in the ghetto. Ritmeyer took her to the ghetto. But Mendl was no longer there. Sensing that her turn had come, she asked Ritmeyer: "Why are you killing the Jews?" "Because of you Jews," he told her, "many Germans are dying, and besides, the Jewish problem is too complicated for you to understand."

But he let her go . . .

•

When Joshua Shelyubsky's house caught fire and it became impossible to hide there any longer, he crawled out to look for another place. As he did so he came face to face with an S.S.-man. Without hesitation he hit him in the face so hard that the German fell unconscious. As Joshua bent to pick up the German's automatic he was attacked by a second S.S.-man. In the ensuing struggle he was stabbed to death.

•

On Zhabinke Street a distraught Jewish woman ran out of a burning house with an axe in her hand. Attacking two Germans from behind, she split the head of one of them, but the other turned and shot her.

•

In Chaim Silberman's hiding-place on Balione Street there were, in addition to his family, Moyshe Mishkin and his brother Joshua, his brother-in-law Nonye and Nonye's young son. They stayed there for seven days and nights without food or water, but not until the seventh day did they discover that the ghetto was burning. On the eighth day they heard a Yiddish conversation above. Moyshe Mishkin cautiously went up to investigate. He found Ayzl the carpenter and a Polish refugee, both of whom were working in a German carpenter artel in Goldenberg's sawmill. They were able to obtain work passes for all the men in Chaim's house and move them into the small ghetto. When Chaim's daughter learned that her children had been taken to prison, she went there to try and get them out, but it was too late. They had all been sent to the Petralewicz ditches . . .

•

Chaim Azef was considered by the Germans to be one of the best leather-workers in Slonim, so he had remained unscathed during all the previous roundups and massacres. As the ghetto was going up in flames he sat at home with his "protector"—the work pass—certain that he was still in no danger. But he was "invited" to go along with all the other Jews, most of whom had never been fortunate enough to have any such "guaranteed" passes.

•

As several hundred Jews were being led through Koshchelna Street, Asher Gendler (who had owned a small leather factory) called over his Polish neighbor Laszewski (a barber) and handed him a package of food. "We shall never see each other again, my friend. You and I have never done each other any harm. Here, take this, I won't need it any longer."

An S.S. man, who noticed this incident, clubbed the Pole unmercifully and then arrested him.

•

At Fyvel Burda's house the flames spread to the bunker. Shprintse Rabinowicz ran out into the street, her hair afire. Unnerved by days and nights of suffering, she ran up to the first policeman she saw and begged him to kill her. He refused to do her that favor. Instead, he led her to the assembly point from where she would have to walk the death-march to the mass graves at Petralewicz.

•

While the Germans were liquidating the ghetto they also "cleaned up" the Jewish enterprises outside the ghetto, for example, Bayarski's textile factory on Panesva Street, where the "director" was the former dry goods merchant Paius. A truckload of German soldiers pulled up there, rounded up Paius, his wife and two children, a member of the Bayarski family and the Jewish gardener Weisenberg, and marched them to Petralewicz.

Weisenberg said to their neighbors, in Polish, "Farewell, these people are murderers!" The neighbors (Tatarke) wiped the tears from their eyes. At Breiter Street the Germans halted the death-march long enough to add the old shoemaker Spitalnik and the electrical worker Kuks, along with a young Jewish convert and her child, to the victims.

•

When the baker Zelik Pashenitski was taken to prison, the Germans, suspecting that he had a treasure hidden somewhere, promised him life in exchange for the money. Under guard they brought him back to his bakery and as soon as he turned the money over to them, they took him back to the mass grave. The bakery was turned over to some new "Aryan" owners.

After the liquidation of the ghetto these new owners noticed that every morning there was a loaf of bread missing from the shelf. For a long time they could not catch the thief, so one night they posted an armed policeman on the premises to solve the riddle. During the night the policeman was startled out of his wits by an "apparition" that crawled out of a hole in the wall. The apparition grabbed a loaf of bread and almost disappeared back into the wall again before the policeman recovered sufficiently to act. The thief was a hidden Jew who had come out to forage, like a nocturnal animal . . .

•

Dr. Israel Sperling and his wife (Quint's daughter and son-in-law) had been hiding in a well-camouflaged bunker until the cries of a hungry two-year-old gave them away. Everyone in the hiding-place was taken to prison. As a physician, Dr. Sperling was later released, along with Mrs. Sperling.

•

During the second week of the massacre, after nine days in hiding, the pharmacist Milikowski, his wife and son gave themselves up. They were issued new work passes, but sent to prison to await their fate. Once a day they were given water, but no food. This was after nine days of semi-starvation. Unexpectedly, a German by the name of Wittman appeared and had him released. An official in the Slonim Health Department had been interceding for Jews, particularly doctors, who were sent to the Beuten camp.

•

Sholem Sweticki, the mason on Skrobive Street, who had been forced to cart the dead bodies of Jews to the cemetery, had noticed that Paula Westerlich, a former employee in the Jewish Home for the Aged, was working there. On this particular day he signalled her that the bodies he was bringing in were of his wife and two sons. With the help of two merciful Christian neighbors, Paula brought out shovels and saw to it that the bodies were well covered with earth, so that the dogs could not get at them . . .

•

In this work of burying the Jewish dead, the Germans also conscripted several Christian municipal workers. One day, carting a wagonful of victims to the Jewish cemetery, one of the "corpses" (a woman) startled them by pleading with them to let her go. They crossed themselves and promised to do so. At the cemetery she ran in a panic toward the Bialystok highway, then returned and begged them to kill her, because she had nothing left to live for. They tried to calm her, but she wandered around among the gravestones half-demented until the executioner Kishko finally appeared and gladly fulfilled her last request.

•

On Tuesday of the second week of the massacre, at ten in the morning, Gerth Erren appeared at the prison and ordered all the Jews to line up in the yard. Under his supervision they were "sorted out." A substantial number of men were selected to stay alive; all the rest were condemned to death. Most of the former were skilled workers, doctors, engineers, sanitation workers. Engineer Wolfstein immediately led them to the small ghetto. The rest were locked up behind the iron gates.

A little while later the trucks pulled up at the prison-yard. As the guards brutally herded the people into the trucks, police appeared and began calling out names from a list. Whenever no one answered immediately to a name (which meant that they had already been killed), others answered instead, and another twenty or so Jews again received a temporary reprieve. Before the beaten and hopeless victims were driven away, the hangmen generously ladled out water for them to drink . . .

As Michal Estrin and his three friends (Polish refugees) were being put into an open truck, they gave each other the signal to resist. At each corner of the truck stood an armed guard. A fifth sat with the driver. The twenty Jews in the truck were compelled to sit in such a way that they immobilized each other's legs, but Estrin and his friends so arranged themselves that one of their legs was free. As the truck neared the forest they leaped at two of the guards and with their combined strength shoved them headfirst over the side of the truck. At almost the same instant they turned and tore the rifles out of the hands of the remaining two guards and cracked their heads open with the butts. The guard inside the cabin instinctively stuck his head out the window to see what was happening. Estrin hit him over the head too. As the driver stepped on his brakes, Estrin and the other three called on the men to make a break for it, jumped off the truck and dived into the woods. Only Feytche Wolkomirski followed them. The others remained in the truck, apathetic and resigned to their fate.

The next morning, by a circuitous route, the four escapees reached the new ghetto. Later they learned from a ghetto doctor that one of the German guards had died instantly, a second was badly hurt and the other three had suffered only minor injuries. After this incident the Germans tightened their security in transporting prisoners. They handcuffed the stronger Jews to each other and put them on the trucks among old people, women and children.

●

When the ghetto was first set up, Sascha Zirinski and his mother Chava lived on Zhabinke Street and worked in Jezerska's sawmill. Up until the third massacre he stayed in his work-place and did not even go into the ghetto at night to sleep. He did, however, often visit his mother there. On the night of June 28 he decided to bring his mother something to eat and to stay with her during the round-ups. His non-Jewish fellow workers tried to convince him not to do this, but Sascha went anyway and was caught in the trap along with hundreds of other Jews.

As the truck carrying Sascha raced toward Petralewicz and passed near Jezerska's sawmill, Sascha noticed his coworker Zhenia Poliakowa there. He called out to her and leaped off the truck, apparently hoping to get to the sawmill and hide there. A police bullet felled him in the church square. The truck stopped, the Germans picked up Sascha's body and tossed it up to the Jews in the truck. They then went and found his mother and brought her to the truck. By that time she didn't even have the strength to climb up into the vehicle. They shot her on the spot.

•

When it became clear to everyone that Jewish blood would flow again in Slonim, Nonye Zirinski discussed the situation with his friend Charitonchik, a Tatar, who advised him not to wander about the city during the "disturbances" but to go to the synagogue and stay there. On June 29, with the ghetto in flames, Charitonchik hid Nonye in the synagogue attic. When the S.S.-men asked him where the Jew was, the Tatar replied, "He's probably lying dead somewhere in the ghetto."

Every day Charitonchik brought Nonye food and news about the ghetto. And that's how Nonye Zirinski was saved. After it was all over, he continued working in the synagogue.

•

The German engineer Wolfstein, who always behaved correctly toward the Jews, also had a good relationship with the local authorities. But one day, when the ghetto was afire, the Gestapo Kommandant suddenly asked him: "Can you show me your passport?"

"Certainly," Wolfstein replied, and handed him the document.

"No!" the Kommandant insisted. "Show me your second passport!"

"I have only one passport," Wolfstein said calmly.

"Good. You're excused."

But Wolfstein left Slonim immediately. With his "true" Aryan appearance, his perfect German, and his false passport, it was easy for him to move around.

A few hours later they came for him and arrested his wife as a hostage, but she escaped through a window in the toilet of the prison. Both she and Wolfstein simply vanished.

(Before the war he had graduated from the Polytechnic Institute in Danzig. In 1939 he came to Slonim along with all the other refugees from Lodz.)

Quint's Role in the Judenrat

The Jewish Councils set up by the Nazis in all the ghettos were really fictions of "Jewish autonomy." Through these organized, responsible bodies the occupying power was able to control the Jewish population, its property and its labor resources.

The Labor Office of the Judenrat was expected to supply the Jewish slave laborers. Through the Judenrat the Germans collected tribute, furniture, furs, warm clothing for the front, and so on. The Judenrat and its "departments" were actually a tool in the hands of the enslaver.

Today, when all aspects of the Holocaust are being researched and studied, the activities of the Judenrate are being weighed on the scales, and the balance seems to come down on the side of their forced "cooperation" with the occupying power. This is especially true of the Councils in the larger Polish cities, where the ghettos were already established by late 1939, before the Germans had even entered Slonim.

Certain Judenrat chairmen have been labeled "traitors" who sacrificed the lives of ordinary Jews in order to save their own hides; membership in the Judenrat was often characterized as despicable and even criminal. None of this, however, was true in Slonim, where all the 25,000 captured Jews in the city, including the two Judenrate, were annihilated. Only a few hundred isolated individuals managed to escape.

The first Jewish Council in Slonim included many old, experienced communal leaders who were ready to serve the Jewish people at the cost of their own lives. After the first Judenrat was "liquidated" there was no doubt that being a member of that body was equivalent to being a front-line soldier in battle.

The second Judenrat consisted of the same kind of self-sacrificing Jews who knew in advance that they were going to their death. One of these was Gershon Quint, head of the Labor Office of the Judenrat. Quint carried out his duties with the time-tested strategy that went back to the days when Slonim was under Polish rule: ransom, negotiations, knowing which oppressor to drink with, in short, anything to gain a little more time. After the execution of the second Judenrat Quint remained the only ghetto official to continue "in office"—until the third massacre.

With the increasing number of ghetto partisans, Quint took them seriously into account and always fulfilled their requests for information, material help, etc.

In Slonim, then, the Judenrat did nothing for which it can be condemned. Its leaders did nothing to "save their own hides." Quint's "court Jew" policy was calculated to keep thousands of Jews alive until the Red Army could liberate them. When the Germans demanded 800 Jews for slave labor in Mohilev, for example, he replied immediately: "You can do whatever you wish with *me,* but I will not provide them."

Quint did have opportunities to save himself, but he never once thought of betraying the thousands of Jews in hiding. He often said he would be the first to place his head on the block, and that is what actually happened. On June 29, 1944, at the ghetto gate, he was the first victim.

All honor to the Judenrat martyrs in Slonim: Wolfe Berman, Jacob Goldfarb, Noah Mintz, Jacob Rabinowitz, Moshe Zackheim, Moshe Jakimowski, Trachtenberg, Joseph Mordecai Ripp, Karpel Ripp, Chomak, Max Rabinowitz, Misha Latz, Hanaan Steinberg, Gershon Bernstein, Jacob Lyuboshitz, Chaim Rujansky, Gershon Quint.

The Small Ghetto

In front of Jezerska's sawmill on Bridge Street and at the corner of Canal across from Shaya's mill, which lies between two suspension bridges, the German authority chose 17 half-wrecked Jewish houses and surrounded them with a high barbed wire fence. Into this miniature ghetto they packed 700 men and 100 women, selected during the "days of life and death" as "useful" Jews. All of them were now unkempt, dirty and tattered. Even their meager ghetto belongings—bedclothes, furniture, utensils, clothing—had gone up in flames and now they were "living" in the bare ruins.

These were the best—the surviving tailors, shoemakers, carpenters, electricians, mechanics, sewing-machine operators, tannery and sawmill workers, as well as the best doctors and medical workers. All these "lucky ones," living in the suffocating, blood-soaked atmosphere of three monstrous massacres, were supposed to give their skills and their labor to the hated German boss. Many of them worked in the city and came back to the ghetto in the evening to sleep.

The first thing that struck you about this "small ghetto" was the utter chaos. There was no Jewish leadership, there was no one to police it. It was obvious that this was a temporary situation. A few days passed this way and then suddenly one morning the air was shattered by the familiar *"Alle raus!"* Ritmeyer and his murderous ilk had come to visit.

When the sleepy, frightened Jews had gathered slowly and warily around him, Ritmeyer announced that he had come at such an early hour in order to distribute work-cards to those that still did not have them and that they should immediately report to him. Dr. Kaplinsky, carrying his young daughter in his arms, showed him his yellow card.

"Why did you disturb the child's sleep!" Ritmeyer bellowed hypocritically. "Get back in the house!"

Nine persons without cards reported to him, among them Lyova Zelikovski (the former owner of the Hotel Victoria on Paradne Street.)

Ritmeyer suddenly turned into an angel. "I'm now going to take you into the city and give you your passes, so you can live here in the ghetto." He "escorted" them onto the dam and then the Jews in the ghetto heard a volley of gunshots. Those were the last victims of the hangman Ritmeyer. When he finished that piece of work, he left Slonim for good.

About 200 Jews lived and worked in the barracks, on the roads and in the sawmills. Another 200 continued working in the Beuten camp and ate and lived in the barracks. The survivors began playing out the last act of the bloody tragedy of Slonim's Jewish community.

A few of the older craftsmen still believed the assurances of the Nazis that they would be left alive because their skilled work was needed for the "Fatherland." But most of the younger Jews kept looking for ways to escape. During the night—and with no contact with the ghetto partisan organization—they tried to join the fighters in the forest. About 20 or 30 young Jews managed to get back to the "Third Reich"—to Ruzany, Wolkowic, Bialystok and other places.

Some did succeed in getting to the partisans. Among them were Dr. Fira Kovarski, Dr. Parestski, Dr. Volkoviski and his wife, Engineer Abraham Orlinski and his wife, and Dr. Cheplove.

Motl Kletzkin, Chaim Peshkin and Rivka Molchaski escaped by riding out of the city in the carts of the outhouse cleaners. By evening they had gotten to the village of Krivici (near Mizevici) and made contact with a sympathetic Pole named Kosakowski, who helped them get to Ruzany.

From the forest, Shiel Fisher sent a note to his former employer Svetitski, a carpenter on Bernardino Street. Shiel urged him to come with his family into the forest, and the sooner the better, because the small ghetto was doomed to extinction. Svetitski sent him a bottle of iodine, two dozen bandages and a verbal reply: "We're not as crazy as Shielke yet, to go out to the forest like he did. Partisan life is for Shielke, not us."

This characteristic reply helps to explain why so many Jews died . . .

Arms for the Partisans

After the third massacre, Israel Sokolik, Yosl Timan, Hillel Mosh-kowski and Abraham Orlinski continued working in their locksmith shop which was located in the marketplace in Peshkin's cellar. Their work consisted in making keys and repairing locks on the houses run by the Regional Kommisariat. They had been issued work-passes that enabled them to move freely about the city.

They would come to the Beuten camp for metal, which they carried out in their tool kits. Working in the camp were also Abiezer Imber and his father Yitzhak. This group agreed on a plan: the Imbers would supply weapons for the partisans; Sokolik and Timan would get the weapons out to the forest. Imber had informed Sokolik that it would be necessary to discuss this with his foreman, Kohn, a Jew who had been an officer in the Polish army. He urged him to try and recruit Kohn into their plan.

Sokolik and Imber made it clear to Kohn that eventually Erren would destroy the small ghetto too, so they must escape to the partisans as soon as possible. They promised to lead him into the forest where he, a former army officer, would train the young Jewish partisans. Kohn agreed, and they asked him merely to "look the other way" when they carried out the weapons.

Sokolik also introduced himself to Eric Stein, who was part of the smuggling "operation." He reminded Stein that he too must be ready at all times to go into the forest. Stein promised to "move" as many weapons as possible. They agreed on a password to be used by anyone else who came to him for weapons.

Abiezer delivered the weapons to workers' houses where hiding-places had been built into the walls. From time to time, partisans from the small ghetto would come, give the password, and pick up the weapons. In this way, the guns moved more freely from the Beuten camp to Milikowski's place on the hill.

Also working with the Imbers, however, were Jews who argued that without the partisans' "provocations" and with diligent labor, they could work peacefully for the Germans and survive the war. The ghetto partisans had to be very careful about what they said or did in front of these fanatics.

A Messenger from the Forest

On the 25th of July, a messenger came from the forest with an urgent request for four machine-gun disks. And while he was at it, he asked for soap, medicaments and a few other necessities. The underground leaders decided to send this material back with Izzy Boretski, Jacob Chatskelevich and Finkel, who were then to remain in the forest with their unit.

In Kunitz's smithy Chatskelevich stood at the front anvil hammering a piece of metal, in order to cover the sounds coming from the underground shop, where Boretski and Finkel were feverishly preparing the disks, and where Abba Yudelevit and the forest guide were testing the weapons. At midnight, all was ready. Abramowitz locked the door of the blacksmith shop and the men, with the weapons loaded on their backs, stepped cautiously out of the secret exit.

Following their guide through the forest at a trot, they reached a village in the early morning, where the partisans were waiting for them with a horse and wagon. A joyful and heart-warming surprise for these ghetto Jews was the familiar "sholem-aleykhem" with which they were greeted by Anshl Delyaticki.

After riding all day through an area in which the partisans seemed to be in complete control, the wagon stopped at a large, unfinished house that stood in an ancient grove.

"We are here!" Anshl happily announced. "This is our detachment headquarters!"

Promising the fighters from the ghetto that very soon they would be met by friends from Slonim, all the partisans and their wagons disappeared into the forest. After a tense hour's wait, they were joined by a group of Jews who suddenly appeared out of the forest, led by a man in a military uniform. He shook their hands warmly and introduced himself as Yakov Fyodorovich, Commander of the Jewish partisan unit that they would be part of.

The joy of the Jewish partisans, especially those who had just left the ghetto nightmare, was indescribable. They sat down to eat and drink, and a discussion developed about getting the last Jews out of the ghetto. For the first time in many months they fell asleep in good spirits.

At dawn they arose and went to join the detachment, passing several patrols that guarded the borders of the partisan "state."

Chatskelevich, Boretski and Finkel, curious and wide awake, soaked up the new life around them. When the Jewish group had advanced deeper into the forest, their eyes beheld a panorama of huts made out of branches.

"Welcome to our city!" their hosts announced proudly.

From the Small Ghetto into the Forest

The work of the Jewish underground did not stop for even a day after several of their leaders had been killed, Shlomo Chaim at the Balione Bridge and David Epstein in prison. Heading the work now were Pesach Alpert and Nonye Zirinski.

The acquisition of weapons was intensified, because in the destruction of the ghetto many guns had been lost in the hiding-places. The underground had to send as many armed fighters as possible into the forest before the Germans made Slonim completely Judenrein.

In Mendl Shelyubska's house on the hill the following carpenters, among others, were still working for the Regional Kommissariat: Zelik Milikowski, Elya Abramowski, Nute Myerson. The house had a large cellar where they had placed several beds and installed electricity. The entrance was through a big closet that stood against the wall.

This house stood at the edge of the city, where the Bialystok, Brisk and Baranovici roads intersect. Nearby were the Christian and Jewish cemeteries, between them a dense woods. Because of all these favorable circumstances, the partisans decided to use the house only for the storing of weapons, and the cellar as an inn for partisans coming in from the forest and for those going out.

Zirinski and Alpert appointed special weapons-carriers who walked from the Beuten camp to Shelyubska's and back, three times a day. Active in this operation were: Itche Mishelevich, Manya Ackerman, Genia Miller (the last two from Lodz), the Malach brothers, Yosl Timan, Nonye Zirinski, Lyuba Abramowicz, Elya Abramovski, Rosmarin Yumek and his wife Rachel, Israel Sokolik and Itche Rabinowicz.

Acting on instructions from the partisan detachment, Nonye Zirinski kept looking for able-bodied young men for the forest. At the end of July 1942, when everything was ready. Zerach Kremien and Anshl Delyaticki came from the forest with the assignment to lead another group of 30-40 partisans into the forest with their entire supply of weapons.

In the cellar, Anshl and Zerach inspected the weapons. The day before the march was scheduled to start, it turned out that certain parts of three machine-guns, as well as of several automatics and rifles, were missing, and that there weren't enough bullets. With a list of these missing parts in their heads, the gang made a lot of "trips" back and forth on July 31st until they "filled the order."

Led by their "foreman" Itche Mishelevich, a group of six left the Beuten camp: Abram Bubliatski, Timan, Manya Ackerman, Zenia Miller, Elya Abramovski and Itche Rabinowicz. Each of them was weighed down by machine-gun disks, automatics, rifle-parts, hand-grenades and bullets. The women stuffed these items into their bosoms; the men into their trousers and blouses. With his customary woebegone expression, Mishelevich looked the least suspicious. A couple of the men had bandages wrapped around their arms or legs, to make them limp a little. Walking slowly from the Beuten camp to the hill, they had to pass the S.D. headquarters on Ulan Street.

The officer on duty there beckoned to Itche and ordered him to take his group up to the second floor of the building to move a chifforobe. The whole mission could have been wrecked at that point, but the group did not lose its composure. After they mounted the stairs, the Nazi officer warned them that if they tipped over the piece of furniture or broke anything they would all be shot on the spot.

They moved it quickly and then took advantage of the officer's momentery absence to make a bee-line for the stairs and march out of the building without anyone stopping them.

At Zelik's they assembled the weapons and hid them in the attic, where other partisans were gathering. That same afternoon around 30 partisans slipped out of the Beuten camp one at a time, so that even the other Jews there did not notice anything unusual. Each person carried a tool of some sort in his hands, as though they were on their way to work. Israel Sokolik, as foreman, came out with his list and gave the "orders" to report at such and such a place for work.

As they reached the meeting-point they ripped off their yellow patches—and immediately breathed freer.

When everything was ready they lined up in a single file and silently headed for the Jewish cemetery. In this group were, among others: Zerach Kremien, Anshl Delyaticki, Nonye Zirinski, Karpl Shevtik, the German captain Eric Stein and his wife Sima and her sister, Itche Mishelevich, Manya Ackerman, Itche Rabinowicz, Lilia Sivash, Rosmarin Yumek and his wife Rachel, Lyuba Abramo-wicz, Nathan Licker, Genia Miller, Hillel Moshkowski, the brothers Rosen (from Optrolenko), Abiezer Imber and his father Yitzhak, Kohn (the former Polish officer) and Zyama Shusterovich.

At the Jewish cemetery they encountered a police patrol who, after one look at this heavily armed company, retreated as fast as they could.

Moving silently in the night, these brave Jews carried a double load—their cache of weapons and the thoughts of the barbarities they had suffered only yesterday. Each one carried also the open wounds of dear ones destroyed and the scores they had to settle with the Nazi subhumans who were poisoning the world. For these Jews escaping from the unspeakable mass graves of Czepalow and Petralevici, the rifle was their avenger, their best friend.

Moshe Yankelevich ("Moyshe Teygarchts") and a few other refugees from Ostrolenko, who were living in the barracks, had arranged to meet the first group at midnight at a place not far from the Kossovo highway. The signal was to be a whistle, but when Zerach whistled, the noise of a rifle-shot came from the spot where the group was supposed to be waiting for them. Zerach and the others took cover behind some bushes and waited, then gave the signal again. Again it was greeted by a shot. Now everyone knew that Moyshe was a practical joker, but in this tense situation, what was there to joke about? They decided to surround the spot and investigate. What they found was a surprising bunch of "inebriated" Jews who told the following story:

They had tried to "appropriate" some rifles from the barracks, but the two German guards—contrary to their usual habit—did not leave their post for a moment, and the time was growing shorter and shorter. Moshe had an idea. He dug out two bottles of whiskey from their supplies and poured a round of drinks for everybody. Than another. The conversation grew livelier—the guards enjoying the company of their prisoners—and eventually their heads dropped to the table and they fell fast asleep.

At that point, the Jews, who had been drinking with them, just to make it "look good," got out of there in a hurry. But the liquor had also loosened them up and even after they had walked to the meeting-point, Moshe's habitual nature had overcome his caution. Luckily the shots had not attracted the attention of the wrong people.

The next stage of the march was not an easy one, loaded down as they were with weapons and gun parts, and since they had to meet the partisan unit at a stated time, they mobilized a couple of wagons from farmers along the road. When they were close enough to their destination they sent the farmers back with their wagons.

Early evening on August 1, they reached the "border" of Shchors' 51st detachment and were greeted warmly by the partisans, who were amazed by the quantity of weapons they had brought with them. At that moment the detachment was getting itself ready to launch "Operation Kossovo." The three machine-guns had arrived just in time . . .

Two Who Were Late

Pesach Alpert had agreed to join the group going into the forest. As prearranged, he reported to the meeting-place near the Jewish cemetery with a machine-gun on his shoulder and whistled a few times into the dark silence. No one answered. But at that anxious moment another human form suddenly rose out of the ground beside him with a rifle on her shoulder. It was Itche Gratchuk's wife. They talked the new situation over and decided to go into the forest by themselves.

Stumbling in the darkness over hilly fields and thorny bushes, they finally reached the Kossovo Road near the village of Skolzici. The final hours of the summer night passed quickly. Near a hut they met a Jewish youngster tending cows. After speaking with him in Yiddish they were certain that his master must be in close touch with the partisans in the area, so Pesach asked the boy to take them to his employer.

The peasant knew at once what these two armed Jews needed. He suggested that they spend the day in his barn and in the evening he would put them in touch with the partisans. Having no other choice, they decided to take the risk. In the barn Pesach found a hole in the ground and set up his machine-gun, just in case they might need it in a hurry. A couple of hours later the farmer brought them some boiled potatoes, cold buttermilk and bread. Hungry as they were, they gulped it all down and began to feel a little less apprehensive.

Pesach nevertheless lay down to rest with the machine-gun by his side and kept an eye on the surrounding "terrain." In the evening he noticed three men approaching the barn, one of them the farmer. When they got close enough, Pesach gave them the customary warning, "Halt or I'll shoot! Who goes there?" They stopped and after a brief exchange it turned out that they were partisans who happened to be riding by in a "matchanke"—a cart with a machine-gun installed. The partisans offered to give them a ride to their detachment. Again, Pesach and Mrs. Gratchuk decided it was worth the risk.

On the way, Pesach cautiously asked one of the partisans what detachment they belonged to. "Vasilievtses," came the reply. This didn't make Pesach too happy. There were rumors that whenever Vasilievtses encountered Jewish partisans they stripped them of their weapons and drove them deeper into the forest.

The cart suddenly stopped at a partisan encampment. One of the men jumped off and ran straight to Vasiliyev, who ordered that the Jews be fed. Near the kitchen Pesach met Herzl Shepatinski, who told him that he was now a scout for Shchors detachment.

They spent the night there in a friendly atmosphere and in the morning Vasiliyev himself invited them to stay in his camp. Pesach thanked him for the great honor, but explained that his wife and two daughters were already with the Shchors detachment, along with about 200 armed Slonim partisans. Mrs. Gratchuk also declined the invitation with thanks, because her husband was with Shchors too. Vasiliyev instructed his men to harness up the horse and wagon and drive them both to their destination.

At the Slonim camp, Pesach was summoned to Commissar Dudko's headquarters. Dudko told Pesach that Wacek Wilchinski had already apprised him of his talent and experience and that he had therefore appointed Pesach Manager of the camp "economy." He wanted to know how they had fallen into the hands of the Vasilievtses and how they had been treated there. Later Pesach learned that Vasiliyev had received strict orders from Pronyagin not to detain any ghetto partisans on their way to Shchors detachment.

Two Tactical Errors

—————————•—————————

Immediately following the successful "Operation Samachowa" the partisan general staff continued making plans for moving the detachment to their new encampment at Lake Vygonov. To this end they sent a series of couriers to the city on the urgent mission of bringing more Jews out of the ghetto and transporting the remaining weapons to the forest, along with leather, soap, medicaments and various other necessities.

Six men—Zerach Kremian, Nonye Zirinski, Abraham Doktorchik, Pavel Krot, Andrei Khvisenia and Parfinovich—were supposed to split up into three teams and do the following: Zirinski and Kremien were to go to Matus Snovski's place for the weapons; Zerach wanted also to bring out some members of his family. Zirinski hoped to find his brother Sasha still alive and bring him out. Doktorchik and Krot were to get the leather in the tannery on Podgura Street. Parfinovich and Khvisenia were to set fire to the hay storehouse on Panesve Street.

Coming out of the forest, they went straight to the cemetery, chose a little burial hut and agreed to meet there when they had all carried out their tasks. In case of trouble or a gun-fight they were all supposed to retreat to this position.

Together they passed the church and the brickyard and then separated. Zerach and Nonye made their way down to Podgura

Street near the old Jurzdik cemetery. Suddenly a white figure loomed up in the darkness and cried "Halt!" They got their backs up against the cemetery fence and Zerach ordered Nonye to shoot at the white figure. Nonye's rifle jammed. When he finally got it to fire, he missed his target, which again cried "Halt!" Zerach then used his automatic and the German stretched out in the middle of the street in his white shroud. (Apparently he lived nearby, had come out in his nightclothes drunk, seen something suspicious and ordered them to "halt"—as though his command alone would be sufficient to make Jews surrender.)

The sound of the shots, however, alerted the Germans all over the city. The clip-clop of horses' hooves grew louder—police patrols were racing in their direction. Nonye and Zerach crawled back up the hill to the meeting-place. The others, hearing the shooting, were doing the same, and they all got back safely to the woods. All night long they heard the sound of gunshots and rockets coming from the city.

For a few more days the group stayed in the forest, still hoping to carry out their mission, but the Germans had doubled the guard around the city. Finally a courier came from the detachment with orders for them to return to the camp, where everything was ready for the move to the Pinsk marshes.

Later they learned that the Germans had printed leaflets announcing that partisans had attacked Slonim but had been driven back by the Wehrmacht, which had killed scores of them in hand-to-hand combat in the streets.

The partisans had made two mistakes. First, they tried to reach Matus Snovski's place through the center of the city, instead of by the Jurdzik gardens, which would have been closer and easier. Then, even more carelessly, they had opened fire in the middle of the night, waking up the whole city. They should have retreated along Podgura Street and let the drunken German alone.

Anshl in the City Again

A few days before the first massacre in the small ghetto, Anshl came to Zelik Milikowski on a special mission: to rescue more Jews from this last ghetto, to bring back type for the partisan print-shop and to discuss with Schlossberg his escape to the forest in a captured Soviet "tanketka" that he had repaired in the Beuten camp.

With the help of Zelik, Abramovski and Moshkovski, he organized another armed group of 25 Jews to go into the forest. They also made arrangements with Schlossberg about the tank. The problem of the printing type was to be resolved that evening.

Late that night Anshl, Zelik and Hillel Moshkovski went to see Julian at Skrobive and Dubianski Streets, where he still ran his print-shop for the Germans. Leaving Milikovski in the street to stand guard, Anshl and Moshkovski knocked at Julian's door. Julian let them in and they proposed that if he would give them a few cases of Russian type, they would get him and his family out to the forest, where he would work as a printer for the partisans.

Julian categorically refused to give them the type or to go into the forest. The Regional Kommissar had promised him safety. The fellows laughed at his naive faith in the mass murderer Erren.

"Don't you know what he did with the other skilled craftsmen to whom he made the same promise? You're living on borrowed time!"

But Julian refused to listen. "I have nothing in common with you and I'll have nothing to do with your partisans!"

He left them no alternative but to pull out their pistols and demand that he show them where he kept the Russian type. They then tied up several cases of the type and as they left, they told Julian they hoped Erren would keep his word.

The same night, Anshl and a well armed group of Jewish partisans marched out to the forest. Among them were: Moyshe Mishkin and his brother Josha, Reuben Mukasey, Jascha Kremien, Golda Gertavski, Avreml Bubliatski and Hillel Moshkovski.

Before Anshl led out this last group he ordered Zelik and Elya Abramovski to stay in the city until the men with the weapons cache had left. Several days later, however, both of them showed up unexpectedly at the forest encampment with the following story:

One evening there was a loud banging at the door of their carpenter shop and someone ordered them—in Russian—to open up at once. Not suspecting anything, they were about to obey the police command when they heard a suspicious whispering on the other side of the door. They both realized at the same instant that they had better get out of there at once.

Zelik began a conversation with his uninvited guests—through the locked door—to give Elya time to collect their personal weapons. Then they slipped out the back door and made a bee-line for the Catholic cemetery. Meanwhile the police had caught on, but it was too late. They ransacked the house, discovered the cellar, took the few weapons that had been left behind and set fire to the house.

The next day, the Byelorussian newspaper carried a story that the police had waged a bitter fight with the Jewish partisans, killing many of the "bandits," their general staff, and captured a large cache of weapons.

After this "incident" the police broke into other workshops, arresting "suspicious" young Jews and shooting them. In that *Aktion* Sheyndl Volpin and Meir Khoroshchanski perished.

The question remained: Who had betrayed the partisan meeting-place?

Schlossberg's "Tanketka"

One of the many buildings in the Beuten camp was a locksmith's workshop where Schlossberg, a member of the ghetto underground, spent a lot of time repairing a small Soviet tank for the Germans. A decision was reached by the partisans to "smuggle" the tank out of the camp and drive it to the partisan detachment in the forest. The plan was a simple one. Schlossberg would take the tank out on the road for a test and drive it to the forest. When the repairs were finished, the camp authorities set the day and place—the Baranovici Road. Schlossberg reported the details to Anshl.

At the appointed time Schlossberg got behind the wheel. Above him sat a German—unarmed. From the Beuten camp they drove past the prison to the highway. Schlossberg turned right over the highway bridge, cut diagonally across Skrobive to Kossovo Road and "stepped on the gas." The arrangements were that the partisans would wait for the tank at a spot five kilometers from Slonim. There they would take care of the German, drape a red flag over the tank and "parade" through the village with it until they reached the "wolf caves" in the forest.

The tank had not yet traveled a kilometer when the German somehow caught on. He jumped off and got word to the barracks. Soon a couple of German tanks were hot in pursuit of Schlossberg. To make matters worse, the engine in the tanketka failed and

Schlossberg had to stop and try to repair it. The partisans had no way of knowing what had happened. And in any case, they were too small a group to risk going out to find him. The German tankists caught up with Schlossberg as he was desperately trying to get the tank to move again.

He was captured and shot.

Slonim Becomes Judenrein

In mid-August a rumor spread among the "luckiest Jews"—the survivors of the third massacre—that a fourth one was imminent. Many had "heard for a fact" that the Regional Kommissar had decided to cut the number of Jews down to 350.

On August 16th, while Matus Snovski was at the office of the Kommissariat, he saw them unloading cases of whiskey, cigarettes and "snacks" from a truck. For him this was a sure sign that the Germans were preparing a massacre; it had happened before—the thugs were being loaded up with alcohol so that they would do their "job" more zealously. With his special pass Matus was able to get to the Beuten camp and warn the underground.

On August 18th at dawn all the Jewish living quarters were surrounded by Ukrainian, Lithuanian and Byelorussian police, led by German gendarmes. It was not difficult for them to find any Jews who were hiding; there were no longer any bunkers to run to.

Early that morning a messenger from Hick summoned Matus to the Regional Kommissariat. Realizing that Hick wanted to hide him from the drunken thugs until the massacre was over, Matus asked the messenger to wait a few moments while he put his tools away in a safe place. He warned his family to stay hidden.

At that moment scores of armed Jews from the Beuten camp were escaping to the forest. Only about 90 Jews were left in the

camp. The German guards took them out to the ditches at Petralewicz and shot them. Then they did the same with the Jews who
were working in the sawmills, the barracks, on the roads, and for
the Regional Kommissariat.

About 25 of the best craftsmen were left alive because, as the
Nazis told them, their skills were vitally needed. Most of them
decided, however, that the "safest" thing for them to do now was
to try to escape.

At the Snovski's house, Matus' father, Reuben, was hiding in a
hole dug under the floor. His mother refused to hide. She sat with
her granddaughter Malkele in the house and waited. His sister
Sarah hid in the hole that Matus had dug under the locksmith
shop. Elya, her husband, hid in the cellar of a neighbor, a Polish
policeman. No one knew he was there. It never occurred to the
Nazis that a Jew would hide in a policeman's cellar.

Around 12 noon Sarah heard the familiar yelling of the police.
Her father surrendered. Then she heard a shot and her mother's
cry of pain, then another shot. The police had asked the Polish
neighbors if someone would take the child, but no one offered
to do so.

Later that afternoon, when the killing was over, a gang of
drunken murderers came into Matus' shop and fell asleep in the
room under which Sarah was hiding.

When night fell her husband crawled out of his cellar and, on
tiptoe, entered the room where the murderers lay snoring. Silently
he lifted the cover on Sarah's hiding-place and silently he helped
her climb out. In her haste she left her slippers behind in the hole.
Unnerved, they didn't know what to do first. Elya led her out by
the hand. Barefoot, in tatters, they hurried past the bodies of their
parents and the child in the garden and ran toward the cemetery
and the forest. All night long they ran, hungry and demoralized,
their feet bloody, until as it was growing light, they reached the
partisan headquarters.

No one knew them and they had brought no weapons with them.
The detachment did not want to take them until Sarah mentioned

that she was Matus' sister. They asked Zerach and a couple of others to verify her story. And that's how they became partisans.

When Matus returned from his "protective custody" with Hick, he found the three bodies in the garden and a gang of drunken Nazis in his shop. Controlling his emotions, he noticed that Sarah's hiding-place was open and that she and Elya were missing. He concluded that they had escaped, which made him feel a little better. He then went to the home of a Polish neighbor with whom Sarah had left her four-year-old boy. With tears in their eyes they told him the grim story of the previous night's tragedy. With their help he was able to obtain a horse-and-wagon and move the three bodies to the Jewish cemetery, where he dug graves and gave them a Jewish burial.

After this agonizing "funeral" he went to the small ghetto and arranged with the other craftsmen there to get out of the ghetto that same night. Then he went to the Regional Kommissariat to "work." Later that evening the Nazi officials shut themselves up in a room for a meeting. Matus put the best automatic he could find into his tool kit, and left. The guard at the gate, who knew Matus as a trusted worker in the Kommissariat, let him pass.

Thanking his neighbors, Matus picked up Sarah's little boy and a package of food they had prepared for him. Cautiously he made his way through the gardens and around the cemetery to Kossovo Road.

Like shadows, a group of the last Jewish craftsmen stole out of the small ghetto into the dark night.

Embittered but determined, Matus marched all night with the child on his shoulders and weapons in his pockets. On the afternoon of August 20th he reached the partisan headquarters around the same time as the 16 other Jews from Slonim.

The day before, the Shchors brigade had left for the Pinsk marshes. Sarah and Elya had gone with them. Matus meanwhile stayed with the 53rd group.

The next morning Hick learned that during the night there had been a series of disappearances—his automatic, Matus, and more than half of the remaining Jewish craftsmen. His men searched all over the city for them, as well as on the road leading to the forest. But they were gone.

The remaining 350 Jews were killed on September 21, the day of Yom Kippur. The Jewish community of Slonim ceased to exist.

Corporal Mutz
and Sergeant Braun

The two officers in charge of the Beuten camp were not like any of the other Germans at all in their behavior toward the Jewish inmates. If anything, they treated the Jews much more leniently than they did the few non-Jews there. Once in a while Sgt. Braun even conducted inspections among the non-Jews and punished them for violating the rules. But they never inspected the Jews, even though they must have known that some of the younger men were stealing weapons from the camp. They simply didn't look too carefully at what their workers were carrying out of the factory. (Aside from weapons, the Jews also carried out potatoes, bread, tobacco, soap and similar necessities.)

Early in September 1941 Mutz arranged for "his Jews" to sleep in the camp because he guessed, or he knew, that a new massacre was being planned. Forty Jews were to stay in the barracks near the captured weapons. Later he permitted some of the women to sleep in the camp. And he posted a guard around the barracks to prevent any roundups of Jews.

Once Braun even took a Jewish couple into his home, a violation that could have cost him his life.

221

During the third massacre, which lasted a few weeks, he and Mutz "covered" for many of "their" Jews hiding in bunkers and in the bushes behind the muddy pasture adjacent to the camp.

At the end of February 1942 a brigade of workers, guarded by gendarmes, was sent from the Beuten camp to the railroad station to load weapons and scrap metal onto the cars. The foreman of the brigade was Eric Stein. By accident, the barrel of a cannon fell on Jascha Shepetinski's left foot and hurt him badly. A couple of the men lifted him onto a platform and Stein rushed to the camp to get help from Corporal Mutz. All this was done surreptitiously, so that the guards wouldn't know what had happened; they had a habit of shooting anyone who was injured at work.

Mutz came immediately in his truck and with the help of a few men lifted Jascha into the cabin. He told the guards that he was taking a worker back to the camp for a special job. The truck sped past the camp, across the bridges and through Skrobive Street to the Jewish hospital on Michalowski Street. With the help of some Jews in the ghetto Mutz got Jascha through the barbed wire fence and into the hospital. When Jascha thanked him, Mutz replied, "It's the least I could do, Yakov."

Dr. Blumovich diagnosed a broken bone and put a cast on it.

●

The Jews in the Beuten camp had various opportunities for "target practice." Corporal Mutz would often invite brigadeers Stein, Sivoch, Yakov Shepitinski and Vova Abramson to the firing range to see "who was the better shot." For future partisans this "contest" was made to order. Aside from learning how to shoot accurately they also learned how to handle a variety of weapons.

●

One of the duties at the camp was the gathering of captured Soviet weapons which Red Army units had failed to move from the front during their retreats. At the end of April, Mutz and Braun arranged such an "expedition" on the Baranovici Road. The guards were Finkelstein, Bergner and Freedman, all Jews. At a certain point, a hail of bullets came flying at the group from all sides. The guards dropped to the ground. Mutz and Braun, experienced soldiers, realizing they were surrounded, raised their arms in surrender. The guards, meanwhile, were shouting in Russian, "Tovarishchi! Hold your fire! We are Jews!"

The partisans came out from behind their cover with angry questions: "And what about the two officers—are they also Jews?"

The guards explained that these were two Germans who treated Jews decently and that it was only thanks to them that the ghetto partisans had been able to carry out so many weapons over such a long period of time. They added their personal opinion that the two officers were probably former German Communists who had been drafted into the army. The partisans released Mutz and Braun and the three Jews received generous portions of wurst from them as a reward . . .

During the massacre in the small ghetto, when the Gestapo rounded up even Beuten camp Jews, Mutz and Braun immediately returned a large transport of unrepaired weapons with the excuse that without the Jewish "specialists" the work could not be done. The Gestapo was forced to return the Jews to the camp, where they survived for a little while longer.

•

After Israel Sokolik was freed from prison he was sent to the demolished ghetto to collect the remaining Jewish furniture for German use. In a house on Breger Street he heard the sound of Yiddish speech coming from under the floor. To his startled "Who's down there?" came the reply that it was the Steinberg family—two sisters and a mother from Ostrolenko. They begged him to go to the Beuten camp and inform Corporal Mutz about their situation.

Sokolik did so. Mutz jumped into his truck and told Sokolik to get in and point out the house. When they got there, Mutz put the three women in the truck and brought them back to the camp.

Mutz and Braun must have known that all the Jews who suddenly disappeared from the camp loaded down with weapons were going out to join the partisans.

After Eric Stein and his wife left the camp and it was clear that the few remaining Jews would be "liquidated," Mordecai Yanish decided to go out to the forest too. Braun gave him a revolver and a pair of boots.

In September 1942, as the executioners were rounding up the last victims in Slonim, the Jews again turned to Mutz for help.

"The only thing I can do now is go with you," he said. "There's nothing more I can do . . ."

Yes, there were various kinds of Germans, too . . .

Zelik Milikowski

Morat Gadzheyev

Shiel Fisher

Avreml Band and his friend Vasya

Anshl Delyaticki
(after the war, 1947)

Zlatka Alpert

Itche Mishelevich and Manya Ackerman

Elka Iznaidin

Matus Snovski

Shimon Snovski

Reuben Snovski

Natan Licker

Natan Licker and other partisans

Nonye Zirinski (1948)

Pronyagin and Zirinski (1974)

Part II
In the Forest

Introduction

Like all peoples, the Byelorussians have their nationalists who dream of independence. As far back as 1915 they collaborated with the Kaiser's army of occupation. After the February revolution in Russia they called a conference in July 1917 which created a "Byelorussian National Council." In 1918 they began active collaboration with the Germans and under their protectorate formed an "independent government."

Simultaneously the White Guard General Bulat-Balakhovich organized a "volunteer army" and, when the Germans were defeated, retreated with them. Bulat-Balakhovich's "national forces" were actually armed bands that vandalized small communities, writing a dark page of pogroms into Jewish history. In 1933, as soon as Hitler came to power, the Byelorussian nationalists organized their own "National Socialist Party" and declared their readiness to help the Germans in the war against Russia. On June 20, 1939 they sent Hitler a 17-page memorandum from Prague swearing fealty to the Fuehrer. In response, Hitler boasted: "In every country we shall find friends to help us." That same year a Byelorussian secret service office and a Byelorussian Self-Defense Committee were organized in Berlin.

When Hitler's troops attacked Poland they captured many Byelorussians who had been drafted into the Polish army. The Self-

Defense Committee located these men and from among them
trained a group of spies, diversionists, future mayors, police chiefs
and guards for prisons and concentration camps.

At the very beginning of the German invasion of western Russia,
along with the "vanguard" of the fascist army, came the "leaders"
of the Byelorussian people. Carrying out the murderous orders of
their Nazi teachers, they followed no norms of international rights
or human morality. Gangs of handpicked thugs, brought up in the
poisonous spirit of racist ideology, acted mercilessly in their destruction of the unarmed population.

All these "saviors of the Byelorussian people" babbled about
establishing an independent nation under German protection, but
the Nazis had their own interests in mind as they annexed large
chunks of Byelorussian territory. What they did create was a small
"General Byelorussian Region" made up of the Baranovici region
plus parts of the Minsk, Wileika, Brisk (Brest-Litovsk) and Pinsk
areas. From Berlin, Rosenberg sent the hangman Wilhelm Kube to
rule over this region. A trusted aide to Hitler's Goering, Kube
offered to place his own men throughout the leading bodies of the
occupation authority, in order to "prove" that Byelorussia was
independent. Then he appointed Ostrowski "President" of the "new
Byelorussia."

The "independence" was a sham, of course. The whole fiction,
which rested on German swords, was of importance only to the
Nazis: it made it possible for the Byelorussians to strangle themselves with their own hands. Placing the entire responsibility on
the shoulders of the so-called leaders of the independent Byelorussia, Kube obliged them, among other things, to collect taxes
and organize a permanent supply of slave labor. On October 22nd
1941 he ordered them to create the "Byelorussian People's Self-
Defense" (Beloruskaya Samokhova) to help the Germans in their
war against the Partisans, to prepare the population ideologically,
to mobilize slave laborers for work in Germany and to select
cadres for espionage, diversion and other terrorist activities. All
these cadres were trained and then shipped behind Red Army lines

or into the forests. For this purpose President Ostrowski declared a mobilization of the Samokhova to last 14 years—and this applied to men up to the age of 57.

With this announcement Ostrowski unmasked his Nazi plan to maneuver the Byelorussian people into killing each other. Into the forest he sent false "partisan" groups who robbed, murdered and burned down villages, thereby compromising the real partisans in the eyes of the peasants. At the same time, they stirred up anti-Semitism by accusing the Jews of betraying the location of partisan camps to the Germans.

For the Nazis it was clear that if the partisans bought food products from the peasants to feed thousands of people, nothing would remain for the Germans, so they persuaded the peasants to resist "the forest bandits who were robbing them." They stationed units of the Samokhova in the villages, providing them with weapons and bunkers. They opened special police schools to train the peasant youth in this murderous profession. Obviously the plan was to kill two birds with one stone: Let the peasants fight against the partisans and the food products would remain for the Germans as a form of tax. One of these schools was opened in the summer of 1942 in the village of Avinovici near Bitten.

Naturally the partisans had to put a stop to this and were forced to wage bloody battles against these Samokhova schools and headquarters. In their own self-defense they had to shut them down and send the young people back to their villages. Many of these groups, still carrying their German weapons, went over to the partisans and became part of their detachments.

Vlasovtses

In the spring of 1942 another source of help appeared for the Nazis in the form of the "Vlasovtses"—armed and trained Red Army men—who went over to the Germans directly from the front lines.

Andrei Vlasov was a major-general in the Soviet army. At the end of 1941 Stalin suddenly summoned him to the Kremlin. Also present at that meeting were Lt. General Vasilevsky and Marshall Shapozhnikov. When the three generals were ushered into Stalin's office Vlasov noticed that "the Boss" was posing as he always did in the propaganda photographs, with his right hand holding a pipe up to his mouth.

After Vlasov made his report, Stalin—still puffing on his pipe —went to a wall map of the Moscow region and described the situation at the front. Vlasov, beginning to feel trapped, was reminded of a tiger stalking its prey. Stalin put his finger at a certain point on the map.

"Vlasov! Here you will stop the enemy's attack!"

"I hear you—" Vlasov said and wanted to continue with a question, but Stalin raised his eyebrows and said:

"I haven't finished. You will organize a new army. We'll give you whatever you need. But it must be done quickly. Do you understand?"

"Precisely, Comrade Nar-kom (People's Commissar)."

Stalin sat down again and Vlasov assumed this was the moment to state his conditions. "Permit me to say something, Comrade Commissar."

"Yes?"

"Please give me the authority to make my own decisions without prior consultation with the political workers." Vlasov knew he was taking a risk, but he had had the bitter experience of the battles outside Lwow and Kiev, where his orders were countermanded by the "politruks."

With unconcealed surprise, Stalin stared at Vlasov silently for a few seconds. Then he said: "You will be given sufficient authority to carry out this task, which is to organize the army and get it ready for battle. The rest will take care of itself."

Vlasov glanced at the other two generals. Shapozhnikov looked frightened and Vasilevsky was holding his breath. Up to this point Stalin had not said a word to either of them. Now he asked them a couple of questions, to which they had ready answers. Figures. Names. But they dared not ask him any questions, though in this kind of situation they were certainly in order.

Vlasov now saw with his own eyes how these high military leaders feared the dictator, but he asked Stalin a few more questions, to which Stalin mumbled some sort of answers. But some of the questions he seemed not to hear. Again he returned to the map on the wall.

"Here it is, Vlasov!" he said. "By the end of the year you and your army must reach this point and hold on to it to the death!" Then he walked around the long table in the middle of the room, held out his hand to Vlasov and the "audience" was over.

Vlasov carried out Stalin's order to stop the German drive on Moscow. He did more. At the beginning of 1942 his 20th army decimated the Germans and drove them back 200 kilometers.

Twice more Vlasov was summoned to the Kremlin and given the task of getting the Second Assault Army in shape on the

Volkhov front that defended Leningrad. But his spring offensive
stalled in the mud of the Volkhov River and his army was routed.
The greatest part of the troops were taken prisoner by the Germans. Hating Stalin's despotic behavior and his "cult of the individual," Vlasov decided that "the Russian people also have a right
to freedom" and that he would therefore fight against the Soviet
Union in order to win that freedom for the Russian people. He reorganized his army in the prison camps into a German military
force and fought fierce battles against his own people.

As a full-fledged Nazi he now introduced anti-Semitism into his
ranks and turned it against the Soviet Union, which branded him a
traitor. Soviet counter-intelligence then "kidnapped" Vlasov and
brought him to the Red Army side of the lines, where he was tried
as a traitor and shot. The Germans, however, continued to use the
Vlasovtses against the Red Army.

Birth of the
Shchors Detachment

Almost 70% of Byelorussia consisted of forests and marshes, especially the western part, which belonged to Poland until 1939. This kind of topography contains all the requisites favorable for the development of a successful partisan struggle.

There is a big difference between the population of west and east Byelorussia. In eastern Byelorussia the Soviets had already been in power 24 years; the population had been brought up in its spirit. Also, in these regions the Nazis arrived later than in other places. These time relationships helped in the preparation of partisan resistance. In the western regions, however, Sovietization had only been in existence a year-and-a-half; a large section of the population had been and remained anti-Soviet.

In the first days of the war the western regions were overrun by the German blitzkrieg. The Soviet authorities retreated in haste, leaving the population behind without any leadership. In addition, many of the local people had immediately gone over to the

Germans and collaborated with them in establishing the Nazi "new order" in Europe.

In the wake of the initial panic, decimated Red Army units and individual soldiers were encircled by the German forces. Some slipped out of the encirclement. For a while, both of these groups managed to subsist in the forests and villages. Gradually they found each other and joined forces. Among the local peasants they found sympathizers, especially activists of the formerly illegal anti-Polish movement who were well acquainted with the mood of the population, as well as with local political-economic conditions. Not far from the Jewish towns of Bitten, Ivanevici and Kossovo (an area 30-40 kilometers southwest of Slonim), in the dense, impassable forests of Okunivo, Bullo and Rafalovko—the "wolf-caves" —four small groups of former Red Army men set up an encampment.

April 25, 1942, representatives of these four groups met for the purpose of forming one detachment under the name of Shchors, a legendary Russian partisan during the Civil War. As Commander they chose Lt. Pavel Pronyagin (a former teacher) and as Commissar, Grigory Dudko. Out of the four groups they formed four companies—Nos. 51, 52, 53 and 54. They decided that as their forces increased they would move their encampment into the Pinsk marshes.

The first partisan groups faced a powerful problem: how to get in touch with and get help from "the big country"—as they called the rest of the Soviet Union, since they were isolated behind the German lines on a "small piece of land." At that time they did not even have a radio receiver.

In the meantime they made "hit and run" assaults on small police garrisons, hi-jacking enemy trains carrying meat, bread and potatoes—provisions that they used to requisition from the Byelorussian peasants. When these raids were successful the partisans would share their spoils with the peasants. After a few such attacks the Germans no longer appeared outside the city in small groups.

The partisans created problems for enemy transport and communications. At first these diversionary acts were quite primitive: separating rails with a screwdriver or cutting down telephone poles with a saw. But even from these small-scale acts of sabotage the Germans suffered big losses and had to double the guards on railroad lines, highways and bridges. The partisans considered this a victory in itself; they had forced the enemy to pull troops from their front lines.

Unit 51,
A Jewish Group

In May 1942 a small group of Jewish partisans from the Slonim area appeared in the forest and, with the rest of the Shchors detachment, took part in the attacks on German positions. When their number reached 40, the staff decided to set up a separate Jewish fighting unit. This unit, whose members were mostly Jews who had escaped from the Slonim ghetto, was given the number 51 and a "Jewish commander." Later it turned out that he was really a Ukrainian and had not had enough training to fill such a high military post.

Finding themselves finally in their own long-dreamed-of unit, the ghetto partisans from Slonim began a new life in the forest. For this they were totally unprepared, but it was a thousand times better than "life" in the ghetto at the mercy of the Nazis.

Around three kilometers from the partisan camp was a clearing in the forest on which stood a half-finished building without doors or windows. The Jews called this place "The Island" and the building "The Headquarters." Through this island ran a network of paths leading into the forest and to nearby villages. Partisans in military uniforms or in peasant clothing, armed with rifles, grenades, knives and other assorted weapons, passed through here briskly in the course of their duties and then disappeared into the bushes.

Every newcomer (except for the armed partisans from the ghetto) had to pass an "examination." This correct decision of the staff was a way to keep out undesirable elements or even German spies. Each candidate had to be armed and of "proper" age—not too young and not too old. He was required to have recommendations from known partisans who would vouch for his honesty and fighting ability. Those who were too old formed a family camp that worked for the detachment. Since there were many newcomers at that time, people had to wait impatiently around the headquarters for several days. Most of these were only shadows of human beings, fresh from the inferno of death and destruction. Hungry and weakened, they rested on "beds" of old straw and withered grass, telling countless tales of incredible horror, but burning with the desire for revenge.

One of the commander's duties was to prepare these newcomers for their "examination." His main instruction was: A partisan without a gun is not really a partisan—find a way to get one. A partisan must be fearless in battle. If you're thinking of sitting out the war here in the forest, this is not the place for you. You may as well leave now.

Strange rumors circulated about these "admission procedures" into the partisans. The peasants in the area said it was done by a commission of Soviet generals, physicians and secretaries. People swore they had seen Red Army tanks and artillery around the "island" and the headquarters . . .

Unit 51 is Reorganized

At the beginning of July, Unit # 51 was reorganized. Scores of new fighters had joined up. There were now 120 partisans with rifles. In addition to the Jews from Slonim there were six Byelorussians from the village of Czemeri, near Slonim: the two Misko brothers, the three Khvyesenya brothers and Yakov Iskrik. All six had been in communication with Commissar Dudko and already taken part in diversionary raids against Nazi transport. They had also been in touch with the ghetto partisans through Shiel Fisher. There were also a few Red Army men: Artiom Avetisian, an Armenian; Sergei Otarashvili, a Georgian; Murat Gadzhaiev, an Azerbaizhanian; Zinovi Vasilyev, a Chuvash, and Vasili Garanin, a Russian. During the first days of the war they had been caught in a German encirclement. Thus the 51st Jewish unit was also a kind of small international.

Around that time the group was assigned a more suitable Commander—Lt. Yakov Fyodorovich, a Jew from Homel, who had escaped from the Germans at Bialystok. Fyodorovich had taken part in the Finnish campaign of 1940, where he was given the Order of the Red Flag for bravery. A professional soldier and a master of field strategy, he understood the psychology of the soldiers under his command and they loved him for it.

Assessing the raw material he had to work with, he began by introducing an atmosphere of military discipline as a way of rebuilding the morale of these former ghetto slaves. Gradually they became accustomed to the forest conditions and grew physically and morally stronger. The new commander divided the 120 men into three companies, and then each company into four units. As commanders of the companies he appointed Lt. Chaim Podolski, Anshl Delyaticki and Archik Band (who later became a staff courier.) In addition to the fighting units, a group was organized to manage the economy of the detachment. Pesach Alpert was appointed starshina (head) of this group.

Commander Fyodorovich had to start from the A-B-C's—elementary basic training for new recruits: target practice, camouflaging positions, "silent" movements from one position to another, "covering" fellow soldiers when necessary, throwing grenades, marching in such utter silence that even a cough had to be suppressed, lest it endanger the whole company. He also taught them to understand the power of the forest and its secret language: how to interpret various sounds among the rustling of the leaves, how to differentiate between a real echo and a simulated one, how to tell the direction a shot came from, how to "read" footsteps—was it a stray cow or a human being out there in the darkness? And above all, to be bold and daring and to abhor cowardice.

While doing all this, he always had in mind the reawakening of Jewish consciousness among these recruits. During moments of relaxation he spoke with them in Yiddish about what had happened to the Jews of Europe. In an uninhibited way, he let them see his wounded Jewish heart. He was always interested in stories about Jewish strivings for Eretz Yisrael. Fyodorovich hoped that after the victory over Nazism Jews would emigrate to Palestine and create a Jewish military force that would fight for a Jewish homeland.

After three weeks of hard work with the recruits, he reported to the brigade general staff that Unit 51 was ready to carry out any task they were given.

The 51st unit was much better armed than any of the other units. It had machine-guns of various kinds, automatic pistols, rifles, hand grenades and a large supply of bullets for all these weapons.

Mariampol is Judged

After the ghetto in Slonim was burned down, the few partisans who were left there had a very difficult time getting to the weapons they had stored away and which now lay buried beneath charred ruins. One large cache was hidden in Tsinkin's building on Breger Street, where Abraham Bubliacki lived.

Jewish work brigades were moving through the former ghetto area, collecting bodies and bringing them to the Jewish cemetery on wagons driven by local peasants. The only possible time to get the weapons out of the ghetto, especially the machine-guns, was when the corpses were being moved. The plan was to hide the guns under the bodies, get them to the cemetery and hide them temporarily in the bushes or in the little structures over the graves. One of the partisans would then keep an eye on them until dark and then move them to Zelig's up on the hill.

There were several obstacles to this plan, however: the Jewish work brigades and the Jewish informer Mariampol, their foreman. After studying all the possibilities the partisans came to the conclusion that only Mariampol could help them. After the third massacre it appeared that his previous feeling of security had grown a little shaky and that they could now take the risk of talking with him.

Bubliacki was given that task. He told Mariampol in unmistakable language that, like Quint, he had nothing to look forward

241

to but death at the hands of the Germans unless he helped the
Jewish partisans smuggle the weapons out. If he cooperated, they
would take him with them into the forest. Mariampol agreed and
promised to "look the other way" for a few minutes while they
loaded the guns into the wagons. The partisans decided to go
ahead with the plan. The peasant who was driving the wagon was
invited to step down "for a smoke." Other partisans moved the
weapons onto the wagon, beneath the corpses. As the wagon
made its way slowly toward the exit from the ghetto, three partisans
followed a little distance behind. At the checkpoint the German
guards, who had never stopped a wagon carrying bodies to the
cemetery, this time ordered the driver to stop while they searched
the wagon. The three partisans made themselves scarce.

Mariampol had done his "last job" for the Nazis. But the partisan
staff decided to bring him into the forest to stand trial. "Keeping
their promise," they arranged for him to be among the next group
of Jews to go into the forest. As the group rested on the ground
near the Headquarters, Anshl spotted him and reported it to the
staff, who instructed him to post a guard over Mariampol, lest he
disappear during the night.

Next morning Unit 51 gathered for the trial. Mariampol's notorious history was well known to most of them, but there were
some who opposed the death penalty for him. "At such a terrible
time, when so much Jewish blood has been shed, Jews should not
kill other Jews, even traitors," they argued. Anshl Delyaticki,
Manya Feigenbaum, David Appelbaum and Itche Gratchuk replied
convincingly that Mariampol had sold his soul to the worst enemy
the Jews ever had. He had sent Jews to their death. In view of the
mission the Jewish partisans had taken upon themselves, senti-
mentality was utterly out of place here.

Commander Pronyagin gave his opinion: A traitor should not be
forgiven even if he is your own brother. This kind of weakness is
impermissible when thousands of our countrymen are being killed
by the savage enemy. At a time like this it is criminal to stand aside
in the fight if one is able to take a direct part in it. How much

worse is it then to forgive a traitor who has beaten hungry, or-phaned children, betrayed out best organizer to the Nazi Security Police and turned over to the enemy a supply of guns for which others have risked their lives. The death penalty is the only just verdict in this case.

The Commander's moving words won everyone over, even those who had previously opposed the death penalty for Mariampol. The prisoner himself took the entire proceedings calmly, as though he agreed he was getting what he deserved. As the trial ended, several Jewish partisans ordered him to get to his feet and go with them deeper into the forest.

The sentence was carried out by David Blumenfeld, a refugee from Poland.

First Test for
the Shchors Brigade

———————————•———————————

By the end of July 1942 the Shchors brigade had more than 500 armed fighters. On June 25th 1200 Jews in Kossovo, a town forty kilometers from Slonim, had been massacred by the Nazis. On August 2nd the Germans decided to liquidate the rest. For that purpose a Sonderkommando of 30 cut-throats came to Kossovo, where a ditch had already been dug.

With the help of the underground activists in the town, Commander Fyodorovich studied the situation and proposed to the general staff that the brigade should pay a visit to Kossovo and do four things: (1) smash the German police force there, (2) empty their arsenals, (3) save the Jews still in the ghetto, (4) test the brigade's battle-readiness. The mission would also bring a political result. It would raise the prestige of the Shchors brigade in the minds of the population in the area and reduce the temporary influence of the occupying power among the villagers. It would also encourage the young people in the villages to join the partisans in the forest.

In preparation for the attack, all the topographic coordinates around Kossovo were carefully researched and divided among the fighting units. A neighboring detachment was also asked to lend a hand. The Voroshilov brigade loaned 50 fighters, the Dimitrov brigade 70. Shchors would supply 360 partisans and the cannon of Unit 54. "Operation Kossovo," scheduled for August 2nd at dawn, would be led by Commander Pronyagin. The signal to begin the attack would be the firing of the cannon.

August 1st a battle-fever gripped the partisans. No one knew exactly when or where he would enter the battle, but the Jews felt that the taking of vengeance for their murdered people was about to begin. That night the detachment made a "silent march," during which each group was given its specific instructions.

Down a hill, past a muddy stream and its frogs scampering in fright, approaching the first cottage in Kossovo, spreading out and taking positions on the damp earth, waiting for the signal to attack. The cannon was positioned on a hill toward the north. A special unit cut all the telephone lines in the vicinity.

The early morning fog had thrown a shroud around Kossovo. Here and there a light burned dimly. Enemy rockets lit up the sky, as if to show that the Germans were not asleep. Having expected this, the staff had positioned the partisans out of range of the illumination. To prevent anyone coming to the help of the besieged Nazis, the Voroshilovs and the Dimitrovs were guarding the roads in and out of Kossovo.

Commander Fyodorovich had positioned the Jewish unit directly opposite the ghetto. Its objective: to reach the center, to storm and destroy the command post and the police. The Commander crawled from one unit to another, giving his final instructions. The machine-gunners were to pour a rain of fire on the barracks.

The first streaks of light in the sky. The horizon turns pink. Armies of birds awake with a noisy chatter. Now it is possible to see the target.

The first cannon shot shakes the ground. The second and third shatter the chilly air. The Russian "Hoorah!" precedes the rhythmic crackling of rifles and machine-guns. The noise is deafening. Fyodo- rovich leads the 51st unit forward. Bullets are now flying in both directions. It is a fight to the death.

The Jewish partisans race to the main street, past the barbed wire ghetto fence. To the left and to the right, the other groups are covering the 51st with a thick cloud of bullets. Suddenly, Fydodorovich's shouted command, "Follow me!"—and the 51st unit storms the police barracks. On the floor, a few dead police. Two live ones, still standing, are holding their hands up high—they don't know that partisans take no prisoners. The other police have retreated to the command post in the church, from which a counterfire is now coming. But the rest of the detachment has laid down a ring of fire around the headquarters.

The enemy, however, is now firing from the safety of the stone church, keeping the partisans pinned down.

"Fire over the church!" comes Fyodorovich's order. But that too proves unsuccessful. David Blumenfeld, on his own initiative, tries to climb over the church wall to attack from behind. A machine-gun blast from the tower leaves his lifeless body hanging on the fence.

The artillery unit brings the cannon down from the hill and fires at the church wall. The machine-gunners fire at the windows and the tower. With shouts of Hoorah! the partisans break into the building and squelch the last bit of resistance . . .

As the shooting died down, the Jewish partisans were surrounded by the exhausted but admiring young people of the ghetto. Many of them immediately picked up the German weapons and begged to be admitted to the partisan ranks. Their first task was to help the partisans find hidden gendarmes and informers in Kossovo. Someone reported that several police and even some Germans were hiding in the hospital. They were soon found and dispatched.

Operation Kossovo ended successfully at eleven o'clock that morning. The Jewish partisans, for the first time, knew the sweet taste of revenge. One hundred Nazis had been killed. The price: seven partisans dead and ten wounded.

Picking up their fallen comrades, the partisans returned to their base in the forest, their mission accomplished. Some of the ghetto population went back with them.

Before they started back, Doctors Blumovich, Lekomzev, Orlinski and Kovarska collected all the medical supplies they could carry.

The next morning a new squad of German police arrived and completed the massacre of Kossovo's Jews. Then they collected their own dead and left.

Two weeks later the Shchors partisans returned to Kossovo and brought back another load of vital supplies that were so badly needed in the forest.

The Military Academy
Around the Campfire

At the end of every partisan workday a campfire was started where
people spent the few free hours before they went to sleep. The
staff used this opportunity to analyze the most recent military
actions. Crowded around the fire, the partisans listened attentively
as Pronyagin, Dudko and other commanders "took the action
apart," looking for its weak points and its strong points. Pronyagin
would praise the deeds of heroism, the smart and correct military
moves, as examples to be followed. But he was merciless in his
criticism of foolish or timid behavior, or of not fulfilling a mission.
These sessions were called "The Military Academy around the
Campfire."

Such an academy took place after the first great victory at
Kossova. Pronyagin had only words of praise for the "cannon unit"
and the artillerymen who hit the target even though the aiming
mechanism on the gun was missing. He also commended the
51st unit for its bravery and mentioned many of the Jewish partisans
by name.

Dr. Blumovich, a staff member, criticized Commander Fyodorovich for the first unsuccessful attack on the church, because it
collapsed immediately under the police counterfire. Fyodorovich

calmly accepted this criticism from a medical man who knew nothing of field tactics, but it left a bad taste in the mouths of the Jewish partisans.

After the "business" part of the meeting, the mood relaxes as the fire is revived with fresh twigs and branches. The shadows frolic on the wall of ancient pine trees as a light breeze plays with the leaves on the bushes. The twigs in the campfire crackle, spraying the air with bright, cheerful sparks that glow in the darkness for a few seconds and disappear . . .

The men kid each other, tell spicy jokes, laugh at the Fritzes and their local lackeys. Those who love to tell tall tales about their exploits find a ready audience here. The "artists" who know how to use picturesque language become the center of attention. Some of the younger people persuade Dadya Vasya to tell them about the bad old days under Polish rule in western Byelorussia. This old fighter against the Polish nobility wrinkles up his already well lined face and calmly spins his yarns. The young people sit quietly, listening raptly, gazing into his eyes with admiration.

The sweet tones of a harmonica suddenly break into the conversation. People grow pensive as they listen to the old familiar tunes. The melodies express everyone's deepest longings, everyone's memories. The musician begins a folk tune and soon a circle has formed in the clearing. Here and there a woman's skirt flashes among the dancers. Some people start singing, making up new rhymes for old songs.

One of the dancers, in the middle of a step, is called out of the circle for an urgent duty. He swears under his breath, tightens his belt, runs his fingers through his hair—and reports for duty.

After dangerous battles with the hated enemy, these hours around the campfire united the partisans into one friendly family and calmed their spirits.

Unreplenished, the fire slowly dies down, the crowd thins out, people retire to their little huts to get a few more hours rest before "reveille."

Summer nights in the forest are short.

Regards from
the Ghetto Partisans

Somehow the scouts of Unit 51 learned that about a dozen Germans in an armored car were touring certain villages not far from the partisan region. They had come to dig up the bodies of their soldiers who had fallen in battle with the retreating Red Army in 1941. Apparently they wanted to give them a proper burial.

Discussing this interesting bit of news, the staff decided that Jewish unit 51 should "handle" this matter. Commander Fyodorovich assigned a group which included Jacob Chatzkelevich.

Taking up attack positions, they set up an ambush and waited for the German car. A long time passed and just as they were almost ready to give up and go back, a cloud of dust rose down the road. The partisans quickly put the car out of commission by shooting out its tires. The Germans tried to retreat on foot toward the village of Devyatkovici, but none of them got very far. Two surrendered. The partisans burned the vehicle and withdrew to the forest with their prisoners.

In accordance with a staff plan, one of the Germans was taken "on a tour" of all the detachments and informed that what he was seeing was only one percent of all the partisan forces. Then the two Germans were ordered to remove their outer clothing and they were sent packing toward Slonim to bring regards to the Nazis from the ghetto partisans and a promise that they were next on the list.

Jews in the
Partisan "Forest State"

After the victory in Kossova "the wolf-caves" hummed with more than the forest breeze. The Shchors detachment had grown into a forest "state" with regular army units and a population of over a thousand. Every day, Jews who had escaped from nearby cities and towns came to the encampment. The Jewish presence was very visible.

Many of the older people among them were still suffering psychologically from their nightmare existence in the ghettos. The younger people, however, quickly came to look upon the forest as their new home, though as partisans they were still green. The able-bodied and armed Jews from Kossovo were taken into the 51st unit. The others were put into the family camp, now known as Unit 56.

With the addition of the Jews from Kossovo, Unit 51 numbered 150 fighters. Abiezer Imber wanted to know why the 51st unit couldn't have its own cannon. After consulting with Commander Fyodorovich, he began a search for discarded cannon parts. In the Rafalovka region he found two wheels and the barrel of a 45-millimeter gun. Eric Stein, Natan Licker and Dr. Blumovich offered to

252

help him and went looking for parts and ammunition left behind
by the defeated Red Army.

Stein, a specialist in weaponry of all kinds, went to work. The
one part they didn't have was the optical scanner, but even a
cannon without that part is deadly enough.

Despite the fact that they were surrounded by Russians and that
racial slurs were sometimes heard, the Jewish partisans spoke to
each other in Yiddish, though Fyodorovich always gave his commands in Russian.

The Jewish partisans in particular were filled with a restlessness
born of national pain and the need for revenge, revenge, revenge.
Relief from this restlessness came only in battle, in victory over the
enemy. The forest became their home, the gun their indispensable,
familiar tool with which they did their work. No longer were they
ghetto shadows condemned to death. Now they fought as equals
with the Soviet partisans against a common foe. And they were
grateful to the Soviet political leadership of the Shchors detachment for giving them the opportunity to fight and take revenge.

Meanwhile, the 51st group set up for itself scores of booths,
made out of branches, around a central clearing with a canvas tent
that served as a hospital for seriously wounded fighters. The
hospital was directed by Czeslawa Orlinska. At one end of the
clearing they built a kitchen, managed by Yitzhak Imber from
Ostrow-Mozoweck. At the other end, a storehouse for weapons,
where Stein, Imber and Licker were busy putting together their
cannon.

The general mood of the camp was a happy one. Phonographs
played Russian and Jewish music. A radio, on batteries, brought
news from Moscow. The good news that the Nazis were finally
being driven back strengthened the fighting spirit of all the partisans.

The Jews in the 56th Kossovo group also built a life for themselves. They may not have been battle-ready—for any number of
reasons, including a shortage of weapons—but they contributed

their usefulness as workers. Almost overnight they built up a whole "combine" of workshops for tailoring, shoemaking, hatmaking, barbering, harness-making and carpentry. For their work they were paid in food. From the 51st unit they received a few rifles, bullets and grenades. From the nearby peasants they bought various weapons for cash and trade. Shmuel Slonimski traded his shoes for a machine-gun, which they traded with the partisans for five rifles. Soon unit 56 had 40 rifles and one automatic pistol.

To administer the affairs of the family camp the staff appointed Yefrayimov as commander and Seryoza Tatarikov as political leader. Their assistants were three non-Jews and one Jewish professional soldier, whose job was to prepare the ablebodied men and women for military duty. Tatarikov and Yefrayimov divided the Jewish camp into six groups. The first two groups consisted of the armed and ablebodied Jews, led by Yefrayimov. They conducted sabotage activities against the Germans and requisitioned food products from the farmers. The third group, led by the Jewish soldier, stood guard around the camp. The other three groups served the detachment in various jobs and administered the "camp economy," which was under the management of Yitzhak Shepetinski from Slonim.

Feeding such a mass of Jews was a big job for the staff. The armed Jews went out to collect food together with the three non-Jewish partisans, so that the peasants would know that the Jews belonged to the detachment. Often, the political leader also went with them. At night the Jews went out to the villages to collect necessities like pots, kitchenware, food. Some of the peasants contributed this willingly, others did not. In every village cottage the partisans found goods that had been taken from Jews—clothing, furniture, dishes, even sacred books, which the peasants used as paper.

In order to avoid conflicts with the poorer section of the population, they at first requisitioned products only from the more well-to-do farmers (the "kulaks"), from those who had relatives working for the Germans, and from former Polish village leaders. After they had exhausted these sources, they began requisitioning food equally from all the farmers.

The more mature the Jewish fighting group became the more the staff used them in various operations. Every night they went out on the roads to cut down telephone poles, or to loosen railroad tracks. One night they captured a German truck along with the driver.

Soon the entire camp began treating the Jews seriously. The economy group did not merely cook meals. They went out to the mills to grind corn, carried the flour to the bakery which the Kossovo Jews had organized in the village of Czizikes.

But the wolf-caves soon became too small for such an army. Military sense warned the staff that in the event of a major German attack there would be no room to maneuver, no hinterland to which to retreat. In addition, the large family camp, which continued to grow because of the steady stream of Jewish refugees, had become a hindrance to the fighting ability of the detachment. To remain a properly functioning military unit, the brigade would have to separate the family camp and leave it in the wolf-caves with a small partisan group to defend it.

Thus the idea grew of moving the encampment. A larger forest was needed with natural defense positions, such as water barriers. The choice turned out to be the Polessye marshes and the Vigonov Lake.

On August 5th Commander Pronyagin sent out a scouting party, headed by Lt. Ignatov, to see what they could find.

Attack on the Police
Academy "Samokhova"

Soon after the victory at Kossovo, Zerach Kremien, while on a mission for the staff, found himself in the Rafalovka Forest, where he met Commander Fedotov of the Chapayev detachment. (His nickname was Borodka, on account of his little beard.) Borodka complained to Zerach that the police school in the village of Avinovici was "a thorn in his eye, right under his nose." Zerach suggested that he talk with Commander Pronyagin about this.

At that particular time Pronyagin had little enthusiasm for another battle with the Germans, because he was in the middle of making plans to move the detachment out of the "Wolf Caves." Zerach, however, described how easy it would be to capture a lot of sorely needed supplies and at the same time raise the prestige of the Shchors brigade even higher among the populace. Pronyagin couldn't help but see that Zerach was correct and he allowed himself to be persuaded.

Precise plans were made and a strategy worked out, as had been done at Kossovo. Fighters were selected from the 51st and 54th units. The Chapayev unit contributed 50 men to guard the roads around the area. The partisans inside the village itself provided the information that the school had recently been moved to the local landowner's palace, which had been "requisitioned" by the Germans. The police force consisted of about 50 young Byelorussians plus a few German instructors. Some of the Byelorussians had been "drafted" by the Germans and it was necessary to teach them some "partisan ethics." The Commandant of the school was a former officer in the Polish army.

On the night of August 9th, just before the march got under way, Pronyagin spoke to the partisans, wishing them a victorious return and a successful completion of all their objectives, for the good of the socialist Fatherland.

In the vanguard rode the cannon of the 51st Jewish unit with its gun crew: Zelik Milikowski and Vasya and Nonye Zirinski. Again the march was long and arduous, avoiding main roads and villages, because no one was supposed to know of their presence before the moment chosen by the Commander. And so far as the partisans knew, no one did see them except the moon, which kept darting in and out of the clouds.

They knew they were close to Avinovici when the village dogs, awakened by the scent of humans, barked out their first greetings. At that moment the moon came out of its hiding-place and faintly illuminated the little farmhouses and, on the right, the big white building that was their target. The partisans dropped to the ground, formed a ring around the place and waited for the cannon to give its signal. Fyorodovich again crawled from one group to another issuing specific instructions.

As the dawn broke on August 10th, a cannon shot shattered the stillness. Then came the accompaniment of machine-guns, rifles and automatics. The police replied in kind, but the sudden attack had confused some of them and they ran into the marshes to hide. They found no safety there. At one point the police spotted Shepetinski's machine-gun, forcing him to move to the left into a potato field. But from his new position he could more clearly see the reflection of the light on their protective helmets. He trained his gun on them.

When Fyodorovich saw that a considerable number of the enemy had been put out of action he called out: "For the Fatherland! Follow me!" The partisans broke into the building. The remaining police surrendered immediately and were met by a storm of Russian curses. Some of them tried to defend themselves—they were not traitors, the Germans had mobilized them, their lives were threatened. "Then why did you shoot at us?" the partisans demanded. They hadn't fired their guns, they insisted. But it took only a moment to examine their weapons and prove they were lying.

Pesach Alpert recognized a few among them who had taken part in the massacres in the Slonim ghetto. A brief interrogation and an immediate sentence liquidated the most guilty of them. The others were allowed to return to their homes on condition that they warn the population what awaited traitors to the Fatherland.

The rich store of food products was taken back to the partisan encampment. Several cows were given to the peasants who had come running to see what was happening at the palace. When it was discovered that the Commander of the police academy had escaped, Vasily Senkov (of the 54th unit) went out to try to take him alive. But the Commander found him first and shot him in the face. The traitor had positioned himself so securely in the attic that it was necessary to set fire to the house.

The partisans also set fire to the sheaves of grain stored near the palace, ready for shipment to Germany. About four hours later the detachment started the march "home" loaded down with food supplies, weapons (including 25 machine-guns), ammunition and medicaments.

Among the many Jewish partisans who distinguished themselves in this battle were: Zerach Kremien, Abraham Band, Itche Gratchuk, Noah Servianski, Anshl Delyaticki, Jacob Chatzkelevich, Pesach Alpert, Nonye Zirinski, Zelik Milikowski, Israel Sokolik, Dr. Fira Kavarski, Nathan Licker, Elya Osak, Itche Rabinowicz, Jascha and Hertz Shepetinski, Mr and Mrs Orlinski, Shabsi Moshkovski, Hillel Moshkovski, Yitzhak Anuchnik, Zedek Derechinski, Mietyk Lustik, the brothers Malach, Joseph Timan, Zenya Eichenbaum, Gute Kagan.

The local population began to acknowledge the partisans as legitimate representatives of the Soviet Union fighting in the hinterland of the enemy, as an arm of the Soviet government that was punishing the Germans and their lackeys. A conflict began with the occupier over the farm crops. As soon as the armed "tax collectors" appeared in the neighborhood the peasant activists notified the partisans, who immediately set up ambushes to hit the Germans as they returned with the loot that they had stolen for the use of "the Greater Reich."

Large estates which the Germans had taken possession of were burned to the ground. The partisan movement grew to such numbers that the Nazis no longer dared to collect this loot with small military units.

German Counter-Attacks

The Nazis, who had found it so easy to put barbed wire around the ghettos, now discovered it was an impossible thing to do with forests. On the contrary, the partisan activities were undermining the "blitzkrieg" campaigns, the front lines were suffering a shortage of weapons and human resources. Smaller German garrisons in their own hinterland were being driven out or destroyed.

For the partisan staffs it became clear that sooner or later the enemy would turn its attention to the "forest bandits." In mid-September 1942 the German command ordered a thorough "combing" of the Byelorussian forests and marshlands in a search for partisans or "escaped Jews." This operation continued without letup and caught the partisans unprepared. Accustomed to attacking, they now had to stand and defend themselves under the most adverse conditions and they suffered heavy casualties.

At this critical juncture the partisans turned to their tried-and-true tactic—mobility. They broke up into smaller groups and hid in swamps that the Germans didn't dare enter. In the end, the German army was defeated here. By and large, all the detachments retained their strength and even stepped up their diversionary attacks. Bold new leaders emerged from the ranks. The Germans, on the other hand, were forced to put a tighter guard around their headquarters and build fortifications to protect their Aryan hides.

On the Road
to Bitter Battles

On August 15th Ignatov returned from his scouting expedition
with a satisfactory report for the general staff. At Vigonov Lake
much more favorable conditions existed for a partisan encampment
than in the "Wolf Caves." The western part of Polesye consists of
wooded marshes with many rivers, streams and lakes. The vast
swamps are natural defenses against enemy encroachment. On
small stretches of land among the swamps and forests live poor,
isolated peasants called "Polishukes" (Polesyans) who speak a
dialect that is quite different from the general Byelorussian language. The Polishukes raise cattle and farm their niggardly plots of
land. By early 1942 a few partisan camps were already located in
this area.

The scouts also reported that almost two regular German divisions, on their way to the front, had been held temporarily at
nearby railroad stations in order to comb the Wolf Caves. Common
sense dictated that the brigade move its encampment at once.
Pronyagin summoned all the commanders and made plans to break
camp no later than August 20. Left behind to feed and defend the
Family Camp would be the 53rd unit and one company of the 52nd.

When this plan became public knowledge there was panic among
the Jewish partisans. The Wolf Caves had become a place of
refuge and a well ordered home for hundreds of persecuted and

defenseless Jews. Many of the Jewish partisans had relatives in the Family Camp. How could they leave them behind in this precarious position?

Nevertheless, on the morning of August 20, 500 partisans lined up to take leave of the Jewish Family Camp and its defenders. The column stretched for more than a kilometer. In the vanguard was the reconnaissance team to "test out" the advance positions. These scouts were the eyes and ears of the brigade. Everything depended on them. (One of them was Avreml Band.) Behind this group, at a distance of almost a kilometer, rode a few men on horseback. Then several motorcycles. The cannons of the 51st and 54th units had been loaded onto farmwagons, together with the staff records and the medical supplies. Finally came the "infantry," carrying heavy loads of ammunition, food and supplies.

Pronyagin, Dudko and the unit commanders ran up and down alongside the column giving instructions, controlling the pace of the march. The march also had a political significance: this region had few active partisan groups; seeing these fighters, the local people would become more hopeful about their own liberation. Some villages thought it was the Red Army returning to the front and greeted them with flowers.

At the same time, the march unnerved the German police garrisons on the way; they either took up defensive positions or they fled. From prisoners the staff learned that the enemy had an exaggerated notion of the strength of the Shchors brigade.

Near the village of Dolgaya the staff chose a suitable place "to do some business." They crossed the railroad tracks between Bitten and Leszno, where the 51st and 54th stretched out on a front of about a kilometer along the road. When darkness fell, the defenders of the railroad line could still see the "forest bandits," but they did not dare challenge such a "huge" army.

Not hearing even one shot from the enemy, the partisans cut telephone lines, wrecked the rails, set fire to every guardhouse they saw. The enemy fled.

After an all-night march, the column arrived intact at the village of Dobromyshl and camped on the bank of the friendly Szczara River. Bone-weary from their long march and their night's work, the army rested, but the staff met immediately with the commander of the local partisan unit, Alexei Cherkov, who knew the area well and who had won the respect of the people there. He pointed out to Pronyagin how important the village of Czemeri was to the Germans, with its wooden bridge over the river.

The staff assessed the situation. The bridge was guarded by about 50 German soldiers, with one machine-gun. Repair shops in the neighborhood were working on their damaged weapons. Cherkov also pointed out, however, that in Ivacevici nearby, there was a large German garrison.

In the meantime, the partisans had set up camp in the forest and begun organizing its "kitchen." Several groups went on a tour of the surrounding villages to "buy" food. (In partisan language that is called "bombarding" the villagers.) They also visited the German mill and "ordered" flour for 500 people. The mill did not resist. The rest was simpler. A few housewives heated up their big Russian ovens. The men chopped some wood and drew some water out of the well. They slaughtered a fat pig and roasted it. And someone sniffed out the location of the village vodka supply.

When the hunger pangs were stilled, the younger men took a dip in the Szczara, then their heads turned to thoughts of the opposite sex and they scattered through the village houses to try their luck.

In the same village of Dobromyshl, as if from out of the earth, crawled three dirty, crumpled Jewish shadows. A father and two young sons, they had been hiding in Yakov's barn. The Jewish partisans from Bitten recognized them and asked Commander Fyodorovich to allow them to join their townsmen in the unit. The commander agreed, and Yudl Berkner and his two children were admitted into the ranks.

At the end of August Nonye Zirinski and four other fellows were sent to Khoroshevici to find and bring back a supply of artillery shells. This was a highly dangerous mission. They had to go back through Avinovici, Zirovici, Albertin and Slonim. German ambushes were everywhere. But the five men returned right on schedule on the eve of the battle at Czemeri, as the staff had planned.

The day after the Shchors brigade marched out of Dobromyshl, the German garrison marched back in and were told by an informer that the peasant Yakov had been hiding Jews on his farm. They dragged Yakov, his wife and their child out of their home, marched them to the bridge, shot them all, and threw their bodies into the river.

That was how the brave "Aryans" avenged their disgrace in fleeing from the partisan attack and showed that they were still masters in the village . . .

Another Great Victory

The last days of August were hot and steamy. The fields turned yellow. Life in the forest moved languidly. Even the little breezes escaped to an unknown place somewhere, leaving the air dry as dust. Bloodthirsty gnats and strange-looking flies swarmed in the thousands and pursued the partisans with a relentless buzzing, awake or aseep. Cigarette smoke was the only thing that kept them at a distance, but you couldn't smoke all night.

August 31 in the afternoon the alarm sounded in the temporary encampment. The partisans picked up their guns and ran to line up. The commanders quickly checked the ranks and the army moved out of the camp. One group, made up of partisans from the 51st and 52nd units and commanded by Lt. Guzhevski (a former flyer) was assigned to destroy the German headquarters in Czemeri. (The Jewish partisans nicknamed him "the shliapke" because of his funny-looking hat.)

Lt. Guzhevski spoke to his fighters. "It is my responsibility to lead you into the battle tomorrow. At dawn we wipe out the German command post in Czemeri. The success of this mission depends on each one of you. We're not going to storm the building, as we've done before. This time we're going to sneak up on the enemy while he's still asleep. Understood?"

"Understood!"

Led by Commanders Pronyagin and Fyodorovich, the rest of units 51 and 52, together with the 54th and 56th and part of Chertkov's detachment would keep an eye on the roads on either side of the village. An especially strong group was assigned to the village of Lubishitz, at the crossroads of Slutsk-Minsk, the direction from which help might come—if at all—for the beseiged Germans.

After a 20-minute rest, the partisans were ready to launch what they expected would be another "easy" battle. Covered by darkness, they approached Czemeri. By pre-arrangement, a few local activists met them at the outskirts of the town to point out the exact location of the targets. A squad went out to cut the telephone lines. The rest of the partisans took up positions and waited impatiently for the first signs of daylight.

At the signal, Guzhevski's group, led by a local peasant, advanced single-file toward the command headquarters. But then, before Guzhevski was able to stop his mouth, a sentry shouted "Halt! Who goes there?" Guzhevski shot him with his Bezhomka (a rifle with a silencer) but as he fell, the sentry managed to fire his gun. The shot awoke the German soldiers inside the building, but it also acted as a signal for the partisans to attack. All the cards now lay open. There was no surprise attack. The battle was joined.

Guzhevski's group broke into the yard. Jascha Shepetinski set up his machine-gun behind the barn and started firing at the building. Chatzkelevich's machine-gun jammed. The partisans were now firing from all sides. Lt. Guzhevski ordered the machine-gunners to move closer to the building. Jascha and Mietyk did so, but the enemy used those few seconds to toss a few grenades into the yard. Shepetinski flew in one direction, his gun in another. Mietyk's legs were blown off. He begged Jascha: "Finish me off!" Jascha's brother Herzl came running over to find out if Jascha were still alive. The intense firing of the enemy guns pinned the partisans down so tightly that they could not even rescue Jascha's machine-gun.

Gute Kagan (now Myerson), Rosmarina (Jumek's wife) and Ida Weisfish (from Warsaw) volunteered to bring in the machine-gun, but both commanders refused permission. Instead, they ordered

Noah Servyanska, Sivash and another Byelorussian to set fire to the building. The men carried out their mission successfully, but not before Sivash, who was covering Servyanska, was killed by a German bullet.

Abiezer Imber and Zelik Milikovski set up their machine-guns opposite the headquarters. To their right was a bridge. In an exchange of fire, Zelik was hit. Imber dragged him to one side and continued firing at the Germans.

The morning light, in the meantime, was proceeding on schedule. Commander Fyodorovich, in view of the unexpectedly strong enemy resistance, changed the battle plan and called for cannon fire. Under cover of the cannonade, Herzl Shepetinski made a leap across the yard for the machine-gun and dragged it to safety.

Meanwhile, Pronyagin's group had burned the bridge and wiped out its guards. A thorough dousing of gasoline and a single match was sufficient. The group assigned to destroy the repair shop and the gasoline supply also fulfilled its mission without a hitch. Three German soldiers managed to escape and were running up the Ivacevici Road, but one partisan caught up with them on his motorcycle and killed them with one grenade. Two German officers, approaching the town in a car, saw what was going on, got out of the vehicle and tried to lose themselves in the bushes, but they weren't quick enough. A few alert "forest bandits" guarding the road caught up with them.

In that operation, about 50 German soldiers and several police were killed.

Drs. Orlinska and Kovarski gave first aid to the wounded partisans. Mietyk Lustik, Sivash and a Byelorussian partisan were buried in the village of Czemeri.

Among the "battle trophies" taken by the partisans were an automobile and a bus, in which the wounded were taken back to the base. As a sign that the partisans were now "in charge," little red flags were fastened to the vehicles.

That evening the detachment gathered around the campfire and discussed the day's battle. With each victory even the most fearful of the partisans lost some of their fear; with their own eyes they had seen that the "supermen" were just as scared as everyone else. One unexpected heartache was yet to come, however. The buzz around the campfire was suddenly silenced by a single pistol shot. Everyone ran in the direction of the sound. Dr. Fira Kovarski had put a bullet into her own head. She had left her old mother behind in the ghetto and could not overcome her depression.

The Cat and the Dog

The temporary "lull" that ensued after the partisan victory at Czemeri was not a good sign. Knowing this, Pronyagin sent out a reconnaissance team to see what they could learn. Among them was Herzl Shepetinski. They set out for Vigonov Lake led by Ignatov, who had recently scouted the area. What they found was German army units camped around the railroad stations at Ivacevici, Ancevici, Telebani and Domanova. On their way to the Stalingrad front, these units had been "detoured" for a campaign against the Shchors partisans.

Together with the local police, the Germans had begun a "search-and-destroy" mission in the forest in the Brisk district. On September 9th a strong enemy force in Dobromici attacked a partisan group and a smallscale battle took place on the banks of the Szczara River. To avoid an open conflict with a force ten times larger than they, the partisan staff left a small group behind to draw the German fire while the rest of the detachment withdrew to Ivacavici. But there they also encountered German troops. After a brief skirmish, the partisans shifted direction and headed for the Somikhina villages.

At Dyadya, not far from the villages, hearing the rhythmic clatter of automatic weapons in the distance, they halted. The reconnaissance team had also met with a strong enemy force. (Joshua

Czapko, a refugee from Poland, was killed in that skirmish.) The situation was critical. At 9 a.m. on September 11, 1942 the report came in: a large German army was encircling the area. The detachment was threatened with destruction. But the enemy itself, which had so far not discovered the exact location of the partisans, gave itself away with its noisy jabbering—in the middle of a forest they were carrying on as if the whole world were their private domain.

Pronyagin made a hard decision. "We've got to dig in here in a circle and take defensive positions. But no one fires a shot until they hear the command!"

Half of the circle stretched for a distance of 600 meters. The 51st unit occupied the right flank, through which the enemy could penetrate the partisan hinterland. Facing the partisans was an enemy armed with the most modern instruments of death. Behind the partisans were the overgrown primeval marshes of the Pinsk swamps, which now represented their last and final hope. The situation could be compared to a rabid dog that has caught sight of a cat. The dog leaps. The cat, backed against a fence, claws at the dog. The dog retreats a few steps and begins circling warily. Taking advantage of this indecision the cat leaps to the top of the fence, then carefully lets itself down on the other side.

The rabid Nazi dogs were firing without letup, advancing step by cautious step. Pronyagin waited until the last possible moment, then gave the command: "Fire!"

Many of the Nazis fell, to lie forever in the Byelorussian mud. The rest, pinned down by intense fire, could not even retreat. That was the end of the first "psychological" attack.

They tried again with a different kind of weapon. Mines began exploding at the top of the trees and fell upon the heads of the partisans, who kept fighting back along the entire defense line. Each time the rabid dogs attacked, the partisan cats clawed at them until they pulled back. When their second psychological attack failed, low-flying German planes dropped hundreds of grenades, most of which exploded as soon as they hit the tops of the trees, but did little damage to the fighters below.

All that morning the battle continued. At noon the enemy attack grew more intense, as if fresh forces were joining the battle. Meanwhile, the partisan ammunition reserve was dwindling. Here and there the forest had started to burn. Pronyagin heard reports from the ranks: "They're choking us to death! We've got to retreat while we can still do so!"

By sundown the firing had gradually subsided, but the enemy was still out there in full force. The detachment could not possibly hold out against such odds. The staff came to a decision: under cover of darkness the cat must jump over the fence.

They buried the two cannons in a deep pit. The two autos and ten wagons were put to the torch. The horses were let loose. The fallen comrades were buried. The ammunition reserves and the bread supply were divided among the units. As a cover for their retreat they decided they would fire a few rounds in the direction of the enemy. The return fire made it very clear that as soon as morning came the enemy would start its "death-blow." The most difficult part of the operation was what to do with the wounded. The more seriously hurt were put on stretchers. The less serious had to proceed on their own power.

Pronyagin studied his compass and took his first steps into the mud, which responded with a faint squish. The units followed behind him, single file. It was probably the very first time the tall water-grasses had ever seen such strange-looking intruders . . .

Forty Hours in the Mud

Thus began the silent retreat of the Shchors brigade, as the thick autumn darkness enshrouded the slow, monotonous forward movement of the armed human silhouettes. The silence was broken only by the swish and splash of muddy boots, which the marchers were barely able to lift out of the gluey swamp. The stagnant air was fetid. At times they could hear the distant, muffled sounds of gunfire and rockets. Here and there they stopped at a little island overgrown with trees and bushes, where they rested or relieved the men carrying the wounded or the machine-guns.

Any march like this demands tremendous effort and concentration, but their weariness and hunger, and the difficulties underfoot, drained the last bit of strength from them.

Commander Pronyagin had a plan to get his army out of the encirclement. His destination was the Oginsky Canal. By late evening the muddy marchers were halted on a good-sized island where they concealed themselves amidst the foliage, leaving camouflaged sentries on guard.

In the morning, as the sky brightened, they could discern the outlines of the place from which they had barely escaped with their lives. They could hear the muffled roar of planes, still searching for them. Only one Jewish partisan, Genia Milyer, had lost her way even before the brigade began its march. They hoped she had not fallen into the hands of the enemy alive.

After a day's rest, the partisan army prepared to move out again. A few of them had tried to find farmers nearby who would sell them food, but they had met with a hostile reception.

On September 13th, the second day of Rosh Hashona, the brigade reached the 10th sluice of the Oginsky Canal on the Szczara River, only three kilometers from Viginova Lake. The next day they were at the dam. For two nights and one whole day, more than forty hours, they had been on the move, without food and with very little rest. Every one of them was soaked to the skin, caked in mud, unshaven. They could barely recognize each other.

Pronyagin immediately sent out three scouts who returned with good news: the detachment had come out of the forest very close to the 10th sluice. The scouts also reported that they had met an old watchman from the Fisheries Artel who told them that five German soldiers were asleep in his house. Commander Merzyakov cursed them out like a trooper for not having finished off the Germans with a couple of grenades. Then he grinned: "Well, we'll have them for breakfast."

The staff took a more serious view of this "oversight" and came to an urgent decision: the five Germans had to be gotten out of the way if the partisans hoped to cross the canal safely.

Bloody Battle
at the 10th Sluice

———————•———————

Against the fiery red sky of morning the scouts could see a group of sleepy, frightened German soldiers wearing helmets. A fat officer was screaming curses at them.

Pronyagin ordered an immediate lineup for the still sleeping detachment. Unhappy about this sudden, unexpected wake-up call, they nevertheless lined up in a hurry and listened attentively to Commander Dudko's instructions. His face was pale and haggard, but his eyes flamed with anger. Brandishing his rifle, he cried out: "Comrades! We're faced with a fight to the death! But we have no other choice! We've got to break out of this damned encirclement!"

Yitzhak Malach, still a very young man, spoke up softly: "Would you believe, fellows, that I've never yet kissed a girl in my whole life . . ." He was not alone in his sentiments at that moment.

The command came to "move out." In the vanguard was Juravlov's 55th group. Then Fyodorovich and his 51st. Then Lyantev's 54th and finally the 56th. The job of the 51st was to attack the sluice and cross the river.

Fyodorovich led his unit in a zigzag across a bare field in which the sluice buildings stood. As the morning fog lifted they saw that they had halted very close to the enemy, who greeted them with a

274

storm of bullets. The Germans defending the sluice had a most favorable position, located as they were with an open space in front of them on the high cement dam. The river split into three here, connected by the little iron bridges of the sluices. In order to capture those bridges the attackers had to cross the inaccessible dams and two water barriers—the river and the canal. The only way to walk on those narrow bridges was single-file. A hundred S.S.-men, armed with light and heavy guns, were guarding this fortress and the approaches to it. Secure in their position, they had not expected the partisans to break out of their trap here. Neither side had anywhere to retreat.

Fyodorovich gave the order to attack. At the same moment, Juravlov did the same. So did the other commanders. Since the S.S. was using tracer bullets it was easy to see that they were shooting blindly. The partisans did not have any ammunition to spare—they had to fire only at targets.

It fell to the lot of the 51st and 52nd units to attack the Germans frontally. Jascha Shepetinski fired his machine-gun at the high dam, where the enemy was shooting from; then at the watchman's house, where German snipers were firing from a window in the attic.

Nonye Zirinski's unit faced a barn built out of big logs. From a high window the Germans were firing without letup. Under cover of the unit's return fire, Yitzhak Malach ran toward the barn, climbed up the logs and grabbed the edge of the window-sill with his left hand as he prepared to toss a grenade into the window with his right. A pistol appeared in the window. Yitzhak fell to the ground, blood pouring from his temple. Zirinski crawled close enough to him to pull him away, but it was too late.

An hour earlier Yitzhak Malach had admitted to his friends that in his whole life he had never yet kissed a girl . . .

In a rage of revenge Zelik Milikowski finished what Yitzhak had started. With unerring accuracy his grenade went straight through the window, killing all the S.S.-men in the barn. This enabled the group to move around the building and get to the sluice bridge, where another squad of S.S. were firing from the dam.

Pronyagin ordered the barn burned down. A few partisans crawled in through the window. Inside, in addition to the dead S.S.-men, was a machine-gun and a case of precious bullets. They carried it out almost tenderly and then set the house on fire from the inside.

At the first bridge a fierce battle was raging. The peat on the dam had started to burn. The smoke floating across the field stung everyone's eyes.

Three times Zerach Kremien, Nonye Zirinski, Archik Band and others tried to storm the bridge, but the enemy fire forced them back.

Pronyagin shouted: "Group 51! Take that sluice! At any price!"

But it was impossible. The partisan attack was stalled. Everyone knew that something had to be done quickly, or it might be too late.

In front of the sluice stood about 20 rowboats loaded with straw, blankets, sacks of food. This was where the Germans slept. Zinovi Vasilyev, a Chuvash, swam over to the boats and tried to claw his way up on the smooth cement of the dam, but he couldn't get a grip to pull himself up. Then he had an idea. Reaching for a blanket, he soaked it in the water and stretched it out on the cement. Now he had no problem climbing up on the dam. His friend Misha Zigan followed. Then three Jewish women from the Slonim ghetto, whom he had been training, also climbed up. From below, Fyodorovich shouted: "Use your grenades!"

They did so, and stopped the enemy fire for a little while. During that interval Fyodorovich ordered Noah Servyanski to cross the little bridge over the canal. Noah succeeded. On the bridge he grabbed a submachine gun from a dead German soldier and emptied it into the bushes, where other S.S.-men were concealed. Zinovi and Misha and the three women hurled their last grenades. The resulting panic among the enemy gave the partisans the opportunity they had been waiting for. Bent over almost in half, Zerach, Jascha Gringaus, Nonye, Jascha Chatzkelevich, and a group of Byelorussians from Czemeri, crossed the bridge and occupied a space on the small island, from which it was now possible to silence the enemy fire, so that the 51st could get across to the second canal.

But on the bridge itself the Germans were making a desperate last-ditch stand. They still had a supply of grenades and were using them unsparingly. The partisans had no more grenades, but the Byelorussians Iskrik, the Khvisenya brothers, Turlai, the brothers Misko, had a solution to that problem too. They snatched up the enemy grenades and threw them back where they came from . . .

A few partisans from another unit managed to swim out of the second canal and approach the enemy from behind, but the Germans noticed them in time and started shooting. The group was about to retreat when Pronyagin stopped them with a shout: "Crabs crawl backward, not partisans!"

Fyodorovich and his group of Jewish partisans raced toward the bridge, firing their weapons, and seized the right branch of the river. From here it would be easier to attack the sluice. The second group attacked from the left. The third group charged straight ahead. Jascha Chatzkelevich was firing his machine-gun for all it was worth. Nearby were Zelik Milikowski, Pesach Alpert, his daughter Chaya, Golda Gertsovski, Anshl Delyaticki, Abiezer Imber, his father Itzhak, Eric Stein, Shabsi Mashkowski, Shiel Fisher, Abraham Orlinski, Itche Rabinowich, Itche Mishelevich, Manya Ackerman, Gute Kagan, Israel Sokolik, Abraham Doktorchik, Nathan Licker, Artiom Avetsian, Sergei Otarashvili, Murat Gadzayev, Vasili Grananin and many, many others.

As Commander Fyodorovich stood up to lead his unit into the final phase of the attack, he was able only to utter the words "Comrades, forward—," when he fell to the ground, his insides torn apart by enemy fire. Dr. Blumovich rushed to his side, but could do nothing. Doktorchik too was hit, but his commander Kremian and Golda Gertsovski pulled him out of range.

Commander Dudko had also stood up and been immediately cut down. Zirinski and Chatzkelovich tore their shirts apart and stemmed the flow of blood from his legs. They carried him away on a stretcher. A few other partisans forded the canal, holding the stretcher high above their heads, and left him on the other side, where the doctors were treating the wounded. The partisans had suffered many casualties that day. Doctors Blumovich and Orlinska worked without a stop, running from one patient to the other.

The Germans were holding onto every yard of ground with their teeth, but eventually their resistance grew weaker. The partisans kept pulling the noose so tight around them that it became dangerous to fire their weapons lest they hit their own people. The S.S. were now firing only from the iron bridge, and then that too stopped.

The partisans raised their heads, listening warily. Then Pronyagin's Russian "Hoorah!" broke the silence and all the partisans prepared themselves for the final attack, but there was no longer anyone for them to attack.

On the other side of the canal three partisans were waving their hats and pointing to three dead S.S.-men who had tried to escape by swimming away. Nathan Licker had caught them. He and the two other avengers were lifted high in the air by their comrades amidst triumphant shouts of Hoorah . . .

It was now well past noon and the sun was warming up the air. Steam rose from the wet partisan clothing and mingled with the sharp smell of gunpowder. All of a sudden, everyone felt the pangs of hunger and fatigue. For more than three days they had not eaten. Three days of fighting against an enemy that was well fed, well rested, well armed. But they had beaten them. Of the hundred S.S.-men, only one was still alive. The fat Nazi officer had sent him to the village of Krivoshin for help . . .

After the Battle

———————•———————

Yakov Fyodorovich's condition continued to worsen. His death was imminent. He pleaded with the doctors to put an end to his suffering. Dr. Blumovich sent one of the partisans to do it, but who could shoot a wounded comrade? Even when it's the enemy, the doctor is obliged to do everything possible. And Fyodorovich was a partisan hero . . .

In addition to Fyodorovich the following also perished in that battle: Yitzhak Malach, Yitzhak Imber, Yakov Gringhaus, Mishe Zigan, Israel Rabinowicz and a young man from the town of Lyobovici. The ninth victim was a Russian partisan. Among the wounded were: Commissar Dudko, Abraham Doktorchik, Golda Gertsovski and Joseph Timan. The partisans buriud their dead.

•

One questioned gnawed at everyone: how had the sleeping Germans learned that the partisans were close by? The only one who might have a clue to the answer was the old watchman. They went looking for him and found him hiding among the bushes near his burned out farm. His face turned white as death when the scouting party caught up with him and brought him in. Pronyagin demanded:

"Why didn't you tell the scouts that there were a hundred German soldiers here? And why did you wake them up as soon as the scouts left?"

The watchman crossed himself but denied nothing.

Pronyagin handed a revolver to Abiezer Imber. "Shoot the bastard! He's the one who killed your father and the other comrades!"

Imber hesitated so long that Pronyagin had to do it himself. Some of the blame for the disaster belonged to the three scouts who had failed to bring the watchman in for questioning. Lt. Merzyakov was also partly to blame because he didn't order the scouts to go back and find the watchman . . .

•

It was a quiet mid-September evening. A pink cloud got itself trappet among the treetops and couldn't move. The partisans loaded themselves down with some of the booty they had won in the battle and headed toward the village of Khatinici. About five kilometers from the village they set up a temporary camp where the doctors could treat the wounded. Several partisans were assigned to protect the field hospital and serve the wounded. Their first duty was to camouflage the place. High up on a tree they constructed an observation post and kept an eye on the surrounding terrain 24 hours a day.

Dr. Blumovich did wonders with his "scalpel"—an ordinary razor. Helping him as nurses were a few young women from Slonim. There were no anesthetics. The "orderlies" had to hold the patient still during the operation. Thanks to Dr. Blumovich's skill and care, all the wounded except Commissar Dudko and Golda Gertsovski were able to return to the ranks.

On September 25th the detachment sent messengers to the field hospital and brought the wounded back to the encampment, which had been set up on a little island in the dense forest. The nearby villages of Novosyalki and Svetici served the detachment as "food stores." Contact was established with the Zharkintsi Brigade which had now been operating in the area for some time.

Meanwhile the general staff decided that the partisans should rest for a while and catch their breath. Pesach Alpert, the camp "administrator," set up a kitchen and organized a crew of cooks and potato-peelers. Temporary shelters were built out of branches. The professional soldiers took advantage of the opportunity to instruct recent recruits in field tactics. In the evenings, around the campfires, the partisans amused themselves with songs and dances and snacks of baked potatoes which they had "pilfered" from the camp supplies.

Special food reserves now had to be stored away for the approaching winter. Deep pits were dug in dark corners of the forest as "refrigerators" for salted meat, flour, potatoes and other "delicacies."

At this most unlikely time the brigade suffered a tragic accident that cost two precious lives. Returning from a food collecting trip in a wagon were Lt. Vasya, acting commander of the 51st unit, Nathqn Paperstein (a refugee from Warsaw) and the driver. Inside the wagon lay a few sheep, tied up with a rope. They were almost back to the camp when one of the animals moved its legs and hit the trigger of a machine-gun that Paperstein had put down in the wagon without setting the safety catch. The bullets killed Lt. Vasya instantly.

For such carelessness with his weapon, Nathan Paperstein was tried and sentenced to death, as a warning to the entire brigade.

During the "lull" in the fighting, many urgent problems emerged. There was a shortage of ammunition for the Soviet guns used by many of the partisans; there was a shortage of medicaments and medical instruments; there was a shortage of grenades and explosives. Where were these supplies to come from? It had become imperative to set up regular contact with the "great country" out there. Up to now the Shchors brigade had remained isolated and unknown even to the center of the partisan movement led by Marshal Voroshilov.

To replace Yakov Fyodorovich, the flyer Victor Guzhevski was appointed commander.

In the Mud Again

The Germans, continuing their assaults on the partisan bases through September and October, needed information about the camp locations. For this purpose they used traitorous characters from among the local population. Two such suspicious persons were caught by the partisans. At their first interrogation they both pleaded innocent—they had "blundered" into the area while searching for a lost cow. As the interrogation continued and they were questioned separately, however, their stories became contradictory and they started accusing each other. Finally they confessed: they had been sent by the Germans . . .

When they failed to return, the Nazis probably guessed what had happened. Two days later, at dawn, they launched their attack.

The partisans were still asleep. Only Pesach Alpert's "breakfast crew" was up and about when the warning shots came from the sentry posts. The enemy had positioned themselves in a semi-circle outside the camp. Their machine-guns crackled in the forest air. For a moment there was confusion among the partisans, but they had been trained to sleep in their shoes and clothing and with their weapons close to hand.

By prearrangement, a few men carried Commander Dudko and Golda Gertsovski some distance outside the camp. Dudko was given a pistol and instructions: if they were discovered by the Germans, it would be better if he first shot Golda and then himself.

Amidst all the noise and confusion Commander Pronyagin shouted "Follow me!" (as he had the last time) and jumped into the mud with a splash. The suddenness and intensity of the enemy attack was causing a near-panic among the partisans in the vanguard, until Dr. Blumovich said coldly: "If we keep on bumping into each other like this the whole damn brigade will be stuck in the mud here all day!"

The march finally got under way, but this time the pace was faster and the water much colder. The further the detachment got from the camp, the fainter grew the sound of shooting. Infuriated by the narrow escape of the partisans, the Germans set fire to the "captured" camp. The marchers could see the black smoke rising above the trees.

When they were a safe distance away, Pronyagin sent back three scouts to check on Commissar Dudko and Golda Gertsovski. They returned in a couple of hours with their report: the enemy had taken over the camp and the surrounding area. There was little hope for their two wounded comrades.

The partisans continued plodding along, their hearts aching. There had been no other way to handle it—to have taken them on the march would have imperiled the whole brigade. Disconsolate, they wandered through the mud all that day until they came to a dense forest. Through the thick curtain of leaves they could see the sky darkening. Commander Pronyagin ordered his troops to "fall out."

Bone-weary and soaked to the skin, the partisans crawled out of the mud to "dry" land, searching feverishly in their pockets for tobacco and anything they could use for cigarette paper. The guards set up watch-posts. A few small campfires were lit, where people could warm up and dry out. Gradually some even managed to fall asleep.

Early the next morning they loaded their weapons and supplies on their backs and started out again. After another day's march they reached the Lan River and again set up a temporary camp in the forest.

As they began to relax a little, the staff discovered that in the panic they had left the brigade archives behind, including the staff orders and even a record of marriages that had taken place in the forest . . .

Two in a Trap

Camouflaged by a blanket of leaves and twigs, Golda Gertsovski and Commissar Grigory Dudko lay quietly in their "shelter" and listened to the clamor of the Nazis as they broke into the abandoned partisan camp. They had each been seriously wounded in the legs. Golda, who was still able to move around a little, sat up and peered anxiously from behind the bushes at the "conquerors."

In the panic of sudden flight the camp administration had left behind a considerable store of food, which the Germans now took for their own use, and then set fire to the makeshift huts. Gertsovski and Dudko were close enough to breathe the acrid smoke. The birds in the foliage retreated to the tops of the trees, then flew away.

All that day Dudko kept his pistol gripped tightly in his hand.

By evening, most of the fires had died down, but the fire in the bodies of the two wounded partisans burned more fiercely as their fevers rose. Their dreams suddenly were filled with inexhaustible drinks of cooling water.

On her hands and knees Golda crept out of their hiding-place and headed toward the smoldering camp-site. Her life and that of Commissar Dudko now hung by a hair. If anything could be done, she would have to do it now, alone. Crawling painfully toward the stream, she banged her knee against a canteen. In one gulp she swallowed the little bit of water still left inside. A bit refreshed, she continued her tortoise-pace amid the charred ruins. As her eyes grew more accustomed to the darkness she could distinguish bits of food on the ground. She found an empty pot and gathered up scraps of cabbage, potatoes, soggy bread. Then she found the stream, drank greedily of its fresh water, filled the canteen and started back.

The Commissar greeted her with angry words about her long absence; his concern had mounted with every passing minute. But when she showed him her "trophies" he thanked her profusely and drank his fill. He still had a box of matches, some German cigarettes and a razor. Golda gathered some twigs and a few stones. They got a little fire going. She heated up some water in the pot, cut up pieces of cabbage, potato and onion and soon they had a "soup." After the meal, feeling a little stronger and a bit more hopeful, she gathered more leaves and made their bed on the hard ground a little more comfortable for the long night.

In the morning Golda found two big branches and with the razor trimmed them down so she could use them as crutches. First she had to teach herself how to use them. Then she dressed their wounds. But there wasn't much else they could do but hope that their comrades would return for them soon. Meanwhile Dudko cursed the general staff up and down a hundred times a day for leaving two wounded, helpless soldiers behind. They could have left a couple of armed partisans behind too, to protect them and tend to their needs.

A couple of days passed . . .

One misty morning, as Golda was searching for food in the camp, she was surprised by two old peasants. It was too late for her to escape. She had to brazen it out. "Halt!" she demanded. "Who goes there?" The frightened peasants stopped in their tracks and explained fearfully that they were on their way home and had taken a short-cut. Golda waved her arms as though signalling for help from friends in the forest. She ordered the two men to keep on going to the right and get the hell out of there fast. She warned them never to come back, if they wanted to stay healthy.

After a few more days their "food reserves" dried up. They fell asleep hungry and awoke hungry. A whole week passed and they gave up hope that anyone would ever come for them. Dudko's wounds had become more painful. He kept waving his pistol around and threatened to shoot the whole brigade if he ever lived to see them again. As his Russian oaths became more and more colorful, they seemed to ease his pain . . .

Expelled from the Brigade

On the fourth day of their wanderings through the Pinsk marshes, the partisans came upon a little village whose wooden cottages and blackened chimneys seemed to have been there forever. They could hear human voices, dogs barking, cows mooing.

First, however, they had to investigate. When they were certain that there were no Germans in the village of Kormoz, they set up temporary camp in the forest nearby. Pesach Alpert and his crew immediately went out among the Polesyan villagers to "buy" food. Soon campfires were brightening the damp grey day, along with the spirits of the partisans, as they awaited further orders.

The next morning the 51st unit lined up before their new Commander Guzhevski, who was not known for his friendly feelings toward Jews. His scowling face boded no good. From a slip of paper he read out an announcement: "In order to strengthen the battle-readiness of the detachment, the staff has decided to separate from the 51st group certain elements such as older people, children and women, who are hampering the entire brigade."

With this as introduction, he then read a list of names, including Itche and Mosye Gratchuk, Elya and Sarah Osak, Yudl Berkner and his two children, Itche Pinski, Sarah Abramovski, Israel Sokolik, Ponyachek, the three Shepatinskis, 14-year-old Nyutke Shelyubski, Itzkowicz, three young men from Lyubovich, Vaksman,

Abraham Bublicki, Israel Slonimski and ten others—a total of 32 people. Apparently the staff, with the help of some "friends of the Jews," had succeeded in compiling a list of "non-battle-ready" elements, but the real reason was that Guzhevski didn't want too many Jews in his detachment.

Israel Sokolik went straight to Anshl Delyaticki.

"Why?" he asked.

"I had nothing to do with it," Anshl could only say.

Sokolik then went to Pesach Alpert with the same question. The answer was: "Why don't you ask Dr. Blumovich—he's a member of the staff, you know."

Blumovich explained to Sokolik: "The staff has decided to separate the weaker fighters, also women, children and old people, who don't fight at all but have turned out to be a burden to the brigade."

This didn't satisfy Sokolik. "To me this sounds like the Nazi selection of 'useful and useless' Jews." Blumovich warned him: "Sokolik, you have a wagging tongue. Be careful you don't lose not only your tongue but your whole head!"

The staff seemed to have forgotten that most of those who were on the list had risked their lives while they were in the ghetto to obtain weapons and clothing for the partisans, that more than a dozen such Jews had been killed in battle with the enemy. Now that there was a whole army of partisans, they could afford to dispense with their services.

At least they let them take their weapons (including two machine guns) and a supply of ammunition. They were also given permission to buy potatoes and bread from the peasants in the area, but not meat.

There can be no doubt that had Fyodorovich still been alive, this anti-Semitic decree would never have been promulgated. The implication of the decision was that only among the Jewish partisans were there individuals who were not "battle-ready." But there were lazy, cowardly, panicky people among the other nationalities in the brigade, and they were never separated. Commander Pronyagin frequently could do nothing about some of his capricious and undisciplined former Red Army officers who acted on their own and had no feeling for the Soviet principle of "friendship of peoples."

The problem, however, was a very complex one at that early period in partisan history. There was no unified command for all the brigades; there was no Party discipline and there was no communication with Moscow. It must also be admitted that there were individual cases of definite laxity among those who had been separated.

Without a plan and without leadership, their hopes disappointed, the separated group left the encampment without a destination. Embittered by such an unexpected betrayal by comrades with whom they had built the detachment, with whom they had fought side by side, they were now faced once more with the prospect of wandering aimlessly through the forest swamps, looking for another partisan group that would accept them.

That evening they found an isolated village where they were able to get a little food. Posting a couple of guards, the rest "retired for the night" in a barn. The next morning they were dealt another blow: Ten of the men announced that they did not want the responsibility of the women and children and had therefore decided to go out on their own. They did, however, permit Sarah Abramovski to go with them. And they disappeared.

So now there were only 21.

But the next morning another seven left—they too did not wish to be burdened with people who were not "battle-ready." They argued about weapons, especially the two machine-guns. The argument grew so heated that it almost came to a violent end. But finally they reached an agreement: the seven "strong" ones agreed to take Berkner and his two children with them—in exchange for one of the machine-guns.

This group of ten went off on its own into the forest, but the next morning they drove Berkner and his children away, leaving them alone in the swamp. Berkner then found his way back to the original group, where he was received sympathetically. Vaksman, who was now the leader of this group, told him, "Stay with us. Whatever happens to us will happen to you."

For two weeks these 14 desolate human beings subsisted on raw cabbage given to them by peasants in the villages. Their fate now depended solely on blind luck. They no longer even bothered to take security measures. Thus, one day they were found by three armed men and became utterly confused. The few weapons that they still had were not even within reach. The three men cursed them out roundly for their negligence. "You could all have been slaughtered, lying on the ground like that! Don't be alarmed. We are partisans from the Vasiliyev brigade. We'll report this to our staff. Meanwhile, be careful."

And they too disappeared.

A couple of days later two partisans brought them the news: permission had been granted for them to come to the Vasiliyev encampment. They were given directions and instructions, and when they got there they discovered that the two "strong" groups had also been allowed into the camp . . .

In that terrible inhuman time, even some Jews were committing anti-Semitic acts . . .

Another Victory
for the Shchors Brigade

On the evening after the 32 Jews were sent into limbo, the detachment marched to the town of Czuczevi to pay a surprise call on the German garrison there. The brigade general staff, having lost its camp site and all its supplies for the approaching winter, had decided that they had to retrieve those losses from the enemy and inflict some punishment besides.

The scouts had reported that the Germans were relaxing in their well-lit barracks, certain that the partisans had scattered like mice to their holes . . .

The 51st group shot out the lights in the barracks. The enemy, leaving many dead and wounded, fled into the darkness. The other partisan groups pursued them. The battle lasted two hours.

The Shchors brigade avenged its honor and replenished its storehouse. The next morning, loaded down with food, supplies and ammunition, they marched toward the east, to a new encampment in the Hotsk forests.

Dudko and
Golda are Rescued

On the sixth day of the march through the mud, near the village of
Hotsk, the staff ordered a 12-man unit to return to the Novosyalki
area and look for the two wounded comrades that had been left
behind. Among that group were Abiezer Imber, Yumek Rozmarin,
Jacob Chatzkelevich, Nonye Zirinski, Izzy Borecki and Moshe
Sofer. The mission of this group was to find Dudko and Golda and
bring them to the new camp, or (if they were dead) to bury them
with partisan honors.

The group had to cover a distance of over a hundred kilometers
in order to avoid German ambushes.

On the eighth day of their ordeal, as soon as the morning light
penetrated the cover of the trees, Golda took up her lookout post
and did not believe her eyes. A "forest person" had appeared
momentarily and then vanished. Her teech chattering with fever,
she told Dudko what she had seen. He laughed at her hallucinations
and cursed the staff. But Golda was sure she had seen a man who
seemed to be looking for something among the trees. She took up
another lookout post and there it was again—but this time it was
two figures, both carrying spades.

Golda's heart almost stopped. She had heard familiar voices, but both men were dressed like German soldiers. She remembered something: after the battle at the 10th sluice, many of the partisans had put on German uniforms. The first pale light illuminated the face of one of the men. Disbelievingly she called out, "Yumek! Rozmarin!" The reply was as disbelieving as her outcry: "You're still alive!" Golda almost fainted.

From amidst the trees came the rest of the group, asking about the Commissar. She put a finger to her lips and with her other hand motioned in Dudko's directon. In whispers she told them how agitated he was, how embittered he was against the brigade, and that he was sitting there with a pistol in his hand.

Nonye and Yakov undertook to pacify the Commissar, since they were the ones who had carried him to safety and bandaged his wounds. Dudko did calm down a bit, but he remained bitter against the staff.

Golda and Imber prepared "breakfast." Others get a stretcher ready for the Commissar. Three of the men took up sentry posts. Then the group rested up for the return march. In the evening they started out. Golda kept up with the others, holding on to one of the partisans. Dudko had to be carried all the way. After two nights and two days they arrived at the encampment. The whole brigade came out to greet them. The doctors examined the two wounded partisans and praised Golda's care, which had prevented the wounds from becoming infected.

"If Golda was anybody else," the Commissar said (he meant that she was Jewish), "she should receive a medal from the Soviet Union for her heroism . . ."

Komarov's
Partisan Unification

———————————————•———————————————

Hotsk is a large village in the western part of the Pinsk marshes. The Germans had not yet reached this area, so the local peasants had not yet had a taste of Nazi occupation. This situation created conditions favorable to a quick partisan growth in this region. Arriving here in October, the Shchors brigade found a great partisan unification movement going on under the leadership of Komarov, amounting to almost an army division. He had succeeded in uniting various wandering partisan groups and in the Zhitkovitch region had created the "Pinsk Division." Strengthening all the scattered forces into one big fist, he was preparing them for serious confrontations with the enemy.

The Shchors brigade immediately joined up with Komarov and began a campaign of continuous hit-and-run assaults on small enemy posts. The intent of these strikes was to drive the enemy out of such villages and small towns as Tuczovici, Zalyusia, Svetici, Novosolki, Czatinici, Hanzevici, Guzevici, all on the narrow rail line. Each battle brought rich booty, but also many casualties.

Very soon the Shchors brigade had become very popular with the local population. New fighters came from Polesye, but because of the shortage of weapons, not all of them could be used.

The staff decided to set up a winterized camp in the forest, 6-7 kilometers from Hotsk. The 51st group was assigned its place and began the hard work of building mud-huts a meter-and-a-half deep in the ground. For this purpose they sawed down scores of fir trees which, as they fell, became entangled with the branches of other trees and then plopped to the ground with a thud. With sharpened axes the partisans trimmed off the branches, leaving only the bare trunk. Each trunk was then sawed into three or four sections. It took two men to carry one of these pieces on their shoulders to the prepared pit.

In Zelik Milikowski's opinion, however, for two men to carry such a "light" log was an insult to his proletarian callouses. All by himself he lifted the heavy, tar-covered log to his shoulder and carried it, at a trot, laughing all the while at the "weaklings" who needed two people to carry one little log. His example was followed by Noah Servianski, Anshl Delyaticki and a few others—to the great amazement of the Russian partisans.

The logs were placed close together in a shallow gutter and fastened together with boards, creating a thick wall inside the pit. When all four walls were up, they put on a cone-shaped roof of the same thick logs. Atop the roof they laid branches and leaves, and over that a thick layer of earth. When the snows came, it would be warm inside these huts. Anyone who found a stove and a chimney pipe would be living in luxury.

For light, they put in a little window. A wooden bunk for a bed. A door and a few steps. At the door a place for weapons. These earthen houses were constructed around a "square" where the partisans could gather and move around.

Pesach Alpert, the camp administrator, worked hard to put up a kitchen and collect a store of winter food products. The partisans went to the villages and supplied themselves with boots, fur jackets, gloves and warm hats.

Gold for the Defense Fund

In the summer of 1942 the government defense committee of the
U.S.S.R., headed by Stalin himself, started a drive to collect money
from the public. Every worker was expected to contribute at least
one month's wages a year to this fund. The money was collected in
installments from the worker's pay envelope.

In the marshes the contributions were made much later and the
partisan command distorted the effort, issuing an order of man-
datory contributions of gold. That is, partisans must turn in any
gold they had in the form of rings, watches, chains, earrings, coins,
etc. Hiding these articles was punishable by death. Even Stalin did
not demand any gold from the population and there were no
threats of death penalties. That was Komarov's own idea.

In the forest near the village of Zhalovich someone reported
that Rebecca Kunitz was hiding a gold watch. They searched her
and found the watch. The trial and execution followed in short
order. Merzlyakov's adjutant—a man named Fedko—personally
carried out the sentence by stabbing Rebecca Kunitz through the
heart with a bayonet.

Even before she was buried Merzlyakov summoned Abiezer
Imber into his hut and said to him: "You're a watchmaker, aren't
you? Is this watch made of gold?"

Imber looked at the case. "No, it's gold-plated silver."

297

Merzlyakov grimaced and said: "You saw nothing and heard nothing! Understood?"

Embittered by this coldblooded murcer of an innocent Jewish girl, Imber muttered, "Understood . . ."

Yes, he understood perfectly. Here in the forest too, Jews were made conscious of their Jewishness. By taking a young Jew's watch and then her life, they "assured" the victory over Hitlerism. Had it been a Russian girl she would have gotten off with a symbolic punishment. But against a Jew they applied the full measure of "war-time law" as a warning to others . . .

Berkovitch

No one knew anything about Berkovitch. No one knew how he had come to the brigade except that he was from Baranovici. Part of a scouting team with two Russian partisans, he was an expert in the Polesyan terrain.

After the battle at Czemeri, Berkovitch said to Pesach Alpert, "Comrade Administrator, come with me and have a drink!" In his hand he held a bottle of vodka. Pesach refused and told him to go away. He appeared to be drunk.

In the village of Korostov the scouts learned from a local peasant that the forest watchman in the area was in the pay of the Germans. Without checking further as to the truth or falsity of this accusation, the scouts went out, shot the watchman and his family and burned down his house. A few days later it turned out that the watchman had been a friend of Komarov's and that he had fought in Spain in 1938 against General Franco.

After a brief investigation, Komarov, who was also a native of Korostov, ordered the execution of the peasant who had informed on the watchman. It was this peasant himself who was a spy and had made the accusation on the instruction of the Germans. Komarov also ordered the arrest of Berkovich, whom the two

Russian scouts accused of "talking them into" this dirty piece of work.

The day after the investigation Archik Band, who was head of the guards, brought Berkovich a meal in his hut. (He had been confined to quarters.) Berkovich told him that he expected to be shot that same day and he therefore wanted Band to have his watch, which was a gift from his father-in-law. "Let it be a memento of me . . ."

Archik tried to reassure him. "They won't shoot you without a trial—"

"I think the trial has already taken place," Berkovich said.

Archik refused to take the "memento."

Later that day, Archik heard a shot. He ran out of his hut and bumped into Merzlyakov coming out of Berkovich's hut. "I just heard a shot!" he cried.

Merzlyakov replied curtly: "Everything's in order. Don't get excited."

He had shot Berkovich in the presence of Commander Komarov. They then removed his boots, took the watch, and buried him near his hut.

This "lynching," plus the execution of Rebecca Kunitz without a scrupulous investigation, as well as the "separation" of the 32 Jews from the brigade, was too much for the Jews in the 51st unit. When they learned that the two Russian scouts had gotten off with three days hard labor, while the entire blame for the crime had been put on Berkovich, they surrounded the staff headquarters, weapons in hand, and demanded that the officers come out and explain why Berkovich had been shot without a trial, while the lives of the two Russians had been spared.

The staff did not come out. Instead, they doubled the guard around the headquarters.

The Jews continued their demonstration. At midnight they were still waiting for an answer. Finally Gyzhinski came out and reported that the next day there would be a rollcall of the 51st group, where everything would be explained. The dawn was breaking when the Jews returned to their earth-huts.

Archik Band went to see Commissar Dudko, a veteran Communist and an honest, objective man. He was worried, Dudko said. The Jews had done something that might have dire consequences. "You are all new Soviet citizens and you don't know yet what Soviet power means. But you didn't do this maliciously, you were excited and all worked up."

In the morning the 51st unit was ordered to line up and place their weapons on the ground. They were surrounded by all the other units in the brigade, weapons at the ready.

Because of the political importance of the incident, General Klyeshchov, military deputy of the Byelorussian Communist Party, was also present. The Jews had heard rumors that it was he who had ordered Berkovich shot.

The entire staff was present. Klyeshchov spoke first. "What you did here yesterday is counter-revolution. In your language it's called a strike. (He used the word *bunt.*) We shall destroy all such strikes and counter-revolutions. Some of you are rich men's sons with soft hands who are constantly breaking discipline." He demanded that those who had incited the rebellion be exposed.

Pesach Alpert held out his hands. "Look at these hands, General. These are proletarian callouses! Where do you see any soft hands around here?"

Others also held up their hands.

"Yes, we are new Soviet citizens," Pesach continued. "We came here to defend our Fatherland. We don't bow our heads in fear, like some others do!"

Archik Band spoke next. He reminded them that the Jewish group in the Wolf-caves had not shot Mariampol without an open trial. "Our reaction here was spontaneous. It was provoked by the secret shooting of Berkovich, so don't go looking among us for any so-called agitators!"

Zenia Eichenbaum threw out a challenge. "What you did here

to Berkovich is anti-Semitism! It is a violation of Soviet law! Everybody knows that anti-Semites get away with murder in Komarov's division."

Zerach Kremien suggested that the 51st unit be dissolved because such a Jewish group is like a voluntary ghetto in the forest.

Speaking for the defense were also Dr. Blumovich, Rozmarin and Doktorchik. All condemned the lynching of Berkovich and exposed the absurdity of the charge of counter-revolution.

When Archik Band finished speaking, he lit a cigarette to calm his nerves. As he did so, Komarov walked over to him and asked politely for some tobacco. "They say you have some fine-smelling makhorka . . ."

For Archik that was a sign that the tense situation had been relaxed.

General Klyeshchov issued a formal order dissolving the Jewish 51st unit and divided it among units 52, 55 and 56. The Jewish group in the Shchors brigade thus existed from July 1 to December 19, 1942.

The position of the central partisan leadership in Moscow was also that it would be better not to have any separate Jewish partisan groups, because it was a mainstay of German hate propaganda among the general population that the partisans in the forests were mostly Jews who had escaped from the ghettos, plus some "non-Jewish bandits." This propaganda, especially in the first chaotic period of the partisan movement, did have a certain effect on the local population and among anti-Semitic partisans as well.

Another Jewish Victim

Time passed and everything changed around them. The sky grew gloomy and drooped above the muddy forests, spilling its snow reserves and whitening all of Polesye. The partisans didn't even notice how suddenly everything had turned white, how their earth-huts, covered with white powder, had become one massive piece of white sculpture.

The snows concealed the Pinsk marshes and the surrounding villages. The wagons were now of no use; the sleighs came into their own.

After carrying out an important mission near the village of Pucici, several partisan sleighs were skimming lightly down a white road and picking up speed. Zyama Shusterovich didn't notice his rifle slipping off his lap until it was too late. In a few seconds the snow had buried it. Zyama searched for it half the night but the snow refused to give up its booty.

For losing one's weapon, the penalty was death.

Once more, Fedka carried out Menzlyakov's sentence.

Eric Stein's Self-Sacrifice

As the brigade moved further into the Polesye region it was continuously involved in fierce battles with German troops. Most of these clashes were of a defensive nature; the main consideration was to safeguard the physical strength of the detachment and get safely into the Pinsk marshes. There was no time to conduct diversionary actions against enemy transport such as the railroad lines.

Early in January 1943 this matter became urgent. Soon Eric Stein was busy preparing new surprises for his former bosses. On the first mission that he organized the unit consisted of Zerach Kremien, Nathan Licker, Shimon Snovski, Zenia Eichenbaum, Berezin and Eric. This action was on the Baranovici-Luninetz line and the Budi station. They had no special explosives for this, so Stein hooked up a detonator from a hand-grenade to a Soviet cannon shell. But this primitive weapon didn't go off. They had to come up with a better "model."

The next time, the unit consisted of Nonye Zirinski, Moshe Yankelevich, Andrei Chvisenia, Michel Sefer, Eric and Berezin (who came from the village of Medvedici and knew the area well.) On a sleigh they pulled two shells of a 112-ml. Soviet gun. About 300 meters from the rail line they left the horse and sleigh among the bushes. The group camouflaged itself and settled down to wait for darkness.

At the proper time, using a crowbar and a pick-axe, they chopped a hole in the frozen earth between the tracks and hid the two shells and a German hand-grenade. They then moved about 75 meters away from the tracks and waited silently in the bushes. A few times Stein put his "stethoscope" to the ground to hear if he could detect the vibrations of the oncoming train.

At last they could see the headlight of the train as it cut through the blackness. A few moments later the roar and crash of the explosion and the flying wreckage astounded even the partisans who had braced themselves for it. For an extra moment they filled their eyes and ears with sweet vengeance and then ran to the sleigh.

While it was still dark they stayed on the roads. As it grew light they found themselves in a deserted area between Hancevici and Kleck, where they decided to wait out the daylight hours. Not far from the railroad they found a barn and slipped inside. Andrei and Nonye kept watch through the slits at either end of the barn. The others slept until it was time to relieve the watchers.

Early that evening the scouts noticed someone walking toward the barn. After a hasty consultation with the others they decided it must be the man who owned the farm. They let him enter and then told him he was "under arrest" until nightfall. A little while later his wife came looking for him and was also "arrested." The same happened with their three children. As soon as it grew dark, the partisans apologized to the family and drove away.

The next day the same group went out on a new mission, but on a dam near Buko they stumbled into an enemy ambush and were forced to retreat. Stein, who covered their retreat with his machine-gun, was hit by enemy fire. He never returned to his group . . .

The next morning they went to the village to look for his body. Peasants there said that the Nazis had carved a Soviet star on his forehead and that they, the peasants, had buried him.

Stein's death was an inestimable loss to the brigade. He and his wife had taken part in every one of its battles.

Early in January 1943 a diversionary group from the Russian side of the front, headed by Lt. Col. Cyril Orlovski, was parachuted into the region of Komarov's united partisans. Communications were immediately set up between the detachment and that group. Orlovski was an admirer of Eric Stein's work. He had come with a plan to put a German uniform on Stein and use him as an "inside man" against the enemy. Now that plan was dead.

Eric Stein was awarded the highest honor: Hero of the Soviet Union.

Hunting the Two-Legged Pigs

Around that time Nathan Licker became friendly with Orlovski, who "recruited" him, Kremien and Berezin into his special group known as "Oriole." The three men learned a great deal from the "detonation experts," especially how to organize attacks on enemy transports. Soon Nathan and Zerach Kremien were also recognized as experts.

January 16th, Licker, Kremien and Berezin, on their way back from a scouting mission in the Ancevici region, stopped at the home of an activist to see if they could spend the night there. The peasant advised against this, however, because early the next day a group of German officers were arriving for a hunting holiday. The regional Kommissar of Baranovici, Friedrich Fenz, was also expected to be in the party.

The three men looked at each other and instantly knew what they had to do. They marched right back, on the double, to detachment headquarters with the sensational news. Orlovski was overjoyed. "They're going to hunt four-legged Byelorussian pigs and we're going to hunt two-legged German pigs!"

The Jewish partisans from Slonim had their own account to settle with the hangman Fenz. A small unit of diversionists went out on this "hunting party" wearing white camouflage cloaks that made them almost invisible. Orlovski, who knew all the paths in the Mashuk forests around Baranovici and Kleck, positioned his fighters so that the Germans would not be able to avoid them on their way back from the hunt, when they would all be tired and probably a little drunk.

At daybreak the first sleigh appeared, carrying German scouts with submachine-guns. After that came a few sleighs with the regional officials and then several more sleighs with S.S.-men and Byelorussian fascists. The partisans gritted their teeth and let them pass.

The day was bitterly cold. The January wind blew the dry snow into the bushes where the partisans were hiding. The snow did, however, provide them with a covering that helped against the cold, which was freezing the tips of their noses and fingers. Their ears were snug inside their Russian fur caps.

Half the day passed and the sleighs had not yet reappeared on their return journey. The fifteen frozen partisans were beginning to wonder whether the Germans had taken a different route home. Orlovski dispelled their doubts. They would stick to their plan: let the scouts go by first, wait for his signal and then attack. After twelve hours they heard the first sound of the sleighs scraping against the fresh snow. They let the scouts go by.

A few moments later Orlovski gave the signal—a firebomb hurled straight at Regional Kommissar Fenz. At the same instant, the other fighters began firing. Orlovski had ruled out the use of grenades because the attack unit was so close to the road that the grenade splinters might have hit them too. The first salvo took care of most of the Nazis. A few tried to jump off the sleigh and defend themselves. The Byelorussians took cover. The surviving S.S.-men began shooting wildly. Orlovski raised his arm to toss another firebomb when a stray bullet hit it. The bomb exploded in his hand. He fell to the ground. Commissar Vashkevich crawled over to Licker and told him what had happened. Licker immediately tried to reach Orlovski, but an enemy machine-gun among the fir-trees was making it impossible. Licker crawled behind a tree and sent a spray of bullets in that direction, silencing the machine-gun. Nathan crawled unimpeded to the commander's side, where Justa Lopez (a Spanish Civil War fighter) was already waiting. Braving a barrage from the remaining S.S., Lopez and Licker successfully carried Orlovski to a safe place.

His right hand had been blown off and the right side of his face badly burned. He needed immediate medical attention. He groaned and opened his eyes. "Nathan," he ordered, "go back there and fight. You're more useful out there . . ." Then he slipped into unconsciousness.

The two fighters carried him back to the Shchors camp, where Surgeon Victor Lyekomzev and his wife (a nurse) amputated his hand—in the middle of a forest, without the proper instruments, without an anesthetic, and with no antiseptic but pure alcohol. But they saved the life of this brave commander.

It was a sweet victory of revenge. Many high Nazi officers had been killed, among them Regional Kommissar Fenz and the police chiefs of three surrounding regions.

In Limbo Again

Quite unexpectedly the brigade staff ordered Lt. Fyma (Chaim) Podolski to return to the Wolf-caves, scout the area and prepare winter bases for the partisans. For this purpose he was given a detail of about 20 Jews and two Russians. Among them were Archik Band, Itche Mishelevich, Ilya Mankowski, Liba Zhagel, Abraham Doktorchik, Rachel Rozmarin, Eric Stein's widow, Abraham Bubliacki, the two Finkel brothers, Abraham Orlinski. The two Russians were Fedka (Merzlyakov's adjutant) and Grisha Khakhol. The whole "operation" was a disguised form of anti-Semitic persecution.

A second group was given the same kind of mission, but in another area of the forest. Among this group were the wives of Fyma Podolski and Itche Mishelevich. Fyma and Itche told Commissar Yegorov in no uncertain terms that if their wives were sent with the other group, they would go with them. For disobeying his order Yegorov threatened them with harsh punishment, but when he saw it would create too much dissension among the Jewish partisans, he allowed the two women to go with their husbands. What difference did it make to him, anyway, so long as they were out of the brigade. The pretext of setting up winter bases was a brazen lie; the brigade had just left the Wolf-caves area because it was too small.

When the group reached the Brisk-Moscow railroad line and discovered it was under strong German guard, they decided to wait for nightfall before crossing it. The two Russians then sent the Jews across the tracks one at a time. When all the Jews had crossed over, Fedka and Grisha turned and disappeared into the forest, hurrying to report to Yegorov that their mission was accomplished.

Incensed, Archik Band ran back across the tracks and chased them for about a hundred meters before he lost them in the darkness.

With this clear evidence of betrayal rankling in their breasts, the small group of Jews reached the station at Leszno (between Slonim and Baranovici). In the Bassin forest on the left bank of the Szczara River, about 20 kilometers from Slonim, they met a group of 15 Jews from the Zeitsew detachment. From them they learned that in a certain village, eight German soldiers reported every evening at five o'clock to stand guard.

Picking ten men from each group they made a plan to intercept the Germans and destroy them. It turned out, however, that the partisans had come too late; even worse, the Germans had somehow become aware of their presence. The next day the partisans came to the village a little earlier, but found a whole German army, including several tanks, surrounding the area. Apparently the Germans had taken the partisans to be an advance unit of a larger detachment. The Jewish partisans ran into a barrage that covered every inch of the area, but they managed to retreat without any losses.

Soon after this "incident" Archik Band found his mother and his sister Matlia and her children. His father Yechezkel had died of starvation. Embittered by the continuous anti-Semitic machinations of the general staff, Archik decided to stay with his family and help them survive. But now they had to hide not only from the Nazis and the Byelorussian anti-Semites but also from the partisans, who were looking for Archik as a "deserter." With his submachine gun he several times fought off all his persecutors and even succeeded in obtaining food from the peasants. Their hiding-place was near the village of Poshkova, in the Wolf-Cave forest, where they stayed from April 27, 1943 to July 10, 1944, when the Red Army drove out the Germans.

Podolski's group wandered around for almost two months before they were accepted by the "Soviet Byelorussia" brigade. In this detachment they took part in a number of battles against Nazi troops and blew up railroad tracks along a 50-kilometer line.

In the spring of 1944 the Shchors brigade with 700 partisans fought bitter battles against retreating German units as large as a thousand men, near the villages of Plyushki, Shutki and Kharovski. Three Jews of the Podolski group were killed.

When they were liberated, the Slonim Jewish group was still based in the Wolf-Cave forest.

Unexpected Battles

———•———

Soviet General Sidor Kovpak (Kolpakov), leading his "United Partisans" deep into Hitler's hinterland, swept through Byelorussia, Ukrainia and the Carpathian Mountains of eastern Galicia and became a legend in his own time. Wherever this force appeared—it included half a regular army brigade—the earth grew red-hot under the feet of the Nazis and their allies. The enemy never took them lightly. Many motorized divisions were moved from the front to oppose him. They even put a price of 50,000 gold rubles on his head.

In early February 1943 the Kovpak army marched through Hotsk and the Jewish partisans from Slonim met some of the 250 Jewish Kovpakites. As part of the regular Red Army, there were never any anti-Semitic manifestations under Kovpak's command, not even in the first partisan period. On the march to the Carpathians he took along all the Jews he met in the forests and even in the liberated ghettos, armed or not. All the able-bodied men and women were taken into the army. The weaker and older Jews were put in the baggage wagons and taken to a safe place where they were hidden with trustworthy peasants—mostly Poles who had sought Kovpak's protection against the Nazis and their Ukrainian helpers.

Kovpak's policy on feeding his army was to do it at the expense of the Germans; whenever he defeated any kind of German military unit he took all their possessions, including food. He was highly critical of partisan leaders who confiscated the last bit of food from local farmers. In July 1943 he organized the 7th company, a unit in which those who knew no Russian were permitted to speak Yiddish.

After Kovpak's army had gone beyond the Hotsk region, S.S. regiments came swooping into the area to exact vengeance, burning, destroying and looting.

On February 11, 1943 Commander Komarov sent 10,000 poorly armed partisans against the Germans in the villages of Hotsk, Starobin, Michalki and Lugi. Allowing the German troops to come very close, he cut them down like stalks of grain, but then the enemy sent a hail of mortar fire against the partisan positions. It became impossible to hold the line against such a mighty force. On the second day the partisans realized that they were almost completely surrounded. That night they decided to slip out of the encirclement. All the detachments retreated to Shvento-Volya except the Shchors brigade which covered the retreat, and it was cut off from the rest of Komarov's army. After a two-day march they came into a new area. The scouts who were sent to reconnoiter ran into a German ambush in a village. After the battle, Shimon Milikowski (Zelik's brother) was discovered missing.

Jacob Chatzkelevich and four other partisans went back to search for him. They found him lying dead on his rifle. The men carried him six kilometers to a nearby village, where they buried him.

Beginning of
Second Partisan Period

Various scouting units, sent by front-line Red Army staffs, began appearing in the partisan "neighborhoods." These regular army groups gradually put some order into the previous chaos. One such party appeared in the Lake Vigonov area, where the Shchors brigade was encamped. A large group, it was headed by Sergei Sikorski, Deputy of the Byelorussian Communist Party Central Committee. With him came a contingent of Pary and youth organizers, two radio men with their equipment, two editors of the newspaper *Zarya* (Morning Star), with a printing press and typesetters, plus a squad of ten armed guards.

Their arrival marked a new phase in the partisan movement in the Brisk region. Their first order of business was to unify all the scattered partisan units in the area. Sikorski assumed overall command. He appointed Sergei Yigorov as Commissar and Pavel Pronyagin as commander-in-chief. Dr. Blumovitch was named chief medical officer. All the detachments were reorganized. The Shchors brigade was broken up into smaller, independent units: the former 52nd group remained the Shchors; the 54th was renamed "Suvorov"; the 55th became "Kotovski"; the 56th, "Budennyi."

Communist Party and Communist youth groups were organized throughout the brigade. Later, parallel regional committees were organized with some participation by the local population.

The first issue of *Zarya* appeared on May First. It reported the reorganization that had taken place and summoned the partisans and the population to a fight to the finish against the Nazis. Around that time the staff of the united partisans moved to the region of the Black Lake, so that it could better lead all 49 armies.

Sikorski introduced a system of strict discipline among the partisans. He sent messengers throughout the forests ordering the partisan leaders to take all the groups into the brigades irrespective of nationality and whether they were armed or not. He reminded them of the slogan under which the entire Soviet people were working: "Everything for the front! Everything for victory!"

This was a welcome development for the Jewish partisans, who hoped that the newly organized Party authority would put an end to the former anarchy and the anti-Semitic lawlessness. They felt that the equal rights of Jews would now be respected. Their only regret was that the Party authorities had come so late.

Among all the partisans joy was boundless when the first Soviet planes appeared and dropped supplies for them: weapons, ammunition, explosives, medicines, salt and other necessities, including even letters from home. Finally they began to feel that they were not alone in this terrible German hinterland, that behind them stood a mighty land.

Early in July the general staff moved to the southern bank of the Dnieper-Bug canal. Not far from the village of Svarin they built an airfield for Douglass cargo planes. (Noah Servyanski and Rivka Moshkovski were among those sent to work there.) The first such planes arrived in August 1943. On their return flight they carried a number of seriously wounded partisans. A regular mail schedule was set up, which worked wonders for the morale of the partisans. Reports of partisan battles were sent to the press back home. Medals and awards were distributed to deserving fighters—by that time 304 partisans in the Brisk detachments had already received awards.

Specialized diversionary groups were parachuted into every partisan zone. These groups always opposed any anti-Semitic practices they encountered. In every detachment there was now a special unit that quietly "cleansed the air" of anti-Semites, German agents, thieves and other criminal and disruptive elements. In a few places such scoundrels were actually shot, which quickly put an end to such behavior among the partisans. The top partisan leadership instituted a single code of behavior for all partisan units: strict military discipline which prohibited alcoholic drinks, card-playing, stealing from the civilian population. The penalty for violations of this code was death. "Every partisan is a soldier who is carrying out Paragraph 133 of the Soviet constitution concerning the defense of the Fatherland."

However, while the attitude toward Jews changed radically for the better during this second period of the partisan movement (from mid-1943 to the defeat of Nazi Germany), the problem of strict military discipline was never completely solved.

The War against the Railroad Tracks

With fresh news of partisan victories arriving every day, a most favorable moment had evolved for widespread diversionary strikes against German troop and supply transport. Many Jews took part in these sabotage missions. Zerach Kremien was the leader of one such group, which included Zelik Milikowski, Zenia Eichenbaum, Henek Malach, Natan Licker, Nonye Zirinski, Abiezer Imber, Jacob Chatzkelevich, Noah Servianski and Berezin.

There was an acute shortage of explosives, however, and the partisans were forced to use primitive methods such as unexploded bombs, which was a highly dangerous method for the partisans themselves. But they had no alternative. In its retreat early in the war, the Red Army had left behind a great many mines, bombs and artillery shells. Detonation specialists now removed the explosive from the casing and made their own mines. When the Germans learned about this they began collecting these abandoned devices in order to keep them out of the hands of the partisans.

Every diversionary mission meant a long march, usually after dark, with the partisans carrying rifles, machine-guns, mines, grenades, ammunition and provisions. The enemy was everywhere and had to be avoided, but unexpected encounters were frequent.

As time went on, the laying of mines on railroad tracks became more and more difficult. The enemy chopped away the trees on both sides of the tracks, they built small bunkers for the railroad guards, they mined the approaches to the rail lines, they dug deep pits along the tracks and camouflaged them, they set up an increasing number of ambushes at crossroads and even in the forests.

In view of this, a plan was organized in Moscow for a "demonstration" in which all the partisan armies would attack German rail lines on the same night. In preparation for this operation, Soviet planes parachuted large quantities of mines into the area. This concerted action, which took place in August 1943, was successful. The partisans blew up tracks along thousands of miles of road. German troop transport to the fronts was disrupted for an entire week.

After the enemy had repaired the damage, the partisan diversionists, with help from Moscow, repeated "Operation Railroad Tracks" several times. These strikes were carefully orchestrated to occur immediately prior to German offensives or when the Red Army was about to begin an attack.

By the end of 1943 the partisan movement had reached its highest point of effectiveness. The entire occupied territory had been turned into one unified partisan zone that kept the ground burning under the feet of the invader. The Germans responded with a new tactic: they simply stopped using the railroads after dark. Freight trains were held at stations until daybreak. Before the trains were released, German scouting patrols combed the area. Then an empty train was dispatched, with a few cars in front of the locomotive. If this went through unharmed, the "real" train, loaded with troops and supplies, was sent out.

The partisans were thus confronted with a problem that had to be solved; they could hardly afford to blow up empty trains. By early 1944 Soviet experts came up with a solution: a mine that let the empty car pass, thus setting a timer in the mechanism. When the ground was disturbed a second time (by the next train) the mine exploded.

The damage to German railroad transport, plus the mines that kept exploding under their cars and trucks on the highways, plus the constant disruption of their telephone and telegraph communication, left the enemy hinterland demoralized and prone to panic. As a result, they kept large military forces in the hinterland. In the larger cities along the railroad lines, hundreds of German troops barricaded themselves behind their cement bunkers, fearful of what the "forest bandits" might do next.

All of this, of course, made things easier for the Red Army at the front.

Underground Anti-Semitism

The winter of 1943-44 was unusually severe. A solid sheet of ice covered the Polesye mud. The partisan encampments were hidden under a white blanket.

In a steadily mounting fury the Red Army kept driving the swastika knights back toward Germany, until the snowstorms temporarily slowed their attack near Kovel. Taking advantage of this, the retreating Nazis and their local allies tried to dig in inside the Brisk partisan zone. The weather hampered the partisans too, except for the diversionary strikes on the highways and rail lines. Up until March 1944 the group to which Nonye Zirinski and Jacob Chatzkelevich belonged had already destroyed eleven troop trains. The summer before that they had blown up the machines outside of Brisk that had been digging up peat for shipment to Germany.

At the end of March, companies of Hungarian fascists showed up in that area, sent ahead by the Germans to "clean out" the forest bandits. The partisans, expecting this attack, took up positions at a stream near a village. Meanwhile they sent a message to the Budennyi detachment asking for help.

Chatzkelevich, trying to move to a better position, stepped out from behind a wall. A sniper's bullet him in the leg and he passed out. A couple of the men carried him to safety. When the Hungarians attacked in force, they were met by the arriving Budennyans and wiped out.

On April 4, 1944 Commander Merzlyakov lined up the entire Budennyi brigade and briefed them on another expected attack by the Hungarians. As they moved to take up their positions, Pesach Alpert and Karpel Shevchik promised each other that if one of them should be wounded, the other would carry him off the battlefield. After waiting until morning for the attack, their group was relieved by another unit.

The next morning Merzlyakov fired his revolver—the alarm signal. The partisans lined up quickly. Alpert looked around for Shevchik, but he had been assigned to guard the horses in the stable. At that moment someone ran up to the Commander and reported that Shevchik had shot Mitka Voronin (the manager of the brigade economy.) The Commander threw Alpert a look that signified: "See what you Jews are capable of!"

It turned out that Mitka, learning that the Hungarians were rounding up cows from the local farmers, had decided to do something about it. He asked a few of the men to go with him and "recapture" the cows. Shevchik refused. Mitka ordered him to go with him on this mission and as he did so he reached for his revolver. Shevchik, who was holding his rifle, fired first, killing him, and ran into the forest. Several of the partisans chased him and killed him.

For the anti-Semites, this tragic incident was a windfall. A Jew shooting a Russian? The fact that the Jew had also been shot and killed was of no matter. But times had changed. A few days later a special bulletin from Sikorski was tacked onto many trees around the encampment. It was a very simple announcement: Anyone who took the Shevchik-Voronin affair into his own hands would be tried as an enemy of the people.

The "hardcore" anti-Semites, however, were not satisfied. Since it was no longer possible to discriminate against Jews openly, they would find other ways.

A few days later the brigade took up forward positions at a ditch. Pesach Alpert took cover behind a fallen tree-trunk. His unit commander ordered him and a Russian partisan to cross the ditch and, as soon as the enemy appeared, to attack with grenades. When they had been at their new post for a while, the commander summoned the Russian, leaving Alpert there all alone. A little later Zerinski came running up to Alpert and warned him to get away from that spot because the Hungarians were very close by. Alpert told him he had orders to stay there and stop the enemy with his two grenades. Zirinski ran straight to Merzlyakov and reported what was going on. Merzlyakov countermanded the order.

At daybreak, when the Hungarians appeared, the partisans were waiting for them and decimated them. Merzlyakov ordered a retreat. At this point, Alpert's unit commander again sent him to the other side of the ditch. Alpert turned and started toward the ditch, but this time the Commissar of the unit ordered him to halt and put his hands up.

"Why are you deserting to the enemy?" he demanded.

"Permit me, Comrade Commissar. I'm only carrying out the Commander's order—he instructed me to wait for the Hungarians and wipe them out with my two grenades."

As the Commissar countermanded this order, Alpert could see in his face that he understood quite well what kind of game was being played here.

After this incident, the unit commander let Alpert alone. But no one knows whether he was reprimanded for his anti-Semitism or only for his stupid military orders.

Although the general situation in the forests did improve, the Jewish partisans were painfully aware that they were subject to various acts of prejudice, subtle or not so subtle.

Liberation from Hitler's Yoke

The spring of 1944 arrived. Hope mounted among the partisans that their life in the forests would soon be over. Radio and newspaper reports continued to speak of victories on all three Byelorussian fronts. From Moscow came an appeal to the partisans that they help the towns and villages being ravaged by the Nazis as they retreated.

The partisans responded. More and more enemy troop trains were blown off the rails. More and more the Germans relied on the highways—but only during the daylight hours. But the partisans were able to change their "schedules" too. Their main objective became to create panic among the retreating enemy troops. As soon as they achieved this, they melted back into the forests.

Soon half of Byelorussia was liberated—Minsk, Vitebsk, Baranovici . . . Slonim . . .

The Germans tried to use the water barriers in the Pinsk marshes as a natural defense position against the pursuing Red Army, but they reckoned without their host. The swamps became their graves.

Finally the various partisan detachments based in the Polesye forests were overtaken by the "front." Traditional partisan activity was practically halted. In its place came the tactic of impeding the enemy retreat. This retreat, however, was accompanied by heavy mechanized equipment. Open battles against this kind of technical superiority were better avoided, but the partisans could not always manage this and suffered many unnecessary losses.

Some detachments were liberated quickly and without casualties. Vasiliyev's detachment, which in 1942 included the 32 Jews from Slonim who had been driven out of the Shchors brigade, had now grown into the "Lenin" brigade. Vasiliyev now led them out of the forest toward Pinsk, where they were supposed to become part of the Red Army. But Pinsk was still in flames. Tanks and artillery were exchanging fire. Soviet planes dropped mines in the path of the retreating enemy and some of them were exploding perilously close to the Vasiliyev positions.

Commander Vasiliyev sent out scouts who knew the Red Army passwords. They returned with good news: they had made contact with forward Red Army positions. All night long Soviet tanks and Katyushkas shook the earth of the streets in Pinsk. In the morning the Vasilyevtses received orders from the Red Army staff to comb the fields and forests for deserters from the German armies—mostly Ukrainians, Byelorussians, Vlasovtses, Hungarians, Letts, Estonians. There was a suspicion that these "deserters" had been given the job of setting up an anti-Soviet partisan movement. If there ever was such a plan, the Vasiliyev partisans put an end to it before it even got started.

The diversionary group of the Budennyi brigade, of which Nonye Zirinski and Jacob Chatzkelevich were part, was isolated from the rest of the brigade and did not know what was going on. One July morning they suddenly heard artillery fire nearby—the first augury of their liberation.

July 29th, on the First of May Square in Pinsk, a mass rally was held of the liberated population of Pinsk and the partisans from the forest. After the rally there was a parade of the Red Army liberators and the partisan detachments, including the Jewish partisans from Slonim. When the parade was over they went to visit their native city, which now lay in ruins. Weeping bitter tears, they recited the *Kaddish* for their fallen brothers and sisters.

Israel Sokolik was still carrying his rifle . . .

Jewish Partisans

Nathan Licker

He was the tallest man in the brigade, but that was not his only distinction. His extraordinary capacity for endurance, plus his daring initiative, made him a "natural" partisan.

After Eric Stein's unsuccessful attempt to wreck the rail line, Nathan, Berzin and Khviespenia (a Byelorussian) tried again in the same month of January 1943. After marching about thirty kilometers to the Baranovici-Luninietz rail line, they waited until dark and then Nathan and Khviespenia crawled out to the tracks, laid the mine, and retreated back to the bushes to wait for the explosion.

But their hearts dropped when they heard the train stop some distance away, apparently suspecting a trap. The three partisans should then have gotten as far away from there as possible, but Nathan could not bear to leave the precious mine behind. As he crawled out toward the tracks, German bullets whistled past his head. A few Nazis were already huddled around the mine. There was only one thing he could do now: he pulled the cord. The explosion wounded a couple of enemy soldiers, but Nathan couldn't forgive himself for having "wasted" the mine for so little damage to the enemy. "It was too great a luxury," he said.

A few days later, however, Nathan and his diversionists placed a mine on the Ivacevici-Telekhany line. Result: a hundred enemy soldiers would no longer fight for Hitler.

On another mission Nathan and a larger group of partisans had been trying in vain for three days to get close to a rail line. The Germans had doubled the guard, day and night. Nathan had an idea. Under the tracks at this particular spot was a large water pipe. He sent the rest of the group about a half-mile away to create a diversion, while he and Berezin stayed behind. The provocation worked, and as the battle grew hotter, he and Berezin crawled into the pipe. The rest of the group retreated into the forest.

The two men, crouching inside the pipe. let the guards and their dogs go by. Then they let an empty train go by. Coming next was a long loop-train pulled by two locomotives. They placed the mine at the right spot and disappeared into the bushes. Waiting until the first train was directly over the pipe, Nathan pulled the cord. The earth shook with the explosion. Trains toppled off the tracks, dumping soldiers and equipment. Nathan and Berezin made it back safely to the meeting-point and were met by the cheers of their comrades.

After this mission Nathan Licker's name was known and respected throughout all the Brisk detachments. The newspaper *Zarya* wrote about him often. Nathan didn't let this go to his head. He remained the same good-natured, affable and friendly guy. His motto was: "A Jewish partisan must always be in the vanguard and never lose his head." He himself was responsible for the wreck of more than thirty troop trains.

Nathan was given three government awards: the Red Star, the Red Flag, and the Fatherland War, first degree. Colonel Sikorski, commander of the Brisk united partisan movement, presented him with the "Hero of the Soviet Union" award.

After the liberation, Nathan Licker joined the Red Army and fought in all the battles from Warsaw back to Berlin, where he was wounded. At the end of the war he settled in Brisk.

Zerach Kremien

In September 1942 Zerach Kremien led a group that burned down two tar factories at the Budi station. At Ostrov (Hanzevich region) and Saveiki (Lyakhovich region) his group derailed four enemy transports. After he was transferred to the Kotovski brigade Kremien and his group, from February to June, carried out strikes against 13 troop-trains on the Brisk-Pinsk line near Drohiti and Antopol.

On the Brisk-Moscow line, at Bluden, Oronchitz and Tevli, his group wrecked a troop-train of 25 cars, carrying Tiger tanks, ammunition and explosives to the forest. They also disrupted telephone-telegraph connections along a five-kilometer line.

Kremien was given the Red Star and two Fatherland War awards.

Abiezer Imber

When the partisan detachments were reorganized, Imber was assigned to the Budennyi brigade. One day he and six Russian partisans were summoned to staff headquarters and assigned to a group led by Sgt. Glochev. (Nonye Zirinski later joined that group.) Up until October 1943 this group destroyed nine German troop-trains at Kartuz-Bereza, Brisk, Ivacevici-Telekhany and other places.

In October 1943 a group of parachutists came from the front with the objective of destroying enemy troops in the hinterland. Their leader, Captain Shumilin, asked the Budennyi brigade for two local experienced partisans to act as guides. One of the two was Abiezer Imber.

The Germans, going on the assumption that the partisans would know better than to walk into the lion's den, had increased their guards on the more isolated railroad stations. Counting on this, Imber chose the large, busy, chaotic stations for the diversionary strikes.

At the end of May, Shumilin's group attacked the Germans at the village of Tarkan near Antopol, on the Brisk-Pinsk line. In that battle Captain Shumilin was killed.

Between them, Imber and Zirinski wrecked at least 28 troop trains.

Herz Shepetinski

While on a scouting mission, Herz Shepetinski was caught in a German ambush and wounded, but the enemy apparently wanted to take him alive. Knowing this, he exploded his grenades, killing himself and a few of the enemy.

Jacob (Jascha) Shepetinski

After the liberation of the partisan forests and the parade in Pinsk, Jascha Shepetinski went back to Slonim with the hope of finding relatives or friends, but there was no one left there.

Thirsting for vengeance, he volunteered for the regular army and was sent to a quartermaster regiment at the Baltic front. Later he participated in the battle at Riga and Vynoda in Lithuania, where thousands of soldiers died on both sides of the front.

Shepetinski now realized that partisan warfare, difficult as it was, paled in comparison to the front, where there were no hit-and-run tactics. The command is given to attack, to follow the green rocket, and the troops move forward, many never to return.

From Vilna, Shepetinski's regiment was moved to the Vistula River where, in the village of Varni, he met Nonye Zirinski and Michel Sefer.

On April 14, 1945, in the battle at Weitwalde, near Berlin, Shepetinski was wounded. After his recovery he stayed in the Red Army as a translator.

Gute Kagan

Gute came to Slonim with the stream of refugees from Poland in 1939-1940. Shortly before the war she married Roman Myerson, a Jewish soldier from Mohilev, who served together with me in one company near the railroad station at Slonim.

June 24, 1941, during the retreat from Slonim, Myerson was sent to Baranovici. At the front, he often used to bemoan his inability to do anything to help his young wife, who stayed in Slonim and suffered the fate of the other Jews there.

Gute eventually joined the partisan youth movement in the ghetto. She and Genia Eichenbaum fought in all the battles waged by the Shchors brigade. In the summer of 1943 she became part of the Kotovski brigade and celebrated her 28th birthday by taking part in a mission that destroyed four German troop trains at Oronchitz (Brisk-Moscow line). On March 23, 1944 she and Genia were fighting side by side when Genia was hit. Gute dragged her to safety and in doing so, was wounded herself.

For her heroism she was awarded the Red Flag and the Fatherland War medal. After the war she returned to Slonim to be reunited with Roman Myerson, who had also been wounded.

They now live in Israel.

Genia Eichenbaum

The young women from Slonim who became part of the 51st group fought together with all the other partisans. Some of them displayed more military prowess than the men. Their conduct was an example to the rest of the detachment.

Genia Eichenbaum, who had worked fearlessly in the ghetto underground, maintained the same standards in the forest. She fought in all the battles of the 51st group and later in the Kotovski brigade. During the first half of 1943 she participated in the attacks against German garrisons at Mienozilesie, near Kartuz-Bereza. At the end of December 1943 her group blew up a troop train between Baranovici and Luninietz.

On the 23rd of July 1944, one day before the liberation of the partisans by the Red Army, in a battle with the retreating Germans, Genia Eichenbaum died heroically at the Dnieper-Bug canal, near Byeloziorsk. She was posthumously named "Hero of the Soviet Union."

Lyuba Abramovich

Lyuba, another active member of the underground in the Slonim ghetto, joined the 51st partisan unit in the forest on August 1, 1942. A few days later she was assigned to a small group that had come from the front to organize a partisan movement in the Lip-chanski marshes, near the Jewish town of Zhetl (some 80 kilometers further west). Out of this group grew the Voroshilov brigade. Lyuba not only served as a rank-and-file soldier in all the battles of the brigade, but in her free time also helped to care for the wounded.

As a gift to International Women's Day on March 8, 1943, Lyuba organized a group of seven women partisans (including herself) that blew up a troop train on the Lide-Baranovici line at the Yatsuki station.

In June 1943, outside the village of Ruda Yavorskaya, she fought against the 115th Ukrainian S.S. that had been harassing the brigade. In that battle, in which the enemy lost more than a hundred men, brigade commander P. Rodyanov was killed. Lyuba, fighting by his side, caught him as he fell. He died in her arms.

In December 1943 Lyuba fought against the Germans near the village of Gyazgela, in January 1944 against the Byelorussian fascists at Zirovici, near Slonim. She helped to derail 18 enemy troop trains on the Baranovici-Lida line. For her bravery she was awarded the Red Star and the Fatherland War medal.

Golda Yakimovski

Golda came into the forest with the refugees at the beginning of August. Two weeks later the Shchors brigade moved to the Pinsk marshes and Golda stayed behind in the family camp as part of the fighting unit. Later she was transferred to the Chapayev detachment in the Rafalovka forest.

During the German raids on the partisan encampments in the Bitten region her detachment joined the 53rd group in the Wolf Caves. At the beginning of 1943 she became part of a diversionary group.

Nonye Zirinski

After helping to drive the Nazis out of the Pinsk region, Nonye Zirinski, Michel Sefer, Andrei Khvisenia and Stefan Parfyonovich, who had fought together in the 51st group, joined the Red Army. They were placed in the 142nd regiment, 47th division, and fought in the infantry at the Magnushev fortifications on the Vistula.

In the Glovachova region, Sefer was hit by a German sharp-shooter and died in Zirinski's arms. He was buried in the village of Vilchkovitse Gurne on the Vistula.

On October 14th, Andrei Khvisenia was killed in battle at the village of Sowki near Warsaw. He is buried in a military cemetery.

Early in January 1945, army units arrived at the fortifications with tanks and artillery. The attack on the German positions began at dawn with an artillery bombardment and the enemy positions were overrun. Two days later volunteers were needed for a tank unit to block the retreat of the Germans on the Warsaw-Radom highway. Nonye Zirinski and Sasha Butakov volunteered.

Toward evening the tanks stopped in a woods. A German tank

column was racing westward on the highway. When night fell, the commander of the operation (a major) gave the order: "Follow me toward the enemy tanks!" As he drew closer to the German tanks he veered his tank to the left and rode parallel to the road for a little while, moving closer and closer to the enemy tanks. When he found a large enough gap between them, he slipped into it. Following his example, the other three partisan tanks did the same.

They moved a short distance down the road this way with the enemy tanks. Then they slowed down. The tanks ahead of them kept moving forward. The tanks in back of them were forced to stop. After a few moments, some of the German tankists climbed out to see what the problem was. At that moment the Red Army tankists opened fire, first with their machine-guns, then with their artillery guns that had been mounted on the tanks. During this battle Zirinski caught a piece of shrapnel in his left leg. Sasha and another partisan carried him to an empty cottage in the village and laid him on a bed.

The Nazi tank column had been cut in half, but the battle continued.

Toward morning the Polish farmers returned to their home. Zirinski introduced himself as a soldier in the Polish *Armia Ludowa,* which was fighting here alongside the Russians. They told him there were still some German troops in the village. He asked them to remove his uniform and give him some clean clothes. They left the room and disappeared.

The pain in Nonye's leg grew worse as his temperature rose. He could not even move to get a drink of water. There was not a thing he could do but lie there and keep a tight grip on his rifle.

Meanwhile, the four partisan tanks received reinforcements and the battle was soon over. Sasha ran to the farmhouse with water and rum for his wounded Jewish comrade. Then two "medics" carried Nonye to a field hospital. From there he was moved to an army hospital in Omsk (Siberia) where the doctors had to amputate his left leg below the knee.

Zelik Milikowski

After the partisans were liberated, Zelik joined the Red Army. In the battle to drive the Germans out of Warsaw, Zelik was killed.

Moshe Mishkin

For a time, Mishkin fought as a partisan in the Shchors brigade. Later he was assigned to a group in the Dzerzinski brigade and fought many battles against the Byelorussian fascists. In mid-July 1944 he fought against the retreating Nazis. He survived all the battles and returned to Slonim.

Abraham Band

Abraham Band fought as a scout in the Shchors and Budennyi brigades and eventually was appointed commander of a group that operated in the Antopol and Drohiti regions. After the liberation he looked up his family and helped his older brother Archik get to Poland. At the end of 1947 Abraham and his sister Malia and her two children also went to Poland.

Berezin

Berezin came from the village of Medvedici, where there was no ghetto. He went straight to the forests and joined the partisans. Before the liberation he was in a scouting unit and at one point they spent the night near Kobrin. Someone informed the Germans of their presence. The partisans were able to beat off the Nazi attack and retreat to a village, but in their haste they locked themselves inside a barn which the enemy quickly surrounded.

There was nothing they could do but give up their lives and make the enemy pay as high a price as possible. When the Germans realized that the group was not going to surrender, they set fire to the barn . . .

Abraham Hirshfeld

On June 23, 1941, one day before our unit retreated from Slonim, many friends and relatives came to the railroad station to bid us farewell. One of my visitors was my brother-in-law Borek, who came from a shtetl in Poland. He hated and despised the Soviet way of life. Even though he was well established as an upholsterer and had a relatively good income for those war years, he was very homesick.

I called his attention to the extremely serious situation facing us: the next day the Nazis were going to take over Slonim. I advised him to retreat eastward with the army, but he resented my suggestion. He would never willingly go to the "land of the Soviets," he insisted.

I still ask myself: Did he change his opinion as he stood at the rim of the ditch in Czepelow?

•

This problem was much better understood by Abraham Hirshfeld, who came from a small town near Pinsk. His last act in life was akin to that of the biblical Samson.

What follows is my translation from G. Linkov's "The War Behind Enemy Lines." Colonel Linkov was one of the Red Army diversionists parachuted into the Pinsk marshes, where he led a small partisan detachment not far from Slonim. (He was known as "Batya.")

Hirsheld Abraham's Mine

Our "unremovable" mines gave the Nazis a lot of trouble. Detonating the discovered mine from a distance wasn't advisable because the resultant damage to the railroad tracks necessitated a great deal of repair work that would hold up rail traffic for a long time. For that reason, the police and the railroad administration tried to find ways of removing the mines without exploding them. This required not only specialists but also volunteers for dangerous experiments—who were obviously not too eager to come forward.

One day, in the area of Mikashevici station, one of our "unremovable" mines was removed, while our diversionists watched. In time we succeeded in confirming details of the operation:

In the Lenin region, province of Pinsk, the Nazis arrested all Jews who were unable to work and deported them to a deathcamp. Ablebodied Jewish men were sent to a camp in Slonim and forced to work in shops according to their craft. All these men were informed that their families had been resettled in Posnan, where they would stay until the end of the war.

In the camp at Slonim there was a watchmaker named Hirsheld Abraham. Having no work for him at his craft, they drove him from one job of hard labor to the next. But one morning they did not send him out to work as usual. For breakfast they gave him a piece of white bread and real coffee with milk. Abraham was suspicious of his "benefactors'" motives—and he was right. After breakfast a Nazi sergeant and a policeman started a conversation with him and finally asked him questions about his competency in electronics. Hirsheld replied that he was able to read electronics schematics and that if they let him and his family live in normal conditions he was ready to serve the government. They promised to give him what he asked and they took him to a certain place alongside the railroad tracks. The sergeant said to him:

"You see that piece of track, Citizen Hirsheld? Under that track there is an unremovable electronic mine. Your job is to remove it. If you succeed we'll bring your family back and you can live with them as you did before. If you fail, you won't need your family anyway. Understood?"

Hirsheld nodded.

"Then go ahead with your work, but give us a chance to get some distance away from here before you start. You see that little mound of dirt between the tracks? That's where the mine is."

Hirsheld stood over the mine and asked himself: "Who put the mine here if not the partisans? And they didn't put it there for me to remove it." Should he simply yank the wires and fly up into the sky? But then the Germans would shoot his wife and children. If he succeeded in removing it, he would be betraying his fellow partisans. What he did not know yet was that the Germans had already killed his wife and children.

The Nazis were now 50-60 meters away, watching the condemned prisoner intently.

Abraham came to a decision. He would remove the mine. He reasoned this way: One, the enemy had already discovered the mine, so it would no longer hurt them. Two, if he did succeed in removing it, it would no longer be an "unremovable" mine and the partisans would realize that they had to perfect it. In any case, the Nazis would sooner or later master the technique of removing this kind of mine, with or without him, which would be a victory for them and a defeat for the partisans.

He bent over and studied the mine—but there was really nothing to study. All he could see were twisted little wires stretched across the rails. The rest of the mind was buried under the dirt. He began slowly to "undress" it. It took him two hours. But finally he lifted out the device, removed the detonator and laid it to one side. The pieces of explosive inside had now been rendered harmless.

He motioned to the Germans.

"Good, Herr Hirsheld! Very good! You will be our instructor, our sapper."

That evening, for the first time in two months, Hirsheld ate a decent meal.

What to do now? The mine had turned out to be removable. All you had to do was disconnect the right wires in the right order. True, one mistake and that would be the end of you. In order to make it really unremovable, it needed one more battery. And the wires had to be connected in such a way that the slightest motion would set off the detonator.

Two days passed. Hirsheld was being given the rations of a regular German soldier. But they had not brought back his family.

On the morning of the third day Hirsheld was standing outside his quarters. Jews were being marched past him on their way to work. When he said good-morning to an old friend, he realized that the man had not responded. Did that mean he was already regarded as a traitor? Another friend passed him without a word but dropped a crumpled piece of paper. Hirsheld waited until the line had marched by, picked up the paper and went back inside, his heart beating wildly.

"Dear Abraham: It seems that you are working for the Nazis and that they are feeding you. But we don't envy you. We interpret your actions as betrayal. Don't you know that all our families have already been murdered?"

A vast emptiness enveloped him. He became indifferent to everything, including his own life. He pulled a letter that he had written earlier out of his pocket and added a few words with the stub of a pencil.

The next day he was back on the railroad tracks with the Germans. He walked briskly as he conversed with a lieutenant of the Technical Corps. Behind them walked the sergeant, the policeman and two sappers. Hirsheld stopped at a mine under the tracks and went to work. The lieutenant and the sappers were brave men who wanted to learn. They bent over him, watching every move he made. When the mine finally lay exposed, Hirsheld invited the policeman too to come over and have a look. As he approached, there was a loud explosion. Only the sergeant survived. He had kept a safe distance . . .

I had known this story before, but not in detail. One week after the explosion someone brought me a packet. Inside was a long letter that Hirsheld Abraham had written, describing the tragic circumstances of his life among the Nazis and explaining why he had first removed the "unremovable" mine. He also included a schematic drawing showing how to make a really unremovable mine. In the postscript, written in pencil, he said:

"I swear by the dead bodies of my family that the murderers will never again force me to remove one of your mines for them."

When we checked out Hirsheld's schematic, we found that it was the only correct way to make that kind of mine.

Sarah with the Blond Hair

There was a young, pretty girl in Slonim whom people used to call "Sarah with the blond hair." Her mother was a poor old Jewish woman. People said Sarah's father was a German soldier from the first war. Sarah had been a student in the Jewish school but now she registered as a German and was on friendly terms with the German authorities. Knowing the Jewish population well, she gave the Germans much useful information.

When the "Aryans" learned, however, that her mother was a Jew and confronted her with it, Sarah renounced her mother and treated her accordingly. When the Germans retreated, she went back to Germany with them.

Dr. Epstein's Widow

For helping the Polish government force-feed political prisoners during a hunger strike, the Soviet authorities had exiled the well known Dr. Epstein to Kazakhstan, but they did not prosecute his wife and young son.

Thanks to her "Aryan" appearance, the priest at the Catholic monastery on Penkevich Street was able to convert Mrs. Epstein. With the help of a prominent liberal German (who also spoke Russian) she managed to obtain an Aryan pass and worked as a nurse in the Children's Hospital attached to the monastery. She and her son lived in a room on Paradise Street.

The Nazis knew she was a convert, but because of her friendship with the German, she survived the massacres. They then contrived to get her friend out of the city, picked up Mrs. Epstein and her son and took them to the ditch on Petralewicz Street.

For converting Jews, the Catholic priest too was shot.

Chaim (Chenek) Praski

Chaim Praski was a brave young boy of 12 or 13. His "good appearance" and his perfect Polish speech concealed his Jewishness and he therefore did not submit to any of the German anti-Jewish decrees. He did not sew the yellow star on his clothing and he didn't walk in the middle of the street. He moved freely among the Gentile population, especially in the marketplace, and was thus able to buy food for the entire Praski family. Until—

Until one day some swine recognized him on the street and raised a hue and cry. A member of the Gestapo stopped Chaim and shot him on the spot.

The Berkowitz Family

Berkowitz's laundry, which was outside the ghetto, was taken over by the Germans, who put Felia Pitkowska, a Polish woman, in as manager. They also hired Polish workers and forced the Berkowitz brothers to train them.

During the second massacre, the Berkowitzes' mother was killed.

During the third massacre, with the ghetto already in flames the older brother ran to the laundry to hide, but the Germans caught him there and shot him. The younger brother, Yankl, succeeded in reaching the partisans in the forest and fought in many battles. After the liberation he joined the Red Army and took part in the destruction of the Nazi beast.

The First German Raid on the Family Camp

The family camp, after separating from the Shchors brigade and moving to the Pinsk marshes, remained under command of the 53rd group (later called the "Soviet Byelorussia" brigade.) Life in the camp continued as before: those who were able to fight carried out all the missions the general staff gave them. One problem soon arose: the very young children (about 30 of them) who had been saved from the ghetto fires. Something had to be done to relieve the monotony of their daily life. Dora Freedman and a few of the mothers organized a sort of kindergarten which kept the children busy, but unfortunately it was not to last very long.

In mid-September large German military concentrations appeared on all the roads around the towns and villages near the partisan encampments. Contact between the partisan scouts and the village activists was almost totally cut off. The general staff did everything they could to avert panic, but emergency measures had to be taken for resistance. Barricades were constructed on all the roads leading into the forest. Potatoes were dug up out of the nearby fields and stored away.

Thursday the 17th of September the German raids began.

Massive military equipment was used to break into the partisan forests. The barricades stopped the tanks only temporarily; the enemy had come prepared. Electric saws began cutting through the barricades. Peasants, pressed into service by the Germans, cleared away the debris. A way into the forest lay open. The enemy attacked from three directions, assisted by reconnaissance planes that hung low over the treetops, reporting the location of the partisan units. Coming from Zhireva, Meremin, Dobribor, Ivacevici, Kossovo, Ruzany, they tightened an iron noose around the partisan zones, cutting off all contact with the outside world.

The small Chapayev detachment, with its 300 fighters, put up stubborn resistance in the Rafalovka forest, but was forced to retreat to the Wolf Caves, leaving 30 dead on the battlefield. Matus Snovski, of Slonim, did not hear the order to retreat and continued firing his machine-gun until he was taken alive by the Nazis and tortured to death.

On September 18th, after the first defeat, both Jewish groups decided to retreat further into the swamps before the Germans reached their camp, because with their little rifles there wasn't too much they could do to protect themselves. Under Commander Yefreymov the Jewish fighting groups took up positions. When the Germans attacked with overwhelming force and several partisans were killed, Yefreymov left the 42 Jews behind and ran after the vanished brigade.

On a little clearing in the forest stood the Jewish family camp with its 360 people. Among them were Zyama Ostrovski, Mina Payevski, the Shepetinski family and a few others from Slonim. With them also was the political commissar Seryozha Tatarikov. That he stayed with the defenseless Jews testifies to his generous humanity and even his love for these people. For their part, the Jews in the camp had faith in his calm assurance.

His plan was this: to cross the stream but to go in a different direction from the one taken by the retreating partisans. Tatarikov led and the Jews followed him through the muddy water until they

reached a little island, where they huddled among the protective
bushes. Then he proposed that they split up into smaller groups
and maintain contact with him.

With the darkness came a lull in the enemy attack, although
they still kept sending up rockets to light up the area so they could
more easily find the "forest bandits." Tatarikov's scouts had noticed
signs that enemy troops had already been here and had gone ahead
beyond this area, so he assumed that they would not be back soon.
But this was no place for the family camp. The sounds of battle
were still too close.

The commissar followed his compass and the Jews followed the
commissar. At one crossroads they were suddenly stopped by
machine-gun fire. They scattered and took cover, then slowly drew
together again when the shooting subsided. When they finally
reached a place where they could stop, they saw that some of their
number were missing. For three days the nursing mothers in the
group had had nothing to eat. The five infants were crying pitifully
and the Germans were screaming *"Halt! Halt!"* and firing their
weapons blindly.

On Sunday September 20th they reached a clearing and decided
to spend the night there. The 150 survivors fell exhausted to the
ground. The five babies demanded to be fed and the desperate
mothers did not know what to do. They looked beseechingly at
Tatarikov as though asking his permission to commit a terrible
crime. He sat silently and wiped the tears from his eyes.

Weeping spasmodically, half-demented, the five mothers suffo-
cated their babies, one after the other, then tore the hair out of
their own heads or beat their own heads against the tree trunks.
Mothers with older children clasped them to their breasts. Everyone wept, and Commissar Seryozha Tatarikov with them . . .

On the third day of the raid two partisans brought word that the
Germans had burned down all the partisan camps, killing many
and taking the boots off dead bodies.

The fourth day, Monday, was sunny and hot. They had no

drinking water. People dug up the damp earth with their hands and strained the water through a cloth.

Enemy planes searched for hidden partisans and rained down bullets. The dead lay everywhere.

Tatarikov decided to go to the nearby villages of Barki for food for the children. With him went Sheyndl Krupenya with two partisans. As deputies in his absence he appointed Zyama Ostrovski and Stankowski (a Pole.)

The next day, Tuesday, the commissar and his party had not yet returned. Wednesday, the sixth day of the enemy attack, the survivors in the camp were so exhausted they could hardly stand. Most of them had become apathetic, completely indifferent to their fate.

Ostrovski and Standowski took a small group and plodded their way to their former camp, hoping to find a little food. On the way they met two armed Jewish partisans who gave them water, half a loaf of bread and a piece of meat. They divided it among the women and children. But the two partisans had also given them some good news—the Germans had left the forest. At the camp they found bread, potatoes, meat, cabbage. They brought back as much as they could carry. Little by little, the Jews regained their strength. Some of the Jews who had been hiding returned. Friday, Tatarikov and his group also returned, but with reports of tremendous losses to the brigades. The two German divisions had laid waste many villages, burning down houses along with the people inside them.

In the period that followed, Tatarikov disappeared for days at a time, and each time he returned he looked more and more distressed.

The Jews Are Always to Blame

One day Tatarikov appeared with a few other Byelorussian partisans and called the Jews together. The surviving partisans had come to a decision, he said. Jews would no longer be permitted to remain in the forest because it was clear that their presence had provoked the Nazi raids.

Pashka Pavlovski then took the floor. He was carrying an automatic rifle and two grenades. He repeated what Tatarikov had said and added another point. Jews who had been taken prisoner by the Nazis had betrayed the names of peasants who had given them food. The Nazis then shot these peasants and burned their homes down. His own wife and children were among the victims. (He lived in the village of Volchi-Nori). "The forest is for the partisans, not for the Jews and their families," he thundered. "The Jews should go back where they came from!"

The Byelorussians then left, except for Tatarikov. The Jews were bewildered and asked a lot of questions. Why were they to blame for the death of Pashka's wife and children? It was no secret to the Germans that he was a partisan. Moreover, knowing that a German attack was imminent, why hadn't he taken his family into the forest with him? And even supposing that a Jew had given the Germans the name of a sympathetic peasant—are all the other Jews responsible for his actions? Wasn't this the same "collective

346

responsibility" policy that the Nazis had used against the Jews in the ghettos? Did these anti-Semites really believe that the Germans had launched this entire massive operation for the purpose of destroying the handful of Jews in the forests?

The commissar explained that the partisans too had suffered great losses and in their embitterment were accusing the Jews of spying for the Germans. In any case, it was now dangerous for the Jews to stay where they were. It was unthinkable, however, for them to go back to the ghetto. His suggestion was that they organize themselves into a few disciplined groups and keep out of the way of the partisans. The Jews agreed to do this.

He divided them into four groups. For his own group he chose about 20 men. For the second group he appointed Stankowski and Shepetinski as leaders. For the third, Shmuel Yudkovski; for the fourth, Moshe Pitkowvski. The four groups then moved to separate locations about two kilometers apart.

The next day, the Germans attacked again. Stankovski and his wife and several Jews were killed. The commissar escaped. The four groups kept moving from place to place, trying to avoid German ambushes. This situation continued until the end of September.

In order to push the Jews out of "their" forest the partisan staff resorted to a tactic of terrorizing and robbing them. Several Jews, carrying on their backs a few pounds of potatoes that they had dug up out of abandoned fields, were held up by armed "partisans" who forced them to sit on the ground, searched their pockets and robbed them of everything they had, including the potatoes. One scoundrel even tore the boots off Beyla Pitkovski's feet.

Koptya Korolyov, who was interested only in gold or money, justified his actions with the following "logic": "The Nazis are already on the outskirts of Moscow and Stalingrad. In any case, they will kill all the Jews, so what's the difference?"

Commissar Tatarikov and Sheyndl Krupenya managed to get away from these robbers a few times, but in October 1942 some partisans caught them and accused Tatarikov of hoarding Jewish gold and money that belonged to the staff. Having no such treasure, he could not give it to them. They held a "trial" and then shot him. His real "crime," of course, had been his humane attitude toward Jews.

One group of partisans came upon Jascha Shepetinski's father and uncle, who had just been given some food by friendly peasants. The partisans accused them of robbing the peasants (with their bare hands!). The penalty was death by shooting.

Shlomo Tchernechovski was ordered by three partisans to give up his rifle. He refused to do so. They shot him and buried him. The following day, they remembered he had been wearing a watch. They dug up the grave and took the watch off his wrist.

Noah Obulianski, Chaim Elya Lyuberski and the Birnbaum family were also killed by partisans.

•

Winter was coming. The surviving Jews were without food or warm clothing, unarmed and without their leader and defender. They were in mortal danger in the forest as well as in the villages. At this critical juncture they were befriended by a group of 20 partisans, strangers, who had been fighting in the Michalin forests near Kossova. One of them, "Vaska-the-machine-gunner," persuaded the staff to allow the Jews to dig up potatoes in the fields at least once a week. After a thorough investigation, they accepted the following Jews into their group: Leyma Pitkovski (who had a rifle and knew the area well), Manya and Mina Galerstein and Golda Yakimovski.

Late in October, Leyma, while on sentry duty one night, was shot by other partisans.

At the end of October the Jews were ordered to leave the forest. The 144 Jews refused to do so and began building earthen huts for the winter. After a month of fighting the cold, the hunger and the hostile partisans, Rachel Rabinowich and the rabbi from Ivacivici gave up. A new Jewish cemetery was consecrated in the forest.

It was now becoming almost impossible to dig potatoes out of the frozen ground even with an axe. Foraging in the forest were also many starving cats from the burned down villages. The Jews caught them, cooked them and ate them.

Around that time a new commander was appointed to head the Soviet-Byelorussian detachment. Vladimir Nikolayevich Bobkov had been a captain in the airforce. He was tall and broad-shouldered and his piercing eyes always stared suspiciously at Jews. In addition to being a brave soldier and an experienced leader, he was also a drunkard and an anti-Semite. Even the formerly friendly Michalin partisans became infected with the anti-Jewish virus. The new Jewish cemetery in the forest continued to grow.

At the end of November, Vaska came to the Jews with the news that the staff had decided to kill all the remaining Jews in the forest. He therefore advised them, as a "good friend," to get away while they could still run.

A Fresh Breeze

Suddenly, on December 8th, 1942 a sleigh came riding up to the Jewish encampment with Captain Bobkov and two Red Army men. The unexpected guests took places around the campfire and summoned all the Jews to a "meeting."

72 men and 63 women and children lined up. Bobkov spoke first. He praised the capabilities of the Jews, but accused them of eating the fruits of the peasants' labor while doing nothing themselves. The Jews answered him immediately: It was the general staff itself that had prohibited Jewish partisans from fighting against the enemy. It was the staff itself that had created a new ghetto in the forest.

Lt. Vladimir Ivanovich again charged the Jews with being informers for the Germans and provoking the raids in which so many partisans had been killed. The response of the Jews to that was to call it untrue and libelous. The discussion grew more and more heated until the third guest, whom no one knew, took the floor. He was wearing the dress of a Russian Cossack and sprouting a new beard. Perhaps a parachutist who had been sent from the front to restore order in the forest.

He had heard many things about the Jews here, he said. He knew that some of the accusations against them were not true. He knew that many Jews were fighting heroically at the front. He knew that Jews were working day and night in the factories back home to produce vital supplies for the front. He believed that the Jews here were capable and devoted partisans who should be used in the life-and-death struggle against Hitler. Whatever had happened between them and the general partisan staff should be relegated to the past. The Jews should now reorganize themselves and become active again in the fight.

Bobkov then reported that the staff had made a decision to appoint a commander who would be in constant communication with them. He was now turning over four rifles and ammunition to the Jews so they could go into the villages for food. Between now and January 10th the Jews must knock out the telephone and telegraph lines on the Slonim-Ruzany highway. By the 25th of January the fighting unit must blow up a train on the Domanova-Lesnaya line. Explosive materials would be supplied. Two days from now the Jews must be ready to move to the Rafalovka forest some ten kilometers away.

The Jews agreed but asked him to postpone the move until the warmer weather. "It's an order!" he insisted.

Yes, it was an order that reflected the struggle then going on within the ranks of the Soviet armed forces as well as in the partisan movement. That struggle had led Commander Rumyantsev of the Grizodubov partisan brigade in Polesye to call a special meeting of the entire detachment at which he castigated all attempts to stir up anti-Semitic sentiment among the partisans. He called it a Nazi diversion against the Soviet Union, whose strength lay in friendship between all its peoples. And he issued a warning: anyone who carries out this diversionary work for the Germans is a traitor to the Fatherland.

But under Bobkov's leadership, all such warnings had not only been ignored but mocked and defied. While the Jews had been building their winter huts, he kept silent. Now that they had been built and the Jews were beginning to thaw out their frozen bones a little, he found that he needed the huts for his own people.

The Jewish partisans, however, decided to meet him halfway. They elected Noah Polonetsk commander and Baruch Yudkovski as his deputy. Noah went to staff headquarters and tried to persuade them to recall their order to move, but he got nowhere. Even the Cossack who had praised the Jews so highly supported Bobkov's anti-Semitic order to drive the Jews out of the forest.

Early on the morning of December 12th, in a wet snowfall, the 135 bone-weary Jews started out on their trek toward a new place of refuge. Their strength was at its lowest ebb. The clothes on their backs were filthy. Cold, hungry and dispirited, they met armed partisans on the way who warned them that German military units were waiting at the Wolf Caves. By that time, however, it made no difference to them—it was all the same, the Germans or "their own" partisans.

Six kilometers from Bitten they lit a campfire in the forest and fell asleep in the wet snow.

The next morning, they examined the rifles. Two of them were useless. The same day, two groups, each armed with one rifle, went into the villages for food. They returned with two horse-drawn wagons loaded with sacks of potatoes and even some clothing. Tied to one of the wagons was a cow. Peasants too have more respect for Jews carrying weapons.

The new commanders divided the Jews into two groups. One group immediately started building winter huts. The second group would carry out diversionary missions against German troops and obtain food and supplies. There was more than enough work for everyone, even though they worked day and night. Scores of small

German garrisons in the area were now operating in conjunction with the larger ones. Communications between them was therefore essential. The more the partisans disrupted those communications the more they would weaken the enemy's front-line positions.

17 Jewish partisans, among them Golda Yakimovski (from Slonim) and two young women from Bitten, mobilized peasants with wagons, saws and axes, and headed for the Slonim-Ruzany highway. Zyama Ostrovski and Yitzhak Plotnik led the group onto the highway. The sharpened saws swiftly cut down the telephone poles. The rest of the "gang" laid them neatly across the road for a distance of about five kilometers. With their axes they chopped the wires into bits.

Flushed with the success of their first mission, the 17 Jewish partisans leaped up onto the wagons and stopped along the way to do some more "shopping" in the villages. The mood had changed. They felt like useful citizens again.

Zyama and Yitzhak gave the staff a full report of their mission. The names of all the participants were recorded. The staff sent out a scouting unit to check the report, who found it true in every particular. The Jews had done a fine job.

As a reward, the staff presented the Jewish partisans with an artillery shell big enough to blow up a troop train . . .

The Second Raid
on the Family Camp

———————•———————

December 20th, when the liaison people went to staff headquarters, they found no one there. From neighboring villagers they learned that a new German attack had already begun. Yet, knowing that this attack was imminent, the staff had not seen fit to alert the Jews, while they themselves fled, deliberately leaving the Jews exposed to certain danger.

The Jewish partisans again separated into groups and prepared a place to take cover. They still had time to bring some potatoes from the fields. A scrawny little horse was slaughtered and skinned, and its flesh cooked and divided. Water was going to be a problem.

December 24th the silence of the cold moonlit night was suddenly shattered by gunfire coming from all directions. Dousing the campfire, the Jews ran to their bunkers—all except nine people, who no longer wanted to live like hunted animals.

Early next morning the German troops came roaring into the camp, shot the nine Jews and sprayed the area with grenades. Then they left. The Jews stayed in their bunkers until December 28th. When they came out, they buried the dead and sent out a reconnaissance team, who soon returned with the news that the partisan camp had again been burned down. From survivors they learned that the Germans had ravaged Okunivo, shot 500 of the villagers and left the bodies in a ditch. The Soviet-Byelorussia brigade had then ambushed the Nazis and a bitter battle had taken place, with many dead on both sides.

By mid-January 1943 the Jews finished erecting their winter huts and were able to organize their lives again. The staff gave them certain duties, one of which was the destruction of the homes of peasants who had been collaborating with the Germans.

Around that time, Baruch Yudkovski's wife and child (Arik), both of whom had been wounded, and a woman from Lodz, were taken to staff headquarters and charged with voluntarily "deserting" to the enemy in exchange for revealing partisan secrets. At the trial, Baruch showed how ludicrous the charges were, and his wife and child were released, but the other woman was sentenced to death. The sentence was carried out by the wife of a Communist leader in Bitten (Misov).

Almost half the people in the family camp were killed in the second Nazi raid. There were now only about 70 Jews left. Shortly afterward, partisans found two isolated, well camouflaged earthen huts in which 17 Jews from Kossova and 13 from Bitten were hiding. They had survived both raids and the severe winter. On March 18th they joined forces with the other 70 survivors.

Attacks by Samokhovtses

On January 18th three peasants rode into the forest on wagons, allegedly to chop down some trees. The Jewish sentries stopped them and reported to the staff that they were holding three collaborators from Bitten. Two of them were the brothers Terpchik (Yanechka and Mikolai), who were known for having murdered Jews. The staff investigated and confirmed that these men were indeed working for the Germans and had come into the forest to ascertain where the partisan camp was located. The collaborators were shot.

The next day another group of Samokhovtses (Byelorussian "Self-help" Organization) came into the forest, apparently looking for their three "brothers." This time they atarted firing at the sentries, killing a young woman from Lodz. Aronchik Yoselevich (a Slonimer) ran for help to the partisans. They sent out a party on sleighs to block the retreat, but before they got there, the Samokovtses had shot Abraham Didkovski (from Bitten).

January 20th in the afternoon, about 80 Samokhovtses from Bitten, led by the Byelorussian nationalist Zmitruchenko, attacked the Jewish family camp in force. In panic, the Jews ran toward the Wolf Caves, with the Samokhovtses in pursuit. Coming toward them, however, were partisans on sleighs, returning the enemy fire. The Samokhovtses retreated, but not before they had captured several of the women and children. Beyla Kantorovich and Mina Galerstein were prisoners in a sleigh with Seryoza Rayka, with whom Beyla had once gone to school. She pleaded with him, to no avail. When the partisans appeared, the two women jumped off the sleigh and started running. Rayka shot them both in the back.

By March 1943 the presence of emissaries from Moscow had cooled off the anti-Semitic "Bobkovs" in the forest and the hundred surviving Jews were able to settle down in the former Family Camp. With spring approaching, they began erecting huts for themselves, but then, out of the blue, they received a warning from the staff that a new German raid was expected at any moment and the partisans were therefore preparing to quit the area.

Left to their own devices again, the Jews built camouflaged bunkers and set up sentries around their camp. One afternoon a sudden salvo of rifle shots "from nowhere" killed Mina Payevski, one of the sentries. The rest of the Jews in the camp ran to the ice-covered stream in the marshes, but the ice was already beginning to thaw and many of them fell into the freezing water.

The intensive firing came closer and continued until nightfall. The smoke from the burning camp warned the Jews that they were again without shelter. The next day the Germans left the forest. The Jews counted heads. 24 people had been killed. Four had been taken prisoner and then executed in the village of Zireva. They buried their dead and again the heartrending *Kaddish* was heard in the forest.

Early in April the brigade returned and set up camp near the village of Bula. This time, however, they instructed the Jews to move their camp next to the partisans'. On April 6th a partisan stumbled upon an earthen hut in which there were 19 Jews from Bitten. 15 of them were accepted into the brigade and fought in all their battles. On the opposite bank of the Szczara River a Jewish detachment of 40 partisans, led by Boris Hyman, was discovered in the Havanovich forest. Most of them were from Slonim, Baranovici and Leszno. They too became part of the Jewish Family Group.

One morning early in July, large contingents of Samokhovtses, armed to the teeth, came roaring in from Ivacevici and Bitten. Although the staff had been forewarned about this raid and taken measures to defend themselves, they were forced to retreat in the direction of the Jewish camp. They ordered the Jews to retreat with them further into the forest.

The brigade took up defense positions. 12 partisans were assigned to a special watch to make certain that the Jews were not caught by surprise again. Unit commander of this watch was David Breskin. Also, under instructions from Bobkov, they were guarding two prisoners—Russian partisans. One of them, Romanov, had been leader of a partisan unit and had apparently been agitating to have Bobkov relieved of his duties. Guarding the prisoners' hut was Greenspan, from Makov. As he took them out to the bushes to relieve themselves, each of them ran in another direction. Greenspan fired at them, but they got away. Bobkov came running out and without any questions shot Greenspan and David Breskin for "dereliction of duty" as he threatened to "finish what Hitler started." He then found Romanov's pregnant wife in the camp and shot her too.

The Long-Awaited Liberation

As the front lines moved closer to the partisan forests, the morale of the Germans and their local allies plummetted, while that of the partisans soared. The Jews in the forest too were cheered by the radio news from the front, especially since they were given more and more weapons. Even the small Family Camp now had rifles, grenades and a machine-gun. All their hopes now lay "in the east," in the victories of the Red Army.

In the wake of the retreating Germans were their servile allies, mostly the Samokhovtses and the Kabardians from the Caucasus. A hundred well armed Kabardians invaded the partisan zone and cut the roads to the villages. Fifty Michalin partisans, led by Commander Penkin, came to the assistance of the local partisans. 15 Jews also volunteered for this battle, but only six were accepted. About 70 Kabardians were killed. The rest fled. The partisans lost eleven men, among them Hilary Januscz, a Jewish refugee from Poland.

The news continued good. Minsk, Vitebsk, Baranovici, were already liberated. Soon the Red Army would cross the Szczara and liberate Bitten, Slonim and other towns. All partisans were ordered to stay at combat readiness day and night. Many peasants had come into the forests too, afraid of what the retreating German troops might do in the villages.

Finally, on Tuesday, July 10, 1944, the general staff ordered all the partisans to gather at the edge of the forest. That evening, Red Army units arrived in tanks, trucks, motorcycles, on foot, on their way to clean the Nazis out of the Bitten-Slonim area. The tanks were decorated with big red stars and the slogan: ON TO BERLIN! In every vehicle the dust-covered soldiers waved happily to the assembled partisans. From one jeep sprang a colonel with a green helmet on his head and a red strap under his chin. After he kissed the staff officers Russian-style, he spoke to the crowd:

"Dear brothers! At last you will see your long-awaited freedom! Your courageous struggle against the enemy was a tremendous help to us through these difficult years. Your achievement will be inscribed in our history in golden letters. Now you are again equal Soviet citizens. But our fight is not yet over. The Soviet armed forces still face a long and bitter war with the hated enemy. You must join us in our struggle until the final victory!"

In response came slogans in praise of the liberating Red Army and the "great leader Stalin."

The partisans stayed in camp for a few more days. The older people were then sent into the cities and towns to reconstitute the Soviet government apparatus. The younger people were instructed to report to various field headquarters.

Zyama Ostrovski, Moshe Pitkovski and other partisans were sent back to the Wolf Caves to remove the food supplies that they had stored up for the winter and hidden in concealed pits.

A hundred Jews came out of the forest in which they had left a cemetery of almost 300 marvelous human beings. Would anyone ever visit their graves? And the hundred survivors themselves— was anyone waiting for them anywhere? None of them even had a house to go back to. Even if it were still standing, it was most likely occupied by people who would stare at them as though they were demented if they came to claim it . . .

After completing their last partisan mission, Zyama and Moshe decided to have a look at liberated Bitten. On foot, weapons and knapsacks on their backs, they stopped first at the village of Gnoina to ask for food. Most of the peasants refused to give them any, with the excuse that the partisans had already eaten enough of their bread. Only in one house did they get anything—a few slices of dried-out bread.

Not far from Bitten they met a peasant woman working in a field. When she saw them she cried out: "Moyshe! Is that really you? You're still alive!" And then she quickly averted her eyes and bent to her work.

As Pitkovski came closer to the house he was born in, he felt as if his heart were breaking. He and Ostrovski walked into the anteroom and were greeted by an old woman: "Thank God, one came back!" Ikons hung on the walls. Her two sons had been Samokhovtses and she was afraid of armed Jews.

Only a few Jews returned to Bitten. The newly established regime treated them well, found jobs for them, but the atmosphere in the town was oppressive. They soon fled Bitten forever.

The Liberation of Slonim

Led by Marshal Rokosovsky, the armies on the First Byelorussian front, after they liberated Baranovici, crossed the Szczara River along a 60-kilometer stretch and continued their pursuit of the enemy with tanks, infantry and cavalry.

It was a scorching July morning. During the night, Red Army tanks had broken into the eastern suburb of Slonim. Other units were attacking from north and south. The enemy's resistance grew weaker and weaker. Thousands of German soldiers and officers were taken prisoner, including General Schmidt of the 9th Army Engineers Corps. The natural barrier at the river, where the Germans had hoped to stop the counter-attack of the Red Army, became their grave.

Three years and sixteeen days of bloody repression came to an end.

In Moscow, after every large Russian city was liberated, 20 cannons fired a salute to the heroes of that particular day. Before the salute, the famous Jewish radio commentator Yuri Levitan read Stalin's order awarding medals and prizes to all the meritorious fighters at the front. On those evenings, thousands of people gathered on Red Square to cheer and applaud. All over the country and at the front, radios were tuned to these festivities.

On July 10, 1944, Levitan's voice could be heard announcing the liberation of Slonim, a victory that opened the way to Brisk (Brest-Litovsk), Bialystok and Poland. In addition to Slonim, some fifty communities were liberated, including Bitten, Babinici, Albertin, Shilovici, Mironim, Czemeri and Domanova.

On one of those sweltering July days a partisan column, led by an army band, marched into liberated Slonim. The road was strewn with the dead of both armies, with the carcasses of horses, the wreckage of tanks and the skeletons of trucks. As they passed their own villages, some of the partisans quietly slipped out of line and went home. Some partisans sang as they marched. The 18 Jewish partisans had nothing to sing about. Arms linked, they felt as if they were returning from a funeral.

After they passed the Jewish cemetery they walked downhill through several small streets and reached the synagogue courtyard. It lay in ruins. The further they walked, the greater the destruction. One of those 18 was Yekhiel Granatstein. At what had been the home of his family he found only two window frames and a crumbling chimney. They continued walking to Albertin Hill, to the ditches at Czepelow, where the bodies of most of the Jews of Slonim lay buried. Their voices choking, they recited the *Kaddish* . . .

A few other Jews came from the forest: Pesach Alpert and his family, Zyama Ostrovski, Itche Michelevich and his wife Manya, the Band family, Shiel Fisher, Lyuba Abramovich, Gute Kagan. Several Jews who had been evacuated early in the war also returned: Meir Iznaidin, Chaim Chomsky and his son Yankl, Abraham and Jochanan Rubinovski, Abraham Karolitsky, Sholem Derechinsky, Motl Kletskin, Zavel Bobrovitsky, Eliezer Rosenberg.

Before the Germans retreated from Slonim they went house to house and shot people who were trying to put out the fires. Thus, on Skrobive Street, they killed Raczka, a Pole, for trying to save his home from the flames.

In Slonim and surrounding communities the Nazis annihilated more than 50,000 civilians. Out of 2342 houses, they destroyed

1380. Out of 62 factories, they destroyed 43. Two high schools, two movie theaters, the large municipal library, the Tatar mosque, the stores on Paradne and other avenues—all were burned to the ground. The seven bridges were blown up. Severely damaged but not totally destroyed were the barracks, two Catholic churches, the Great Synagogue, the power station, the waterworks, the railroad line, and many, many streets.

As soon as the Nazis liquidated the ghetto and its living inhabitants, they turned to the Jewish cemetery. Using Soviet prisoners of war, they totally vandalized it. They tore out gravestones, dug up graves, sent the marble and granite to Germany. The inferior stone was used to pave roads. The brick wall around the cemetery was also torn down and used to erect a wall on the S.D. building on Ulan Street. The wall still stands today as a tragic reminder of Hitler's New Order in Europe.

Nothing was left of the Jewish cemetery in Slonim. Even the ground was plowed under. Here and there an ancient, deeply sunken gravestone stuck out of the ground. In parts of the cemetery, peasants planted corn.

Today, no longer a cemetery, the land is part of the rebuilt city.

Help for Jews
from the "Aryan Side"

As I have previously indicated, there were very brave, noble Christians who refused to succumb to the Nazi poison. They too are part of the total picture of that terrible time.

Shiel Fisher worked for a Polish farmer so that he could get his work permit extended to go outside the city. As he walked from the village of Azginovici to Slonim, he stopped at Polish homes; everywhere he was received in a friendly manner and given something to eat. One woman even repaired his torn coat. Often these Byelorussians would rage against the German persecution of Jews. "Don't be afraid of us," one of them said to him. "We are not Nazis!"

•

Jacob Chatzkelevich and Nonye Zirinski never concealed their Jewish identity. Quite the contrary. One day in 1943 they were eating a meal in the home of a friendly peasant near Drohici. The conversation turned to the "Jewish Question" and they volunteered the information that they were Jews. The Byelorussian refused to believe it. Knowing a little Yiddish, he gave them a "test." When he had convinced himself, he confided a secret that he had been harboring for a long time: he knew of a Jewish family that had been hiding in the forest for almost a year.

Jacob and Nonye asked him to take them there at once. Soon they were staring at a group of walking skeletons: a man, two women and a three-year-old child. They had survived on raw potatoes and melted snow. There had been another Jewish family there, they said, but they had starved to death.

After some coaxing, they agreed to follow the partisans to the brigade camp. They were housed in the village of Mianerze, where they were given a cow, and the man was put to work as a tailor for the partisans. The women knitted scarves and gloves.

•

Crossing the "Royal Canal" on a scouting mission in the Kovela area, Jacob and Nonye stopped at the village of Novosolki. As soon as the village school-teacher learned that the two partisans were Jews, she too confided a secret to them: she knew of a Jewish girl who was hiding in a small, isolated village deep in the marshes.

Despite the great risk this entailed, the two men decided to try and find the girl. Practically wading through the deep mud, they eventually reached a little island and spoke with a Byelorussian peasant. At first he denied knowing anything about a Jewish girl, but when they finally won his confidence he told them that during the winter he had found Leda from Antopol almost frozen to death in a haystack. He pointed to several young women working in a field—his daughters. Among them was Leda, but the two partisans could not pick her out.

Leda herself did not trust them until they began speaking with her in Yiddish. She then agreed to go with them. On the way back they accidentally met Zerach Kremien, who was then in the Oriole brigade. They agreed that Leda should join this brigade because they were not at all certain that their own brigade would accept her.

•

Late one evening in September 1941, Anshl Delyaticki was transporting weapons from the Beuten camp. Coming suddenly upon a German watch near the prison, he turned instantly and stopped outside a house. Having no choice, he gambled and rapped on the window. Inside appeared a woman who wanted to know who he was. Anshl replied that he was a Jew being chased by Germans and needed shelter for only a few hours.

The woman thought for a moment, then let him in. He looked around to see who else was in the house. There were two other rooms, in which two children and an old woman were sleeping. He apologized for frightening her and thanked her for her hospitality.

All night long he sat looking out the window, his finger on the trigger of his pistol.

•

Felya Druzbalska, a Polish woman, became a widow on the day the Germans occupied Slonim and shot her husband. She was of great help to Anshl. After the war, he went to live with her and help her raise her two boys.

•

At the end of 1942, when the ghetto in Slonim had already been burned down, three Jews came to the Polish woman Bronislawa Kosiakowska in the village of Mizhevici (near Ruzany). One of them was Motl Kletskin, whom she knew. She guided all three of them "across the border" to Ruzany.

When the Nazis began rounding up Jews there too, Motl came back to Bronislawa's. It was a bitterly cold morning in February; he was so cold that when the warmth of the house hit him he passed out. When he came to, he asked the family to take him to the Germans, because he no longer had the strength to go on living. They calmed him down, gave him some warm clothing and for three days and nights he lay close to the wall oven, sick with typhus.

When he felt a little better they moved him to the barn, where he constructed a good hiding-place for himself. Four times a day the Polish family brought him food in the bucket they used for milking the cows. Motl did whatever chores he could—threshing the grain, milking the cows, etc.

Somehow the Nazis became suspicious and came with their dogs looking for "the Jew." The Kosakowski's young daughter saw them coming and ran to warn Motl. He disappeared into his hiding-place. The Germans, who had been watching her through binoculars, came after the little girl and began to interrogate her. Why had she run to the barn when she saw them? Who was hiding there? How long had he been there? She replied coolly that she had gone to the barn to play with her two new puppies—which she was now carrying in her arms.

The Nazis turned the barn upside down and finally decided she must be telling the truth.

Motl hid there a year-and-a-half, until the Red Army came and liberated him.

•

Three kilometers from Bitten, not far from the village of Zlatova, in an isolated cottage, lived the Pole Juzef Zalenski. In early August 1942 he hid nine Jews who had escaped from Bitten.

Tanya Galerstein, on her way to meet the group, was wounded by a policeman's bullet, but managed to hide in the bushes. As darkness fell, she made her way to the Zalenskis, who dressed her wound. Juzef then took her to a nearby woods, where two other Jews were hiding. He advised them that it would be safer to hide in his house, but they insisted that he lead them to the forest. He knew, however, that at night the roads were especially well guarded by the Germans and he did not wish to risk his life as well as theirs.

He could not convince them, so he led them to the Domanov highway and pointed them in the direction of the forest.

Tanya was able to reach the Shchors brigade, where Dr. Blumovich treated her wound. She stayed with the brigade until it moved to the Pinsk marshes. Because the wound had not healed completely, she stayed behind in the family camp and survived the German raids.

•

Vasya and Sonya Orbelik, young Byelorussians, were very helpful in getting Jews through the forest. Vasya had an instinct for locating enemy ambushes. He and Sonya often risked their own lives to help Jews and refused to accept any payment or reward in return.

•

At the end of the first German raid on the Family Camp, Leyma Pitkovski crossed the Szczara River and went to Selz, where a Polish friend of his named Panakar lived. Panakar hid him in his barn and brought him food for a few days. When Velvl Obulianski and David Briskin also came to him for help, Panakar asked them all to leave, but gave them a supply of bread and flour to take with them.

•

My own family lived for many years on lower Skrobive Street (near the Baranovici highway), surrounded by non-Jewish neighbors with whom we were on very friendly terms. We often helped each other in various ways. When the ghetto was established, many of these neighbors continued to treat us in the same human, sympathetic way. Adam Bairoshevski, whose family lived across the street from us, was often sent by his parents to visit my older sister Tsirl and her family on Michalovski Street with fruit and potatoes from their garden. In return, Tsirl would do sewing for them.

Stiopa Milkamanovich, a Tatar, frequently used to bring food to our elderly parents, who were trying to stay alive in a dirty little room near the river. Stiopa used to cry as he looked at my father Pinchas lying unconscious on his deathbed, and at my mother Pearl, her body bent double under the weight of all her troubles. My mother suffered terribly watching my father die before her eyes, without proper food and medical care. In that whole fiendish world, there was no one else to help them . . .

Instead of an Epilogue:
Erren and Schultz on Trial

———————————•———————————

Because former Regional Kommissar Gerhardt Erren and Chief of Police Lothar Schultz were arrested in Germany, Israel's Department of Justice interrogated Dr. Noah Kaplinsky in Tel Aviv. In 1972 the German court invited Dr. Kaplinsky to testify at the trial. Kaplinsky declined the invitation but asked the court to find Hans Zeifel, the courageous student who, when the ghetto was already in flames, persuaded Ritmeyer to release Dr. Kaplinsky so that he could take care of his patients in the municipal hospital. Kaplinsky assured the court that Zeifel, an honest German, would prove helpful in the investigation.

Zeifel was located in Germany and did indeed testify. The court then sent representatives to Tel Aviv who took a deposition from Dr. Kaplinsky himself. His testimony served as factual, decisive evidence in the prosecution's case against Erren.

Lyuba Abramovich's Testimony

In the summer of 1972 Lyuba Abramovich, who lives in Minsk, was invited to testify against Gerhardt Erren. She agreed to do so, but the Soviet plane took off later than scheduled and she arrived at Hamburg a day later than planned. At the airport she was met by an interpreter who informed her that they were going straight to the courthouse because she was scheduled to be the first witness. Lyuba was taken aback. She had expected to rest up after her long flight, and here they were taking her, suitcase and all, directly to the courthouse!

She didn't fret long, however. She reminded herself that when she was a partisan she had fought without resting, without a shower and often without breakfast. She had fought when it was necessary, not when it was convenient. And this trial was a continuation of the partisan fight.

As she took her place in the witness box, she immediately recognized Erren and Schultz. She was a bit surprised that she recognized Schultz, but in his eyes she could see that he recognized her too. Erren looked at her blankly, since he had not known her.

To the court's question whether she recognized the accused, she therefore replied yes and identified them.

A defense attorney tried to provoke her by hinting that she must have known them rather intimately if she recognized them after so many years. The prosecutor immediately objected to the insult implied in the question. The court sustained the objection.

The accused were then asked if they recognized the witness and they both replied that they did not.

Lyuba told the court that she had worked in the cellar of the Regional Kommissariat's building, cleaning, sorting and repairing weapons. Through a little window in the cellar she could see into the courtyard, where she very frequently saw the defendant Erren.

"From the cellar you cannot see the yard!" objected the defense attorney as he waved a plan of the building.

The court studied the plan. The prosecutor contended that this plan had been drawn many years after the time in question. It was now a warehouse and the windows had been walled up. The court asked the witness if she remembered the windows clearly.

"Yes," she replied, "they were small windows right up against the ceiling." She had often worked by the light from those windows because the electricity in the cellar was not always on.

The defense asked if she remembered what color uniform the Regional Kommissar wore.

"It was a German officer's uniform and the color was green."

The attorney placed two swatches of green cloth before her. Which of these two is the color of the uniform that the Regional Kommissar wore?

There was a hush in the courtroom as Lyuba studied the "exhibit."

"Neither one," said Lyuba. "It had more yellow in it."

The prosecutor smiled.

Lyuba Abramovich continued her testimony:

Before she started working in that cellar the Jews were driven out of their homes and rounded up in the marketplace with their bundles. Erren had appeared there with a big whip in his hand. He stopped near the Abramovich family and struck her father in the face with the whip. Then he grabbed her grandfather's beard and yanked it brutally.

At this point Lyuba turned to the judges and asked if she was permitted to ask a question. "Does German law consider it a crime to pull an old man's beard?" She added that unfortunately the court could not call her family to testify because they were later killed by order of the Regional Kommissar.

Lyuba testified further:

One day the Germans were rounding up Jews in the ghetto and a young boy tried to run away. The Regional Kommissar shot him on the spot.

The defense wanted to know what the boy's name was.

"I don't know," Lyuba replied.

How did she know it was a boy? the defense attorney insisted. Perhaps it was a little girl. Or maybe even an adult. And maybe it was someone else who shot him. She might have imagined it. After all, she was then in a very depressed mood.

The prosecutor intervened and instructed Lyuba that she was

not obliged to answer insulting questions. But Lyuba said she·
wanted to answer the question.

"I was indeed in a depressed mood. But I have never suffered
from hallucinations. I saw it with my own eyes."

The prosecutor turned to Erren and asked if he acknowledged
the fact.

"No!" the accused replied.

Lyuba then told the court how Erren once shot a wounded
partisan named Chaim Labovitch when he could not get any information out of him.

Concerning Schultz Lyuba gave this testimony:

At the end of each workday he used to search the workers to see
if they were carrying anything out of the place. But very often he
"searched" with his fists. For "soiling" a machine-gun he beat one
young man and left him lying half-dead on the ground. Yet despite
this kind of brutality, Lyuba and her friends still managed to outwit
him and take many gun-parts out of the place.

Lyuba testified that Schultz had sought out Miriam Finkelstein,
a very beautiful young woman in the ghetto, and promised her that
no harm would come to her if she would be "nice to him." But then
the Gestapo found out about this and arrested him for "defiling the
race." Regional Kommissar Erren had "punished" him with a two-
week jail sentence. When he came out, Miriam was no longer
among the living.

Schultz objected strenuously that he had already been punished
for that. The prosecutor examined the records and found it to be
true. To which Lyuba commented.

"Yes, they punished him with a couple of weeks in jail for dis-
gracing the Aryan race, but there is good reason to believe that he
murdered her before he went to serve his 'sentence.'"

The prosecutor asked the court to consider this as evidence of
the moral turpitude of the accused and the competence of the
witness.

At this point the judges adjourned for a brief conference. Several moments later they returned with the decision that the witness would be permitted to testify under oath and that the court would reconvene after lunch.

What that meant was that everything up to that point had been a rehearsal. After lunch it would begin all over again.

Lyuba went out to the buffet and sat down at a table. The prosecutor sat down at the same table, ordered a small beer and told Lyuba that she had behaved in an exemplary manner, that her statements were very important for the prosecution's case and that the court's consent to having her testify under oath was "our first victory."

Lyuba asked what he thought the outlook was. "Uncertain," he replied, because Erren has good connections. His daughter is married to an influential official in the government. His experienced attorneys know how to drag out the trial, which is now in its third year. For a few months at the beginning of the trial Erren had even had the privilege of eating in expensive restaurants and going home for weekends.

"Now I understand why the trial is being conducted in such a petty way," Lyuba said. "They keep talking not about the monstrous ideology of the accused, not about their crime of annihilating the Jews of Slonim, as well as tens of thousands of Byelorussians, but about trivial things and petty details."

"I am a fervent anti-Nazi," the prosecutor assured her, "and I hate the Brown Plague which besmirched the German people and caused so much tragedy. But what is one to do? German jurisprudence regards these Errens and Schultzes as innocent because they only carried out the orders given them from on high. That's why we're seeking to prove crimes that the accused himself committed, so we can punish him in some way."

When the court reconvened, Lyuba took a civil oath and began her testimony all over again. The defense attorneys, now knowing she would be a hard nut to crack, tried to entangle her or to engage her in long discussions that would confuse her and nullify her testimony.

The hearing ended in the late afternoon with the prosecutor looking jubilant.

After she had showered and rested, two women knocked at the door of her hotel room. They introduced themselves as Irma and Liselotte and shook her hand almost worshipfully.

"We were at the trial today," said the younger one. "We came to express our appreciation and our sympathy. And our apology for all the evil things you had to endure at the hands of the Errens and the Schultzes." They told her about their widespread organization that devoted itself to exposing the Nazi criminals and bringing them to justice. In this particular trial they had played an important role.

"We've got to uproot everything connected with German fascism and again become a great cultural people. We've got to make sure there is never again a place for such vile Hitlerites."

Lyuba thanked them and wished them well in their work.

The next day, when Lyuba came to the airport, Liselotte was waiting for her with a bouquet of flowers.

For Lyuba it was not the end of her testimony. As the prosecutor had warned her, the defense had challenged her testimony about the windows through which she had allegedly seen Erren in the courtyard. Representatives of the German court and the Minsk prosecutor's office therefore went to Slonim with her to take a closer look at the building. She could find neither the door nor the windows. On the site stood a new building. All the neighbors were new too, and no one could remember what had been there before.

Were these things figments of her overactive imagination? Had her testimony been for naught, after all? The defense had a plan of the building which showed no doors or windows in the basement. A plan? Then there must be an older one, someone suggested.

And there was. It took several hours of searching in the hall of records to find it. But when they studied it they knew exactly where to look for the evidence . . .

The Testimony of Israel Sokolik

In November 1962, Israel Sokolik read in the Yiddish press that the court in Hamburg was seeking witnesses against Gerhardt Erren and Lothar Schultz. Both men had been arrested.

Sokolik was happy to learn that these murderers would finally be punished for their bloody crimes. He went immediately to the West German consulate, where they asked him many questions. Early in 1963 he received an invitation from the Hamburg criminal court to come to the consulate again for a meeting with a Dr. Lindenman, a representative of the investigator's office.

The deposition took place in a very cordial atmosphere. Dr. Lindenman did her utmost to ask the questions in such a way that Sokolik would not become agitated in recalling those horror-filled days. After he told her about the burning ghetto and described many details of the tragedies that resulted, Dr. Lindenman suggested that they take a recess and have a cup of coffee.

Following the brief recess, she showed him several photographs and asked him to identify anyone he recognized. Without any hesitation he pointed to the accused, pronounced their names and spoke of the part they played in the massacres of Jews. Dr. Lindenman wrote down everything he said and assured him that he would be a good witness for the prosecution. She added that they would meet again soon in the Hamburg court.

Ten long years passed. In April 1973 he received an invitation from that court to appear on August 30 as a witness in the trial.

As he walked into the courthouse he recognized the two murderers in the corridor. The sudden confrontation unnerved him. His throat tightened and his mouth grew parched. But his eyes continued to meet theirs until they dropped them.

At precisely nine o'clock a court bailiff opened the doors to the courtroom, a bare, dimly lit hall. The same bailiff called out Sokolik's name and showed him to his seat. The two defendants and their attorneys sat down at a table nearby. A young woman came over to Sokolik and introduced herself as a court interpreter from German to English. A few moments later a side door opened and through it came the judges in their long, black robes. Among them was Dr. Lindenman. They sat down at a long table on which lay the list of charges against the accused. Next to that table was a smaller one at which sat the prosecutor and his secretary.

The President of the court asked Israel Sokolik several questions: Was he Saul Sokolik? Was he in Slonim at the time of the German occupation? Does he know the two defendants? Can he point out which one was the Regional Kommissar?

Sokolik pointed to Gerhardt Erren and said: "This is the chief murderer of the 25,000 Jews of Slonim."

The defense objected to his reference to the defendant as a murderer when the court had not yet confirmed his guilt. The objection was sustained, but the President of the court said to Sokolik: "We understand that it will be very painful for you to recall that time when your closest relatives and friends died. If you wish, we can excuse you from giving further testimony."

Sokolik thanked the court and explained that he had sworn never to rest until the murderers were brought to justice. "I have waited for this opportunity thirty years . . . I am ready to relive the past . . ."

"What can you tell us about Gerhardt Erren?"

Step by step Soikolik described the arrival of the Regional Kommissar in Slonim on September 1, 1941 and how he immediately began tormenting the Jews. How he had exacted tribute from them. How he had ordered the massacres at the Czepelow ditches . . .

"Did you see all this with your own eyes?" the defense asked. "Were you yourself present at those ditches?"

"No!" replied Sokolik.

"Then how do you know all those details about the massacre?"

"That terrible night a few Jews came out of those ditches who had been wounded but not killed. They told us everything. And then the Nazi police came to the ghetto hospital and took the wounded back to the ditches and shot them again . . ."

"Did Gerhardt Erren take part in this?" asked the prosecutor.

"Yes! That same day, as I was returning from work, the Ukrainian police were checking work passes at Third of May Street. A black car with little swastika flags on it rode by—in it were three tall officers. One of them was Gerhardt Erren. The car drove to the ditches and they observed what was happening. After the second massacre Erren ordered the barbed wire put around the ghetto area. No one was allowed to leave the ghetto without a special pass."

"Did you yourself live in the ghetto?" asked the prosecutor. He unrolled a map of Slonim and asked Israel to show the court where he was living when he saw these things happening.

The witness did so, to the court's satisfaction. Then he told the court how the Germans had discovered his hiding-place and how they had driven out seven people and taken them to prison. The judges were visibly shaken by his description of how Jews were driven out of their hiding-places, how they ran to the canal like living torches, with the clothing on their backs in flames.

"Did Regional Kommissar Erren take part himself in the destruction of the ghetto?"

"Yes. During the selections the German factory managers would come and select the best craftsmen and doctors to work for them. Engineer Wolfstein selected me, and it's thanks to him that I'm alive. But the German medical supervisor selected Dr. Bregman to work for him and told him to hurry and get his wife, who was standing in the line that was going to the ditches. Erren noticed this and ordered one of his men to 'catch the Jew who was attempting to escape.' Then he took a club from a Gestapo man and started beating Dr. Bregman over the head until he fell unconscious to the ground. And Erren ordered his men to throw the doctor on a truck that was carrying Jews to the ditches."

As Sokolik finished this grisly story Erren leaped out of his seat and screamed that it was all a lie, that he was not even in Slonim the day the *Aktion* took place. Then he fell to the table with his head on his arms. The court immediately called a recess. A doctor examined Erren and determined that he had had a mild heart attack.

Fifteen minutes later Erren issued a statement: He could prove that he was on leave at the time in question and could not have been in the prison. His attorney then asked Sokolik if he remembered the date he was in prison. Sokolik replied that the Jews hiding in the bunkers beneath their homes soon lost track not only of the calendar but of whether it was day or night.

At that point, exhausted, he asked the court's permission to step down.

The court asked the defense if they had any further questions for this witness. Their reply being in the negative, the court excused the witness.

On June 26, 1974 Gerhardt Erren, age 73, was declared guilty and sentenced to life imprisonment. Lothar Schultz, age 66, was sentenced to three years in prison.

Department of Religious ̄ ̀ ̀ ̈̈̀s
Moore Reading Room
University of Kansas

SLONIM
in the Region of Belorussia—Lithuania—Poland

סלונים
בתחומי בילורוסיה—ליטא—פולין

קנה המדה: 1 : 2.000.000

עבד ושרטט א. וינשטיין